MW01200521

THE
Enchanted
SEASON

*The Detroit Tigers' Historic
1984 World Series Run and
My Life as The Big Wheel*

Lance Parrish
with Tom Gage

TRIUMPH
B O O K S

Library of Congress Cataloging-in-Publication Data

Names: Parrish, Lance, author. | Gage, Tom.
Title: The enchanted season: the Detroit Tigers' historic 1984 World
   Series run and my life as the Big Wheel /Lance Parrish with Tom Gage.
Description: Chicago, Illinois: Triumph Books, [2024] | Includes
   bibliographical references.
Identifiers: LCCN 2023058089 | ISBN 9781637275641 (hardcover)
Subjects: LCSH: Detroit Tigers (Baseball team)—History. | World Series
   (Baseball) (1984) | Parrish, Lance. | Baseball players—United
   States—Biography.
Classification: LCC GV875.D6 P369 2024 | DDC
   796.357/640977434—dc23/eng/20231221
LC record available at https://lccn.loc.gov/2023058089

This book is available in quantity at special discounts for your group or organization. For further information, contact:
   Triumph Books LLC
   814 North Franklin Street
   Chicago, Illinois 60610
   (312) 337-0747
   www.triumphbooks.com

Printed in U.S.A.
ISBN: 978-1-63727-564-1
Design by Patricia Frey
Photos courtesy of Lance Parrish unless otherwise indicated

To my beautiful wife, Arlyne, and our three amazing children: David, Matthew, and Ashley. Thank you all for your love, your sacrifices, and support that allowed me to live my dream. I love you all and thank God for you every day.

—L.P.

To Lisa, my love, my inspiration, and my support.

—T.G.

Contents

Foreword

I took great joy, and had the immense honor, of being associated with Detroit's last two World Series-winning teams—the Tigers of 1968 and 1984.

In 1968 I was a player. In 1984 I was a coach, and both were tremendously enjoyable experiences. Little did I know that when the Los Angeles Dodgers traded me to Detroit on December 15, 1965, for pitcher Phil Regan that I would spend the next 30 years with the Tigers—first as a player, then as a minor league manager, and finally for the last 24 years of my tenure with the franchise as a major league coach.

It wasn't until I went up to the front office on the third floor in 1995 to speak to the new people in charge after a changing of the guard—when I ran into someone who asked me who I was, what was I doing there, and what was my role with the team—that I decided it was time to leave. I remember thinking to myself, *I've been here 30 years, and nobody on the third floor knows who the heck I am. I think it's time for me to go.*

But what a wonderful time it was.

Both World Series teams were very talented. The 1968 team had great players and a lot of underrated players, but we had emerged from the 1967 season thinking we were the best team in the American League—yet hadn't won. So from spring training on, we had one objective in mind, as was the case with our wonderfully balanced ballclub in 1984. In spring training of both those years, we thought we were good enough to win.

Think of the great players we had in 1984.

- **Kirk Gibson:** a volatile, very emotional player but a great kid. Extremely aggressive and mouthy in the clubhouse but a team guy with a knack for the dramatic.
- **Alan Trammell:** steady as a rock, someone who could do it all, played great defense, always a tough out in a jam, an outstanding shortstop, fundamentally without peer.
- **Chet Lemon:** not the best of baserunners but a hitter who could get hot and an excellent center fielder who caught everything, someone we had really needed when we traded for him.
- **Lou Whitaker:** a second baseman who should be in the Hall of Fame. Nobody could throw like Lou, and he never made a mistake on double plays. Plus, he had learned to hit with power.
- **Lance Parrish:** the leader of the team, though quiet, a player who'd grown into the role. One of my favorites. When Lance spoke, everybody listened.
- **Jack Morris:** a wild-eyed guy at times who was unhittable when he had his splitter working. Excitable, someone with his own ideas, and durable. And don't try to take him out of a game.
- **Dan Petry:** an outstanding pitcher for us. He wasn't as emotional as Jack, and his self-confidence wasn't as strong as Jack's, but whenever he had his good control, he would give the other team problems.
- **Willie Hernandez:** we had Pittsburgh Pirates manager Chuck Tanner to thank for Willie because when he heard in spring training that we might be interested in him, Chuck said, "If you can get him, get him!" The rest is history.

Sparky Anderson was the perfect manager for the 1984 team. He wanted the players to play, but he had ironclad rules—like how you can't wear your socks down at your ankles, you have to wear a shirt and tie on the road, you can't have facial hair—but the players accepted them. He was very conservative as far as behavior was concerned, and the players liked that.

My best friend on the 1968 team was Dick McAuliffe. I admired the way he played, but he was a strange guy. He was crazy aggressive to the extent I called him "Mad Dog." But he almost hated baseball. He didn't enjoy it as much as he should have, but he could play. And I would tell him that.

It wasn't about having a best friend on the 1984 team, though. I was a coach, not a player. I felt more responsibility in 1984 than in 1968. I probably had the most interaction with Trammell and Whitaker because they were infielders and I had played defense all my life.

One of the strengths of that club was that they didn't give away many games. They were smart players.

The first year I was in Detroit though, we lost two managers during the 1966 season. Charlie Dressen had a heart attack, then Bob Swift was diagnosed with lung cancer. I wasn't playing as much as I wanted to play. So I went to general manager Jim Campbell and said, "Don't turn down any opportunities to trade me."

He said, "I want you to be patient. Let's see where this goes."

This is where it went: 30 years with Detroit. Nobody outworked me. I threw batting practice my last day in uniform. I'm proud of that. It was a good ride. But a big part of it being a good ride was my time with the team about which this book is written. So please enjoy remembering that great season of 1984. I sure do.

—**Dick Tracewski**, *the longest-tenured coach*
in Detroit Tigers history and a mentor to Lance Parrish

Introduction

He came to be known as The Big Wheel.

Not just for his size, which was physically impressive, but for his steadying influence and for his contributions on the field. Behind the plate, and within the confines of the Detroit Tigers' clubhouse, Lance Parrish kept his team focused. His personality wasn't flamboyant, never has been. Easygoing and affable, he was slow to anger, but he could get fearsomely agitated if prodded—once saying he should have punched a famous opposing manager in the nose after thinking he had instructed one of his pitchers to hit him while Parrish while batting.

In team brawls Parrish wasn't the Tigers player throwing punches as often as he was the one shielding his colleagues from the fists of opposing players. He was the epitome of a dependable teammate, a watchful eye so that no one strayed too far from concentrating on the task at hand, and always a listening ear for those who needed one.

He had some huge moments throughout his Tigers career. In the second game he ever started for Detroit in 1977, for instance, he had three hits, scored four runs, and knocked in four—not equaling the sum of those parts in a single game again until 1989 when he played for the California Angels. He was a six-time All-Star for the Tigers, eight times overall, and a three-time Gold Glove catcher—one who regrets, to this day, that he ever left Detroit as a free agent after the 1986 season. Drafting him in the first round in 1974, the Tigers were his home, his high regard for them reflecting the essence of his soul.

Beam your thoughts back, however, to 1984—the fifth game of the World Series at Tiger Stadium against the San Diego Padres. It's the possible World Series-clinching game for the Tigers, and they're leading 4–3 in the seventh inning. The players were excited, the city of Detroit was holding its breath. The Tigers weren't yet on the brink of becoming baseball's champion, but they're on the brink of the brink. The majestic home run off Goose Gossage by Kirk Gibson, for which the team's eventual triumph is well remembered, was still an inning away. Even now, we can see it in our minds and relive it in our hearts. We can also hear the words of the moments leading up to it: Sparky Anderson gesturing to Gibson from the Tigers' dugout that Gossage "don't want to walk you!"

And to Goose's everlasting chagrin, he didn't walk Gibson.

But for those heroics to take place in the eighth inning or for there eventually to be a victory celebration that day, the foundation of the clincher had to be laid. And in the sixth inning, it was another home run that did so, albeit a quieter home run by a quieter hero but one that proved vital to the eventual outcome.

Up in the broadcast booth, to describe on national television what was about to take place, it was Vin Scully at the microphone with Joe Garagiola at his side. Enjoy it once more…"The Goose is here," Scully said, "and they've clocked him at 95 miles an hour warming up. Well, Lance Parrish will face him with one out in the seventh, 4–3 Detroit."

First pitch: "Fouled away [for strike one]," Scully said.

Next pitch: "And he lines it to left! Back goes [Carmelo] Martinez… GONE!"

What the broadcasters, as well as the entire crowd, had just witnessed was a bullet off Parrish's bat into the stands, vanishing so fast on a low plane that a startled "GONE!" was Scully's only reaction. There was no time for him to say anything else. As Parrish rapidly circled the bases, he clapped his hands. After crossing the plate, he raised one arm into the air, not two. Again, it was a quieter home run by a quieter man.

But the score now was 5–3 Tigers. With Gibson's home run an inning later as the cushion, they had provided themselves with enough runs to withstand Kurt Bevaqua's solo home run off Willie Hernandez in the ninth inning. Enough runs, in other words, to win the game.

But not just the game, the first World Series championship in 16 years for the Tigers and only their second title in the last 39 years.

Parrish emerged from the dugout after his home run for a short wave to the appreciative crowd. Darrell Evans gave him one more hug. Up by two runs instead of one, the Tigers had journeyed past the brink of the brink.

They could sense it now. They could feel it.

Still appreciating just how hard Parrish hammered the ball, Garagiola said, "If you let a fastball hitter sit on a fastball, you can't throw a bullet past him. Sparky said before the game that Parrish would hit a home run."

Sparky was right. Delirium was about to roar in the D!

—T.G.

In the Family's Words

Hi, my name is Ashley Lyne. I'm three days old. I don't know that I am only three days old, of course, but that's how old my parents will someday tell me I was while bundled in their arms on a plane flying across the country to California. That's right. I'm in my father's arms as he walks up and down the aisle past people who are smiling and having a good time. There is a lot of joy on this airplane. I'm little and sleepy, but I can feel it. There was a lot of joy on the ground, too, as we all gathered before we headed to the airport.

Older people than I were watching a game being played on television, a baseball game, I would later learn. Again, I didn't know at the time it was a National League playoff game. Being only three days old, I wasn't really aware of what anything was. My parents will tell me years later what was happening. But for now we're jetting across the country. And I'm in my dad's arms.

I'll find out later that we were on our way to an event called the World Series. No wonder the people on the plane were happy. No wonder they all were smiling as they peered into my face and made baby sounds. In fact, there is a heavyset man with a big round face doing that now. I heard someone call him Jim Campbell. I heard someone else refer to him as "the boss." There's also a smaller man with silver hair. He's very energetic, very active. He's up and down the aisles, talking a mile a minute, and shaking hands. A woman, who must be related to him, leans over to the aisle from her seat and says rather sharply, "Sit down, George!" But he doesn't sit down. He keeps on talking. She tries again with no luck.

There's a young man with a boyish face who seems to be very happy as well. "Hey, guys, I'm headed back to my old stompin' grounds in San Diego," he says to the other young men.

"Yes, we know, Tram," replies the one they refer to as Jack. I didn't know his last name.

As I said, I don't entirely grasp why we're all on the plane. I won't know the importance of the moment or the World Series until I'm older. All I know is that I'm getting sleepy in my father's arms as he walks me up and down the aisle. With the sound of the plane—the rhythm of the jet engines—gently lulling me, I can hardly stay awake. But before I fall asleep, the man with the silver hair approaches my father and slaps him on the back. "Great job, Lance," he said. "We did it. We're headed to the World Series, Big Wheel."

That's my dad, I guess, the one they call The Big Wheel.

He answers by saying "Thank you, Sparky." The man with the silver hair apparently is nicknamed Sparky. But he's George to his wife, who gave up a while ago on trying to get him to sit down.

The engines of the plane drone on. I finally fall asleep.

If I didn't before, let me more formally introduce myself: I'm Ashley Lyne Parrish, three-day-old daughter of Detroit Tigers' catcher Lance Parrish, and we're on the plane from Detroit to San Diego for Game One of the 1984 World Series. Lance Parrish, The Big Wheel, is my father. But once upon a time he was a newborn. Isn't that right, Dad?

Dad, where are you? Oh, my gosh. Time has somehow reversed itself for you. You're suddenly the infant now, not me. You're the one wrapped in a blanket. So, take yourself back to when you were three days old. And allow us, Dad, to share your thoughts as a newborn.

It is June 18, 1956, and I'm in the arms of my loving parents, Otto William and Dolores Parrish. I was born in a hospital in McKeesport, Pennsylvania, near Pittsburgh, and one day my baseball card will list my hometown as

McKeesport. But that's incorrect as my mother will quickly tell anyone who will listen. "You're from Clairton, Lance, not McKeesport. All your people are from Clairton. Remember that!" she'll say. "It only says McKeesport because that's where the hospital you were born in was located."

"I hear you, Mom," I'll say. "I'll get the baseball card changed when I can. You're right. I'm from Clairton."

At three days old, though, all I'm doing is looking into the eyes of a strong, hardworking couple who are thrilled to have a son. My mother is the daughter of a bricklayer. Her father was also a hunter who often brought home a critter or two for the dinner table—a rabbit, a squirrel, or something bigger. We were never quite sure what was being added to the soup or spaghetti sauce. My grandparents on my mother's side, Thomas and Ann, raised vegetables, as did their neighbors, which helped them get through the depression and war years.

My dad was the son of a self-employed egg salesman, who also sold chickens. He didn't raise them—he didn't have a farm, if that's what you're asking—he just sold eggs and chickens. One of my earliest memories was of going over to my grandfather's house, and there'd always be eggshells lying around. I enjoyed going to his house as long as I didn't step on any eggs.

With an Otto as my father (his nicknames were "Bud" and "Oot") and an Otto as my grandfather, I always figured there was German lineage somewhere in my background. My dad was Otto William Parrish Jr., son of Otto William Parrish Sr., but not his first son. They named their first son Thomas for another family member. Both my parents grew up in the Pittsburgh area, but they met in Quantico, Virginia, when they were both in the Marines. My dad fought in Korea but never talked about the war. My mom, meanwhile, remained stateside.

Both were very disciplined people, though, achieving the rank of sergeant. And when their military days were over, they returned to Clairton to settle down. My mother became a homemaker, raising me and my sister Cheryl, who was two years older than I (but died in 2011). We lived in an area called Woodland Terrace where we had a lot of room to run around and get into trouble as kids. I remember liking to climb a big ol' nearby tree. I especially liked to climb high but didn't always hang on as securely as I should have. One time, I took a nosedive right out of that tree and broke my collarbone.

Dad was a police officer, walking the beat in Clairton. He was good at his job and liked it, but the Pittsburgh winters were long. I think he got tired of the snow and cold weather. So, one day when my mother was speaking on the phone to her brother and a cousin who lived in Southern California, they mentioned to her that there were openings on the police force in Los Angeles. It wouldn't be easy for my parents to move; it meant leaving many of their relatives in Pennsylvania, but after a discussion about their future, they decided to do it.

My father blazed the trail. He went out to California by himself, and when he graduated from the sheriff's academy, we flew out to join him. Departure day was on my sixth birthday—June 15, 1962. I had never even seen an airplane up close, let alone been on one. But I remember that day well. Off we went—my mom, my sister, and me. At the other end, Dad was waiting for us with our new life.

Among the keepsakes my mother took to California was her love of the Pittsburgh Pirates. She was a huge Roberto Clemente fan. So I became one, too, as a little boy. Roberto was her favorite. For years, the only time we went to Dodger Stadium as fans after we moved to California was when the Pirates were in town to play the Dodgers, so that my mother could cheer for Clemente.

Clairton was fading in our rear-view mirror by then, however. There aren't any relatives back there now that we keep close tabs on. But that wasn't always the case in those early years. My parents missed their families, so one summer we loaded up the station wagon and made the long trek back to Pennsylvania—all the way from California.

I'm not sure what summer it was, but it was super humid driving across the country and boiling hot in a car with no air conditioning. It was miserable. After we got to Clairton, it was great seeing everybody, of course, but only after we got there.

Dad died in 2007. We never made that trip again.

That's what I remember about Pennsylvania—living there, being young there, then leaving there. I didn't know, when I was three days old, looking up at my parents, what the future had in store for me.

But I knew it and had lived it by the time Ashley Lyne was looking up at me as her dad on the plane to the World Series.

I'm Dolores (Dee) Parrish, Lance's mother, speaking about his early years.

My father grew everything you can think of: tomatoes, parsley, carrots, anything we could put on the table with supper. My mother baked constantly, and my grandmother raised chickens and cows, so we had a lot to eat that was fresh. I don't think we went to a store for years to buy anything. Plus, one thing we could rely on is that my father would always find mushrooms in the woods near our house. He was able to tell the good ones from the bad, but I could not stand the smell of any of them. To this day, I won't eat a mushroom.

I met Lance's father in the Marine Corps. I joined when I was 18. But even by the time we got around to dating and then to get our marriage license, I had no idea his first name was Otto. We always called him Bud or Oot.

Normally, Lance was a very careful boy, so the time he fell out of a tree and broke his collarbone was just an accident. He never cried much, though, even when he fell out of that tree.

Leaving Pennsylvania for California was simply a decision that was best for us. When my husband passed the test to join the police force in Los Angeles, it was kind of like, "Well, okay, that's that. We're going."

We left Pennsylvania on Lance's sixth birthday in 1962. I remember him enjoying the flight. But I can't really think of anything he didn't enjoy as a boy.

Until he was in junior high school, I had no idea he'd get as big as he got. He hadn't been a big baby or particularly big as a little kid, but as he grew up after we moved, he loved being outdoors, bringing things home. I never knew what kind of snake or frog would be next. Participating in the

4-H youth development program was a great activity for Lance. He had a cow named Florence that he was attached to. At 4-H shows he often slept in the stall next to Florence.

When Lance got into sports, I never missed any of his games. I remember vividly the time I sat behind home plate and was yelling at the umpire. Lance turned around, glaring at me with a shut-your-mouth look that quickly got my attention. Believe me: I hushed up in a hurry.

To me, though, part of the enjoyment of a game was in yelling at the umpire. I wasn't being unrefined, just having a good time. But Lance didn't feel that way. He didn't want me embarrassing him. So, I was quieter from that point on.

For the rest of that game anyway.

Chapter 1

1983—Getting Good

We took a big step toward becoming an excellent team in 1983. Before you can be considered an excellent team, you must first become very good and—after years of inching upward—we finally were very good in 1983.

We didn't win a World Series or even get there.

We didn't even win a division title, but we did win 92 games—third best in the majors—and at the end of the season, we felt that we were on the brink of becoming something special.

In most areas where we'd been lacking, we no longer were. After being a bad road team in 1982, for instance, we were greatly improved in 1983. After 13 walk-off losses in 1982, an amazing number, we had only three in 1983. And with a combined 37–19 record in June/July, we were in a contending position as August began.

It was a fun, encouraging season, in which many players contributed. Jack Morris won 20 games, Dan Petry won 19, and Lou Whitaker—coming into his own—led the team with 206 hits while hitting .320. Other .300 hitters on the team that year were Alan Trammell at .319, Enos Cabell at .311, and Larry Herndon at .302. I chipped in by knocking in 114 runs while winning my first Gold Glove for defense.

We also turned the corner in 1983 in believing what we could accomplish. The Baltimore Orioles won the division, but we played well against the Orioles, which helped our confidence going into the offseason. Tram always said the seed of 1984 was planted the previous season, and, no question, that was correct. "One of the reasons for our success was the confidence we came out of 1983 with," Tom Brookens said. "We felt we were right there as a contender. So, we went into the '84 season with a little chip on our shoulder, having something to prove."

What especially helped in '83 was limiting the length of our losing streaks. The most games in a row we lost were four after losing at least 10 straight games in each of the two previous seasons.

Starting with a six-run first inning on Opening Day in Minnesota and scoring 20 runs in our first two games against the Twins, the season got off to a rousing start. We were still feeling upbeat when Milt Wilcox took to the mound on a chilly Friday night at Comiskey Park in Chicago. It was early in the year, April 15. The season was barely underway; the game was just our ninth. Milt had lost his first start of the season—6–3 in Detroit to the White Sox, but while allowing just one ball to leave the infield before the seventh inning, he could not have been sharper this time out. And by the end of the seventh, the countdown for a possible perfect game, not just a no-hitter, was well underway.

Wilcox had six outs to go, entering the bottom of the eighth, and none of the three scheduled hitters coming up for the Sox in the eighth had presented problems for him in the earlier innings. Nor did they this time. He struck out Greg Luzinski for the second time, retired Ron Kittle on a fly ball to center, and then also struck out Greg Walker to get through the eighth.

Then he had only the ninth inning ahead of him with Carlton Fisk, Vance Law, and Jerry Dybzinski as the scheduled batters.

Wilcox was under 100 pitches heading into the ninth, and we'd given him a 6–0 lead, so there wasn't any major game pressure on him as the Sox came up to bat. Fisk had had two hits, including a triple, in Milt's first start of the season, however. At 35 he was still a dangerous hitter. But Wilcox got him on a first-pitch fly to left to begin the inning. Lefty Mike Squires then batted for Law. Squires was an experienced pinch-hitter who was hard to strike out. He usually put the ball in play. Taking a ball on a 2–2 pitch was an example of his veteran patience, so on the subsequent full-count pitch, Wilcox needed to throw a strike, which he did. Squires hit it weakly to Rick Leach at first base for the second out.

But the Sox weren't out of pinch-hitters yet. They still had Jerry Hairston in case they needed him—and down to their last out, it was time. They needed him. In Wilcox's favor was that he had retired Hairston as a pinch-hitter in his first start against the Sox that season. But we knew that Hairston was a hitter to be wary of. After all, he had hit a pinch-hit, walk-off home run off Dan Petry on July 8 of the 1982 season. We knew he was fully capable of coming through for the Sox. And it would not take long for him to come through again. On Wilcox's first pitch, Hairston hit a clean single up the middle to end the exciting perfect game bid. Even the partisan White Sox crowd of 19,483 groaned, which was understandable. It had come so close to witnessing history.

It's a running joke between me and Milt now because I still give him grief about that particular pitch. The consensus on Hairston was that he was a dead fastball hitter. He'd be up there looking for a fastball right away. Plus, he was just a good hitter. I opted to call for Milt's splitter on the first pitch because it had the arm action of a fastball and I thought we might get Hairston leaning on his front foot and maybe come over the top of the ball, hitting it into the ground. But Milt, because he had a perfect game in the works, just wanted to get ahead of him. So, he threw a fastball that Jerry smacked right back up the middle for a base hit.

Well, that put the end to that.

It was nothing new for Milt to shake me off. That's for darn sure. At times I couldn't get on the same page with him. But I've always kidded him that if he had only listened to me, he would have had his niche in history. I'm sure he gets tired of hearing it. In fact, I've even heard him say, "Lance never lets me forget."

It could have gone either way in that at-bat with Hairston. With a pop-up Milt would have had his perfect game. I'm not saying any of this to impugn him in any way. He pitched with his gut. If he had something in

Fuss

As a versatile player, John Wockenfuss had some solid seasons for us. He would do a good job defensively wherever you put him—outfield, first base, or behind the plate. So, you could throw him out there almost anywhere and count on him to do a good job. But what stood out for me, and probably for everyone else, was his weird batting stance.

He'd flutter his fingers while holding his bat, then face the pitcher with a closed stance. But he could hit the ball to right field with the best of 'em, making him probably the best batter on the team to hit-and-run with. He was often successful at shooting the ball the other way.

Fuss also was someone who kept us loose in the dugout with a wisecrack. Initially when he got traded to the Philadelphia Phillies in the spring of 1984, I thought, *What the heck are we doing?* John had been a steady contributor for several years, and also in that deal, we sent Glenn Wilson to the Phillies at a time I thought he was part of the plans for our future. But that trade, for Willie Hernandez and Dave Bergman, obviously turned out great for us.

I could write a book just about Wockenfuss, though. There were so many sides to him—some of them humorous, others not so. He was a practical joker, for instance, but we had guys on the team who didn't always take to practical jokes. That occasionally caused problems because Fuss never minded getting under your skin, but he was an interesting guy all the same.

For instance, there was the time John pretended to be angry with something in the trainer's room and threw what some of us thought was a bat weight—one of those donut-shaped devices that fits around the base of a bat—at Kirk Gibson, but it was only the plastic covering of the weight. It hit Kirk squarely in the chest, though, and would have hurt him had it been the weight, so we gasped when John threw it, but it was all a joke to Fuss—something to get a rise out of his teammates. Well, Kirk was not a player who enjoyed being the target of practical jokes, so he angrily chased John out of the trainer's room and let him know it in no uncertain terms.

his head about a pitch he wanted to throw, he went with it. But pretty much that ball was right down the middle.

A lot of people don't think of the catcher when a perfect game is on the line. All the credit would have gone to Milt, and deservedly so. I wanted it for him, but I also wanted to be a part of a historic moment. I wanted to be able to share in it—to feel I had helped him at least a little bit through the process.

But it didn't work out.

Wilcox retired Rudy Law on a grounder to first for the final out, so he still came away with a one-hit shutout, an outstanding game, but not one for the record books. Not the perfect game from which he'd been only one out away. Milt would throw another shutout later that month against the Seattle Mariners, but it wasn't the flirtation with history this game was. In fact, he never came so close to pitching a game for the ages again.

We had a lot of fun in 1983, mostly because we played a lot of entertaining games that went our way collectively—but also individually. In other words, I think we all helped out from time to time. For instance, on May 3 I hit a home run in the 11th inning to beat the Mariners 2–1 in Seattle, but the icing on the cake was that I ended the game by throwing out pinch-runner John Moses on a steal attempt of second base. It was my third caught-stealing play of the day.

I don't mean to sound like I'm bragging, but I generally had pretty good success throwing runners out. What I can also say is that our pitching coach, Roger Craig, was a huge help to me. He made it a part of our pitchers' schooling to understand the importance of a quick delivery so I'd have a chance of throwing out a runner. I always thought that if they just got me the ball, I'd be successful because I had a lot of confidence in my ability.

Plus, Roger was extremely talented at calling pitchouts. It was almost as if he had a sixth sense about them. I was awed by his skill, thinking, *How does this guy know every time that someone's going to try to steal?* It seemed like every time he called a pitchout, the runner took off. I'd have an open lane to throw, and *bang*…he'd be out. That made my job easier.

As a team, though, most of the time it just seemed like everyone on the roster chipped in, such as on May 14 in Kansas City, when we came back to beat the Royals 11–10 after falling behind 7–0 in the first two innings. We got three innings of shutout relief that game from Aurelio Lopez, who was amazing. He didn't always look like he was in the best of shape, and his fastball was straight as a string sometimes, but Lopez's consistency was absolutely incredible. He had a rubber arm, wasn't a flamethrower, but he could throw strikes all day long. He was a huge contributor to our cause.

Despite losing out on his perfect game bid, it didn't take long for Milt to come through again. On May 19 he wasn't perfect, but he went 10 innings in a four-hitter to beat the Texas Rangers 2–1 at Tiger Stadium. John Wockenfuss drove in the winner with a sacrifice fly.

Batting for Kirk Gibson, Fuss also had a pinch-hit grand slam in a 10–1 victory against the Orioles on July 3, halting one of our two four-game losing streaks.

Despite struggling much of the season, Gibson had some memorable moments. On June 14 he hit a home run completely out of Tiger Stadium, well over the roof in right, in a game against the Boston Red Sox. The ball, which landed on the roof of the Brooks lumberyard across Trumbull Avenue, traveled an estimated 540 feet. It was the first of three times in his career as a Tiger that Gibson cleared the roof in right.

One of the biggest games of 1983—I'd never be so bold as to call it the biggest—occurred on July 10, a 5–3 victory against the Oakland A's in Detroit. I hadn't done anything in my first three at-bats, but in the ninth, when the A's brought in Jeff Jones to pitch to me with the bases loaded, I smoked a pitch deep into the left-field stands for a walk-off grand slam. This was the home run I kidded Jonesy years later about when I was asked in his presence what the biggest moment of my career was. We'd become good friends by then as coaches for the Tigers.

With the help of Herndon's five hits, we beat the Angels the next night 12–6. Hondo was always one of my favorite teammates. Often, he hit behind me and was a quasi-hitting coach for me. When he was on deck, for instance, he would notice subtle things I was doing differently when things weren't going well for me. He was so astute at identifying my bad habits, in fact, that I eventually asked him to watch out for them. Trammell was the one getting five hits against the Angels in Anaheim on July 24, a game in which I hit a home run in the top of the 12th inning to win it. Tram's five hits marked the second time in two weeks that one of my teammates had accomplished such a feat. To me, it really was a feat. I was always jealous of guys getting five hits in a game because I never did it.

By mid-August of 1983, our fans were really into what was happening at Tiger Stadium. In front of a crowd of 44,565 on August 12, we rewarded them with a 7–6 walk-off victory against the New York Yankees that put us into a tie for first place. Tram hit a home run in the ninth to tie it, and Herndon drove me in with a single in the 10th to win it. At that point, we were right in the hunt, so I think we all stepped it up. Sparky Anderson made everyone aware of the situation by saying, "We're in it, boys. We're in it. But let's put the pedal to the metal because we have a chance to do something special."

The next night we took over sole possession of first for the first time since April 6 with a 6–3 victory against the Yankees, giving us a 65–49 record. With 50,016 on hand, Morris got the better of Ron Guidry. Close to being at his best, Jack struck out 12 while not allowing a walk.

Not long after that, we showed some additional grit, scoring seven runs in the last two innings of a 10–4 victory in Kansas City—after losing 18–7 the night before. It was always a dogfight going up against the Royals. They had an explosive team. Things could get out of hand against them in a hurry. Sparky had told Petry before the game that he needed a complete game from him because Lopez was down with the gout, and the bullpen had been roughed up the previous night. After a shaky start, Petry held the Royals scoreless on one hit after the fifth inning. When it was all said and done, Sparky called it "the biggest game he'll probably ever pitch."

The month ended with what seemed like a meaningless 5–1 loss to Texas, but it wasn't meaningless to me—for it was the only game that season in which I made a run-scoring error in a loss. On my bad throw while trying to catch him retreating to the bag, Dave Hostetler of the Rangers scored all the way from second base. Dang it! That was one of only four errors I made the entire season.

Generally speaking, most position players get more excited about what they do offensively, but it was just as important to me to have a good game defensively. I always tried to remember that whatever I did behind the plate made just as big an impact as whatever I did at the plate.

I took a lot of pride in my defense. I worked very hard at trying to be a good catcher. But more than anything, I took a lot of pride in working with our pitching staff in trying to call a good game.

As the years have gone by, the guys on those good Tigers' teams have had quite a few discussions about just how difficult it was back then to win the American League East division. At one point (from 1981 to 1986), six different teams won it six years in a row. And when we went back into first place that August of 1983, five teams were within two-and-a-half games of each other.

Toward the end of the season, there were three more games worth mentioning. On September 14 for our sixth victory in a row, Glenn Abbott beat the Cleveland Indians at Tiger Stadium 5–0 with a four-hitter, all singles. Glenn had been acquired just weeks before and would not be with us for all of 1984, but he did pitch some excellent games while he was a Tiger. I thought he was a great fit. He competed his butt off. Glenn was a down-to-earth, good ol' country ballplayer, someone who was fun to have on the team. He often put a smile on our face because he always had some crazy little saying for every situation. One time he came to the dugout, calling a curveball he'd just thrown "a real bowel locker." In other words, he'd just tied someone up in knots with a breaking ball.

Six days later came our biggest splurge of the season: we scored 11 runs on 11 hits in the first inning against Baltimore, sending 16 batters to the plate. Orioles starter Dennis Martinez lasted just one out. We won the game 14–1, but weather limited its length to five innings. John Wockenfuss pinch hit for me on my second at-bat in the first inning not because I was hurt but because we were already ahead by so many runs. It was a weird feeling to be out of the game that early, though. Then, to complete our season of playing well against the eventual division winner, winning five of seven against them down the stretch, we beat the Orioles 5–4 on September 22 at Tiger Stadium. Whitaker delivered a walk-off single in the 10th after tying the game in the ninth with another of his four hits.

At the end of that season, I remember thinking it had been the best year I'd had. As late as July 11, I was hitting .300. My batting average against right-handers in 1983 went up 20 points from 1982 (from .259 to .279) and way, way up from 1981 (from .198 to .279). I ended the year with 36 doubles off right-handers, twice as many as I had in any other season of my career and 14 more than the number of doubles I had off righties in 1982 and 1984 combined. For whatever reason, I locked onto something that season. I know everyone's goal as a hitter is to hit .300—and, well, I never hit .300. Something always caused me to taper off, even if I was still at .300 well into the season. But in 1983 I felt really good at the plate, like I could hit anybody at any time. Sure enough, though, my average fell off again. I ended up hitting .279. But it was a fun year for me…a good year.

Better yet, it was a fine year for the team. We had significantly improved and were already looking forward to spring training when the season ended.

Chapter 2

Spring Training and the Trade

I always enjoyed spring training because it meant we were getting back to baseball after a long offseason. We were returning to what we do. But the feeling in Lakeland, Florida, in 1984 was different.

We came to camp with much more than hope. We were returning with genuine confidence about the upcoming season. For the first time in my career as a major leaguer, I could say that we knew we were going to be good. For one thing we were coming off an encouraging 92-win season in which we proved to ourselves, as well as to other teams, that we could not only compete, but also contend.

The Baltimore Orioles finished first in 1983 and eventually won the World Series. They were an outstanding team. But we played well against them. We were not intimidated by them. We felt we were at least their equal. Beyond feeling good about how we played in 1983, we patched some holes. We needed more power from the left side, so we signed Darrell Evans as a free agent. He was excited to be here. And we were excited to have him, as well as his long-ball potential—especially at Tiger Stadium. Coming off a 30-home run season for the San Francisco Giants, Evans was a good fit.

Darrell's addition was viewed by everyone as the first big free-agent signing we had ever made. I don't remember any player coming in with more fanfare. As a team we'd been looking for additions that would make a difference and we all felt this one fit the mold. We needed a hitter who could be an offensive force. As it turned out, Darrell wouldn't have his best year at the plate in 1984, but he made huge contributions all the same. He was a very verbal, knowledgeable baseball observer, exactly what we needed, and someone with experience to give our young players direction. He was the total package, almost like being a player/coach. The input he had off the field was extremely important to our development.

As spring training began, however, it was also essential to remember that the core of our team had been kept intact. Starting pitcher Milt Wilcox filed for free agency and initially thought the Tigers didn't want him back, but he ended up returning, saying he has been through "the bad" with us and wanted to be around for "the good." Or as he put it when he arrived in Florida, "I can put a lot behind me. I'm here, I've signed, now it's time to look ahead." The decision to bring Milt back was huge. It was the right thing to do. He still was a very good pitcher and a good fit for our ballclub.

Relief pitcher Doug Bair also filed for free agency and he, too, returned. That was another good decision. Doug always seemed to do the job we asked of him. He made our pitching staff stronger. In search of more playing time, however, outfielder Lynn Jones left as a free agent. We all liked Jonesy, but there were casualties to every offseason. While roster decisions weren't always popular, you just needed to accept them and move on. To this day, though, Lynn Jones remains a great friend to a lot of us who were on that team.

Enos Cabell filed for free agency as well and wanted to come back, but the signing of Evans made him expendable. He eventually signed with the Houston Astros, one of his former teams. We'd miss Enos. He was a good teammate. Everybody loved him. He kept us loose. Evans was an addition we needed to make our lineup stronger, however. Obviously, it was a big move.

But at this point in mid-February, we were still looking for a left-handed reliever. We needed a lefty because manager Sparky Anderson required balance in his bullpen, especially in later innings so he could make his percentage moves at the mound but also because Aurelio Lopez, who had been such a reliable force for us for several years, displayed some vulnerability in the second half of the previous season. Part of it was because he had some nagging health issues such as gout. No matter what, we needed assurance that our bullpen was going to be stable this season. I know for a fact that we were searching for it.

On top of all that, we had a new owner in Tom Monaghan, an enterprising, energetic businessman from Michigan who founded Domino's Pizza. John Fetzer was an excellent owner, a traditionalist who took immense pride in owning the Detroit Tigers. And I'm sure Mr. Fetzer would not have sold his team to anyone who didn't value the future of the franchise as highly as he always did. I didn't really know Fetzer, though. He never came around. I think I was in his presence only one time. To the players he was a ghost figure. When he sold the team, he said, "I'm looking for 30 more years of stability." With Monaghan in charge, it became a different era. That was a palpable reality as spring training began. Enthusiasm was everywhere. As his predecessor described him during the ownership transition, Monaghan "is an avid fan."

To us players, the new owner being a fan proved to be correct. Monaghan wanted to be around his new ballclub—and to interact with us from simply watching our games to playing catch with us. After seeing him around for a while, I sensed his genuine excitement. I do think he was shocked, however, at some surprises—such as the amount of "cussing in baseball" as he put it. Since he was religious, I know it didn't sit well with him, but as Sparky informed him, that kind of language is the reality of the game. You could tell Monaghan was looking forward to his first season of owning the team, though, and he quickly picked up on the fact we were excited, too.

Most of all, we were optimistic because the nucleus of the team not only was back, but also had fully matured into being a cohesive, talented unit. Alan Trammell and Lou Whitaker were unmatched as a double-play combination. Larry Herndon had been consistently productive since coming over from the San Francisco Giants two years before, and Chet Lemon had shown that the deal for Steve Kemp, though seen by some as a gamble at

Difficult Goodbyes

My biggest disappointments of spring training in 1984—and I say this fully admitting you never know how things are going to play out—involved a couple of my closer friends on the club. Glenn Wilson was traded to the Philadelphia Phillies in the deal that landed us Willie Hernandez and Dave Bergman, and on the same day, Rick Leach was released. I had a great relationship with both those guys.

In Rick's case, it's one thing to get traded, but when you get released with a week remaining in spring training, that's difficult to swallow. I thought very strongly and very highly of how hard Rick worked while concentrating on baseball after playing football at the University of Michigan. For him to get released was tough for the rest of the club to deal with when it happened. I was happy for him when he signed and did well with the Toronto Blue Jays. "They told me my contract was too big for me to play at Triple A," Leach said about the Tigers. "Unconditional release, that's rough."

I didn't know that much about the guys we were getting in the trade, but at the time Wilson went to Philly, I thought he had become an integral part of what we were building. In my opinion, he had a bright future, which I imagined was going to be with the Tigers' organization. When we let him go, I was stunned. He was overjoyed, though. "It got to a point," Wilson said, "that I couldn't wait to get to the ballpark every day, hoping this would be the day I got traded. I really wanted it because I'm going to get a chance to play. That's the best news I can get."

John Wockenfuss was also traded in that deal and he was a talented guy, though I know some people liked him while others not so much. So, at that point in parting with those players, it was just a matter of waiting to see what we received in return. *How good would Hernandez be? How useful was Bergman?* I didn't have a crystal ball. I didn't know those guys.

Well, it turned out they were incredible additions. And once again, I had to tip my hat to the decision-makers like general manager Bill Lajoie. They brought in two players who made a definite impact on the 1984 Tigers. It was a great trade. But at the time of the deal, I remember thinking *I hope they know what they're doing.*

As it turned out, they did.

the time, was wise. Chet was an excellent center fielder. Plus, he was a solid hitter.

Kirk Gibson didn't have a good season in 1983, but he still has abundant potential. We were not down on him at all. Al Kaline would work with him on improving as a right fielder. "I've always found him eager to learn," Kaline said.

"I'm not expecting Kirk to be a polished right fielder by Opening Day," Anderson said, "but I do look for a lot of improvement."

The starting rotation was in good hands with Jack Morris, Dan Petry, and Wilcox. We also planned to give unsung Juan Berenger more starts than the 19 he made for us the last year. Juan was an intense competitor. And in whatever role Sparky decided to use him, we still had good ol' Rosie—Dave Rozema—to contribute as a swing man. He could both start and relieve.

As for me, I was coming off what I considered my best season both offensively and defensively. I'd like to think the Tigers had no worries about my position as the team's starting catcher—or about my spot in the batting order.

As I looked around, I saw a good solid, skilled team. We had a shrewd general manager in Bill Lajoie, and you never knew if he might make a deal or two before we broke camp. One of our teammates, John Wockenfuss, had already begun to campaign for a deal, however. He'd seen his name connected to early trade rumors that would send him to the Philadelphia Phillies, where he'd be playing close to his Delaware home. He wanted it to happen. John said he had never asked for a trade in his 10 years with Detroit but would welcome one, even adding that the Tigers "would be doing me a favor." "I've been playing for this club for 10 years and I can't make the average salary?" he said. "That's what I'm angry about. I feel dumped on. I'm not afraid to say these things. You bet I would welcome a trade. My wife saw my name in one of the Philadelphia papers. I guess the Tigers are looking for pitching help. I don't know if it's anything more than a rumor, but like I said, I hope it is."

Even the chance of a trade added a degree of uncertainty to the roster as spring training slid by. *Would there be a deal or not? Who was safe? Who wasn't safe?* It would take a few weeks to find out. But deal or no deal, we could already see ourselves getting better by the moves we had already made. We were going to be a stronger ballclub.

The answer to the lingering trade question arrived on March 24. We made a deal that day, a big deal. And even if we had thought something was going to happen, it came as a shock when it finally did. We sent Wockenfuss and outfielder Glenn Wilson to the Phillies for left-handed reliever Willie Hernandez and Dave Bergman, a first baseman the Phillies had acquired earlier that day from the San Francisco Giants. Some respected names were shocked by the deal. "Willie is on the verge of breaking through," said Cardinals manager Whitey Herzog. "I'm surprised the Phillies traded him."

It was a trade we felt completed us as a team, though we didn't know to what extent at the time. Bergman was a great addition both on the field and inside the clubhouse, while all Willie did was have the greatest season of his life, winning both the Cy Young and Most Valuable Player awards. "No one could have envisioned how much Willie would help, certainly not me," Tom Brookens remembered. "When we first made that trade, I thought, *What the heck did we just do?* It didn't make a lot of sense to me. But it soon did."

As it turned out, everybody we brought in fit into the chemistry of the club. Everybody got along. Everybody pushed one another. Bergie and Darrell were the two lead dogs in helping to hone our mental makeup and our approach to the game. Instantly respected, they assumed somewhat of a leadership role. For instance, they were not afraid to speak up and say to anyone screwing up, "Hey, you need to pay attention to what you're doing!" It was a good thing to hold each other accountable. It made us stronger.

But as Opening Day approached, it was time to briefly look back instead of ahead. As it turned out, we went only 11–17 that spring of '84, our worst spring record in 15 years, but it wasn't indicative of unsolvable problems. In fact, it didn't bother us at all. With the way Sparky ran spring training, winning the games was not important. Sparky just wanted to prepare the team for the season, and part of that approach was for him to look at as many guys as he could in different situations. Obviously, you need to get game ready. But our preparation for the season itself took place on the practice fields away from the exhibition games. Our fundamental drills were essential but became so monotonous. We did them over, and over, and over again. There seemed to be no end to them.

Sparky heard everybody bitching about them, of course. He would listen, then he would pull everybody together and say, "Look, here's the deal. We're *not* going to make any mistakes during the season. We're *not* going to beat ourselves. We're going to make the other teams make mistakes. When game situations arise, you're going to know what to do automatically. To get to that point, if we need to do these drills every single day, that's what we will do so that when the season rolls around, there will be no mistakes made either physically or mentally."

And you know what? It worked.

The preparation for the season was more important than the spring training record. Coming off the 1983 season, a lot of us felt we were knocking on the door, we were ready to compete for a championship, and I think Sparky felt the same way. It wasn't as important in his mind to win spring games as it was to excel at fundamental drills.

Knowing the personalities on our team and watching us going through the preparation for the season, you could feel it coming together in a unified way despite our won-loss record that spring. You never know how quickly you're going to jell. But I believed we would be ready when the bell rang.

Chapter 3

Growing Up in SoCal

We didn't immediately settle in Diamond Bar when we got to California. It was a couple of years before we moved into a house there. The first place I remember living was in a house Dad rented in the town of Rosemead. Like Diamond Bar, it was a considerable distance from downtown Los Angeles. One of the reasons I remember living in the Rosemead house was its location. It was right across from a company called La Victoria Hot Sauce. So instead of running around and climbing trees as a six-year-old—as I remember doing in Pennsylvania—the property of the hot sauce company and the wild smells coming from the factory made for an interesting playground.

The great thing about acclimating to life in California, though, was that we had relatives there. So I had cousins on my mother's side that I got to hang out with. She had a brother who had three children, and shortly after we moved, my mom's sister also moved out from Pennsylvania with her husband and two kids. Suddenly, there were several familiar people around. That made relocating a lot easier.

We eventually moved into a house in Diamond Bar where the entire subdivision had been built on a former cattle ranch, the Diamond Bar Ranch. They just took the name from the ranch and named the town after it. As I recall, there was a housing development on the north end of Diamond Bar and another on the south end. In between was where I hiked and roamed around. Since it wasn't an area for climbing trees, I took up other pursuits like bringing critters home and catching just about everything there was to catch. I caught more snakes and lizards out there than I can remember. I didn't have any tools to catch them with, mind you. I just caught everything with my hands. I drove my parents crazy with what I'd bring home because some of the snakes were poisonous. It's not as if we were looking specifically for anything like rattlesnakes, but if we found something catchable, my pals and I caught it. I built more cages for lizards, toads, and snakes than you can imagine when I was younger, using every scrap of extra building material my dad had. I was always bugging him to buy more screen. The one rule was that I could not bring what I caught into the house. I had to keep my critter collection in the garage or backyard. Luckily, my dad always had a lot of building material lying around.

It wasn't a big house that we moved into, just a small little place, but Dad was good with his tools and he eventually added two rooms onto our house. He could do everything, and what he didn't know how to do, he would read about. He'd get literature on the topic, eventually leading up to having stacks of books lying around on how to do this, how to do that. He tore our house apart and rebuilt it, irritating my mom because it took him quite a while. But when it was done, it looked tremendous. He did an awesome job.

I didn't play organized sports until I was old enough for Little League in Diamond Bar. With my cousins in Rosemead, I had played a lot of pickle and assorted yard games that we invented but nothing organized. Depending on the number of kids available, we'd just make up games. But we were always outside. That's how I was introduced to sports, though. Even at that young age, my cousins brought out the competitor in me. But then we moved to Diamond Bar, and everything was pretty new like the baseball diamonds, and that's where I got into organized baseball.

My first team was called the "Seven Ups." I don't know if it was sponsored by 7UP, the soft drink, or by someone who liked to drink it...or was just a play on words. Even then, I could throw pretty hard, so they let me pitch a little bit. In my first year of Little League—maybe even at the first practice—our coach asked us, "Does anybody here want to catch?" When I looked around, nobody was raising their hand. So, I said, "I'll do it!" I'd never caught before or knew what was involved with playing the position, but I volunteered to do it because I knew I could catch a baseball. I also pitched, but for the most part, that's when I officially became a catcher.

The only elementary school in Diamond Bar was about a mile from our house, maybe a little more, and back then bus service wasn't what it is today, so I basically had to walk to school and back. At least for the first and second grades I had to, but when I was ready for third grade, they had built a school right behind our house.

I loved our neighborhood in Diamond Bar—especially at Halloween. It was the very best area for trick-or-treating. When I got old enough, it became a late-night affair to go from house to house on Halloween, covering some serious ground. I wouldn't come home until I couldn't drag my pillowcase around anymore. I never weighed it, but it was always heavily loaded with candy. My parents also got into the swing of things at Halloween. One year, they had a party with my dad dressing up as Frankenstein, but like everything else he did, he really got into it with a mask, cut-off sleeves, and a pair of platform shoes that made him much taller than he really was. Not only did he go to the party as Frankenstein, though, he handed out candy at our house as Frankenstein, which turned out to be hilarious. Half the kids who came to our door ran away scared.

On weekends or in the summer, my parents also would take us to a lot of Disney movies at a nearby drive-in theater. Drive-ins were big back then—especially in Southern California. You'd roll down the window and place the speaker on it. It was great fun. Plus there'd always be a trip to the snack bar between features to get a treat.

As a young boy, I also remember camping trips my parents would take us on to the Joshua Tree National Park. We'd spend a few nights out in the desert, which was great because I was an outdoorsy kid. There were a lot of giant boulders you could climb over at Joshua Tree. From a safety standpoint, it probably wasn't ideal, but for an active boy, it was a blast. I loved it.

Meeting Arlyne

Arlyne and I didn't get married right out of high school. In fact, we kind of grew apart. She went into the Coast Guard, and I was off playing baseball all the time. So our paths didn't cross for a while after graduation.

Years later, she had come back home and, just to say hello, phoned my mother, who told her the family was going down to the California Angels game that night because the Detroit Tigers were in town. This was in 1978, my first full season in the big leagues. Arlyne was working that day, so my mom said they would leave an extra ticket at will call for her. I knew nothing about these plans, though.

Well, Arlyne got to the ballgame in the first or second inning, but I wasn't playing. I was down in the bullpen in the left-field corner when suddenly I heard someone calling my name. The other guys looked around to see who was calling to me, and they pointed out it was some pretty girl up in the stands. I looked over…and it was Arlyne!

Man, I was absolutely stunned. She was the last person I expected to be there because it had been a few years since we'd seen each other. But we reconnected after the game and stayed in touch from then on. One thing led to another, and the rest is history. It proves you never know who you're going to run into at a ballgame. Even then, we didn't get married right away. We didn't get married until after the 1978 season, in fact. I was playing winter ball for the Mayaguez Indios in Puerto Rico, and Arlyne was there with me. Sheldon Burnside, a pitcher who eventually made it to the majors with the Tigers, was also pitching for Mayaguez, and his fiancé, Cindy, had flown down to join him.

Arlyne and I were planning to fly over to St. Thomas in the Virgin Islands on an off day to get married. So we asked Sheldon and Cindy to accompany us to stand up as our witnesses. They agreed to do it, but on the morning of the flight, they announced they were going to get married, too! We had learned that a judge in the territorial court building could legally do it, so we all flew to St. Thomas. Before the ceremony we bought wedding bands in one of the zillion jewelry stores there are in Charlotte Amalie, the capital city, and we all got married in T-shirts and shorts. Arlyne and I went first. Then we switched spots with Sheldon and Cindy. They were our best man and maid of honor, and vice versa.

We had our post-wedding meal at a nearby Dairy Queen. The wedding cake was whatever you wanted off the menu. I probably had a hot fudge sundae. Sheldon and Cindy live in Montgomery, Alabama, and are still married to this day. They had three kids and now have a lot of grandkids just like we do.

Arlyne remembers how we met a bit differently than I do, though. This is her version of it: "So Lance has told you how we met, that our lockers in high school were next to each other. What he might not have told you is that he was very flirtatious and friendly. I was the quieter one. He was always slamming his locker door to get my attention. Plus, it seemed to me like he had a different girlfriend every week. I was a junior varsity cheerleader the year we met, then moved up to varsity my last two years in high school, so I saw all his games in all his sports. By the time he was a junior—don't let him fool you—he was the best athlete in the school.

"I was always close to his family. I had even lived at his house for a while when things got rough for me at home. His mother, Dee, and I remained close—more like girlfriends instead of two women 21 years apart. She knew the situation at my house, which sometimes wasn't good. She told me to always consider their home as my place of refuge. I never forgot that. And we remained close even in the post-high-school years when Lance and I didn't see much of each other. I just always loved her spunk. I have to say, though, she's a sports fanatic, someone who loved the Pittsburgh Pirates back in Pennsylvania. When she was young, for instance, she was so saddened when Pirates slugger Ralph Kiner got engaged that she said she wore her hair ribbons in a way that, to her, resembled half-mast. Dee could get pretty noisy at games, though, yelling at umpires. Sometimes it was better if she sat in the outfield bleachers or on the grass, where the umps couldn't hear her. She was an umpire's worst nightmare. Lance agreed."

And she did, too. "I would embarrass him royally," Dee told the *Midland Times-Herald* in 2007. "But I come from the East Coast. We yell."

What I also loved were my experiences with the 4-H Club. I had a friend named Steve whose family was involved with cattle ranching. I enjoyed going out to his house just to do the chores. I was the hang-around buddy who helped with just about everything they did with the cattle. I loved being around the livestock so much that Steve's family contacted my parents about me getting involved with 4-H. That would mean I could buy my own steer and enter it into nearby shows like the L.A. County Fair, which I did for a number of years.

It really was a labor of love. I had several different breeds of cattle over the years, a different animal each summer, and when the show was over, I'd sell it like everyone else would do. Parting with a living project I'd grown close to and cared for wasn't easy, though. I never came close to finishing first for showing my steer, but I sure learned a lot and one year I finally did win a ribbon for how my steer looked. Even now, I remember it being a great looking Hereford. I loved 4-H because it was a wonderful teaching tool for kids. When my parents told me I could get my first steer, that might have been the happiest moment of my first 15 years.

I didn't like the selling part of raising a steer, though, because after you had cared for it, fed it, and groomed it like a pet, you had to sell it, knowing it would get butchered. One year some good friends of my parents were the ones who bought my steer, and when they eventually invited us over for dinner, they said it was my steer that we were eating as steak. *My steer!* I couldn't do it. That would be like eating your own dog. I refused the steak they gave me. I just couldn't do it.

The saddest moment of my younger years was probably when my sister Cheri, short for Cheryl, was diagnosed with rheumatoid arthritis in just the fourth or fifth grade. I was younger, so I didn't fully understand what it meant at the time, but I could see how the disease affected her physically. She'd always been as active as I was, but it meant her ability to keep up would change. When I saw what the onset of arthritis was doing to her, that was one of the most difficult times of my childhood. I went on being active, but she slowly declined. And she's now deceased.

I always thought of myself as being physically fit, but I don't think I actually worked out until I got to high school. My introduction to weight-lifting was the summer before my freshman year. By then I was playing all the sports. I considered myself an athlete, but I can't say any of them could be called my first love. As time went on, baseball became the sport I enjoyed more than football or basketball. All things considered, I was better at baseball than the other two.

I wouldn't ever say I was the best athlete in school, but I was one of the better ones.

When I got into professional baseball, it always seemed I got criticized for being too laid-back. I had never been a guy to jump around and bounce off the walls, but in high school, I actually was pretty high-spirited. I was very active and aggressive. In basketball, for instance, I often got criticized for being too aggressive. Opposing coaches would yell at the refs to call fouls on me. As a result, I got into a few scuffles playing sports when I was younger, but nothing you'd call a knockdown, drag-out fight. It was more or less a difference of opinion I had with other guys.

I can't say I ever was a great student because for me my focus was elsewhere—mostly on time out of the classroom. Schooling to me was a pain in the butt. I probably should have dedicated more time to it. My parents were pretty strict about homework. I was expected to do it, and if I didn't, I would be reminded in one way or another that I needed to get it done. Looking back, though, I did just enough to get by. I was an average student. No better, no worse.

Getting my driver's license as soon as I could was huge because it gave me the freedom to get to and from my school, Walnut High School, which was about 10 to 15 miles away from my house. There were times before getting my license when I had to walk home from school because my mom didn't drive at the time, and if I couldn't hitch a ride, walking home was the only way to get there. Not that it was like walking home in a foot of snow, mind you. I mean it was Southern California, so it was no big burden, but it did take some extra time.

When I got my license, my dad bought me some cheapo car that he fixed up. He sanded it down and painted it himself, and I probably shouldn't refer to it as a "cheapo" car because it wasn't cheap to him. Money wasn't exactly growing on trees for us back then, and I couldn't have cared less how it looked or how old it was if it enabled me to get to and from school, which it did. Just a few weeks after I got my license, though, I smashed my dad's car pretty badly. He had a Toyota and one night he let me drive it to a friend's house as long as I was going to be home by 11:00 PM. I said that was no problem, but I wasn't wearing a watch and I lost track of the time. There was no traffic that night, but I still wasn't sure what time it was on my way home when I came to an intersection where I was going to turn right. A car going from my left to right went through before I turned, but as I turned right, I tried to glance at the time on a wall clock in a gas station to my left. My head was turned away from the road in other words. Then all of a sudden—bam!—I smashed into something.

It freaked me out for a second because I didn't know what had happened. There had been like no traffic at all, but the one car, which had gone through the intersection before I turned, had pulled over and come to a stop near the corner. So, as I was looking left to see the time, I plowed right into him. Well, the other driver freaked out and started yelling at me. To make matters worse, my radio, which was blasting out, had jammed in the collision. So this guy screamed at me to turn my "damn radio down" and also yelled at me because my car had locked bumpers with his, meaning he couldn't move. The scene was complete chaos.

As it turned out, he had no insurance, so he didn't want the cops involved, which I agreed to, even though my dad was a cop. I thought my father was going to kill me anyway for smashing up his car, but it turned out he was cool about it, and we eventually got the car fixed. That just represented his overall temperament, however. I never can recall him losing his temper. That's the way he handled things. Maybe he was disappointed to see the damage, but his reaction was first to make sure everyone involved was unhurt—and then to get the car out of there. He never yelled at me. The other guy in the accident, though, had the nerve to claim he had suffered whiplash in the collision and tried to sue us, so my driving career didn't get off to a real good start.

I met my future wife in high school, even though we weren't in the same grade. It took a few years, though, before we got married. Arlyne was a year ahead of me, but because her last name was Nolan, and mine was Parrish, our lockers, which were assigned alphabetically, were close to each other. That's how we initially met—at our lockers—and I'm sure she made a much better impression on me than I did on her. She was beautiful, always dressed great, was fun to talk to. But because she was a sophomore and I was just a freshman, I felt I had no chance of connecting with her. It shows you, though, that you never know what might happen.

I think it helped that her brother Linton played sports and was in my grade, so at least we had that in common. Anyway, by the time I got out of high school, the direction of my life was taking shape, both personally and professionally. At least, I hoped it was. After all, following graduation, the baseball draft was only days away, and one team seemed very interested in me.

Chapter 4

Feeling a Draft

The team I thought was interested in me was the California Angels. But even when it was approaching my senior year, I had no real knowledge of the baseball draft. I was very naive throughout the entire process. I tried to take it one step at a time, but that was sometimes difficult. I had players from other teams coming up to me, saying I was going to be a first-round pick: "This is the amount of money you should ask for. Don't take anything less."

But all of that was the furthest thing from my mind. All I knew as the draft approached was that I had signed a letter of intent to play football at UCLA. But I also planned to play baseball there because both sports were important to me. I was still very much a high school kid. But my whole senior year was interesting, to say the least—interesting and busy—with me competing in three sports (football, basketball, and baseball) plus going on football recruiting trips and knowing there were scouts in the stands watching my baseball games. I also went to some local workouts for the top area players that were conducted by various major league clubs.

The last workout I went to was held by the San Diego Padres. There were a lot of talented players there, guys like Garry Templeton and Lonnie Smith. As events would unfold, they both were drafted ahead of me in the first round, and Garry and I would end up years later on opposing teams in the World Series.

What I knew at the time about my baseball future—and, believe me, it's all I knew—was that on all my football recruiting trips I stipulated that I also intended to continue playing baseball. That luckily wasn't a problem for any of the schools I visited. And it turned out that all of them—UCLA, USC, Cal-Berkeley, Arizona State, and Nebraska—offered me letters of intent.

I was 6'2" or 6'3" my senior year and pretty fit, not small in other words, but I remember thinking on those trips that the college football players I saw looked like monsters compared to me. I wanted to play quarterback, but I was recruited as both a quarterback and defensive back. In high school I had played on both sides of the ball.

Cal-Berkeley wasn't all that high on my list, but I seemed to be high on theirs. Their football team came down to the L.A. area my senior year to play UCLA at the Los Angeles Coliseum, but that game was going to be on a Saturday, and my high school team was playing on Friday night against one of our rivals. The coach recruiting me arranged it—I don't even think it would be legal today—for the Cal marching band to play during our half-time program on the field. He said they needed the practice anyway so it might as well be at my high school game.

I ended up not seeing it because I was in the locker room at halftime, but I was told by my friends and family who were in the stands that, suddenly, out of our end zone came the Cal-Berkeley marching band, one of the best in the nation. My dad was sitting with a friend of his from Pennsylvania who had no idea what was going on. After halftime he turned to my dad and said, "That's one of the best high school bands I've ever seen." He thought the Cal-Berkeley band was our band. My dad got a big laugh out of that.

To be honest, though, I really wasn't interested in going far away from home. So my decision came down to UCLA and USC. It was the connection I made with the people at UCLA that convinced me to favor them, but I paid attention over the years to which school had the better teams in the two sports, and it always seemed to be USC.

I thought I had a really good workout for the Angels at their workout day. Everything went well for me, but while not knowing if I was going to

Tina Turner

Back in my minor league years, I had a financial advisor who also counseled some celebrities and movie stars. I was home in California one winter between baseball seasons when, out of the blue, he called me and asked if I was available to help him with something that could be fun. I replied that it all depended on what "something fun" would be.

He said there was an opportunity for me to go down to the television studios in Burbank where they were filming *The Hollywood Squares*. One of his clients, Tina Turner, was going to be on the show, but because she and her husband Ike were going through a difficult divorce, she felt she needed a bodyguard. I said, "Are you serious? I've never done anything like that. I wouldn't know the first thing about how to be her bodyguard."

But he assured me it was nothing that would put me in harm's way. I was still pretty wary about it, though. I mean, isn't being in harm's way the very definition of being a bodyguard? "No, no, no," he answered, "she just wants someone to walk with her from her dressing room to the set where they are filming the show, a short walk, in other words."

The plan was for me to stand by her dressing room door, then escort her to the set…and maybe meet a few celebrities. I still wasn't sure, to tell you the truth. It didn't sound like something I wanted to get involved in. But he kept insisting it would be fun with no threat of danger, so I ended up saying, "Why not?"

When filming day arrived, I went to the studios in Burbank. To this day, I can't tell you who else I met. They didn't make a lasting impression on me. And after one day, it was over. I was never her official bodyguard.

It must have been before my rookie season in the big leagues because I remember going to New York for the first time the next year, and when the media gathered around my locker, instead of asking me any baseball questions, they just wanted to know what it had been like to be Turner's bodyguard. It was kind of embarrassing, to be honest with you. This is what I told them, and this is what I still say about that episode of my life: "Trust me: Tina Turner wouldn't know me if she fell over me on the street. It was one day and out. I never saw her again."

For years, I downplayed it when someone would bring it up, but I couldn't escape it. I don't know how it got around so fast because I never said much about it after it happened, but it's like I've told the story a hundred times in the years since.

get drafted by the Angels or anyone else for that matter, my focus remained on going to UCLA. Then on draft day, I was in algebra class when my baseball coach knocked on the classroom door, asking if he could speak to me in the hallway. I walked out to see what he wanted, and he quickly shook my hand, telling me I had been the No. 1 pick of the Detroit Tigers. I was both shocked and disappointed, to tell you the truth. I thought, *so much for thinking I'd made a good impression on the Angels*, my hometown team. They drafted a shortstop from Louisiana, Mike Miley, at No. 10 in the first round—he was later killed in a tragic automobile accident—and I went No. 16 to the Tigers.

I was excited about being drafted, sure, but I knew nothing about the city of Detroit or the Detroit Tigers. At the time I had never even heard of Al Kaline. I remember going down to my school's athletic building after classes that day, and some of the coaches down there asked me what I thought about possibly playing for Ralph Houk, the manager. With a blank look on my face, I replied, "Who's Ralph Houk?"

They looked at me like I was a creature with four eyes. But that's how naive I was about professional baseball. It was a different time with no cable, no ESPN, no Internet, and just one game a week on TV. I didn't even read the sports pages. I knew about a few players, but Houk? I knew nothing about who the managers and coaches were on any team in the majors.

The only time I'd ever had any reason to think about the Tigers was on the day I worked out for the Angels at the stadium in Anaheim. We used the visiting locker room and in the hamper, where the dirty uniforms were thrown, was one belonging to Bill Freehan on top of the heap. It turned out the Tigers were in town on the same day as my workout in 1974.

I had pitched and caught my whole career from Little League to high school, but I was drafted as a third baseman. The way that came about was because we had needed someone to play third my senior year. I had injured the middle finger of my throwing hand, so I couldn't catch for a while, and because we didn't have anyone else to play third, my coach threw me out there. I think I made throwing errors on the first three balls hit to me. I airmailed every throw over the first baseman's head because of my finger injury. I didn't switch back to catcher until I went to the instructional league in Florida after my rookie season in the Appalachian League in Bristol, Virginia. Despite hitting only .213 for Bristol and making 20 errors in 55 games, I was the All-Star third baseman because I hit 11 home runs in just 253 at-bats—the most home runs by any third baseman in the league. There were three hitters in the league with more home runs, but all of them were first basemen.

Well, the next thing I knew after getting drafted was that I had an area scout, Jack Deutsch, at my house negotiating with me. It was happening that quickly: I was facing the decision of wanting to go to college or playing professional baseball. It was a huge decision. It really was. I didn't know what to do. I loved playing baseball, but I was going to get that chance in college as well. A conversation with my dad helped before any money was mentioned because he told me not to rush into it and to do what I really wanted. If that meant professional baseball, I should go do it. This was my golden opportunity.

It was an exciting time but also nerve-wracking. Sports were huge for me, but they weren't my everything. When I wasn't competing in some game or other or practicing, I was out roaming the wide, open spaces or working at the 4-H club. When I was doing that, my mind was 1,000 miles away from whatever sport I was involved with at the time. That's how I lived my life. It was almost like being on a farm. I loved playing sports, but I had other interests as well. There was a decision to make, though, and I wasn't 100 percent confident about the best thing to do. My mom was pretty much on board with what my dad was telling me. She just wanted me to be happy with my choice. In her wise opinion, it wasn't as if there was a bad decision to make. Either one was going to be all right.

Deutsch was the first person from the Detroit club to contact me after the draft. He was sent to my house to negotiate with me and obviously to sign me. But it's not like I was ready to negotiate. The whole process was totally foreign to me. Anyway, my dad and I were in the living room when he showed up. After some small talk, he told me what the Tigers were about to offer me, which was $60,000. It sounded to me like a lot of money, but I had no idea how it compared to any offer the other first-round picks were getting. That kind of information simply wasn't available at the time. The words one of my coaches had said kept coming back to me. He was among those cautioning me not to take anything less than $100,000. But that amount was way beyond anything I could comprehend. He might as well have been talking about $1 million.

The thing is I still hadn't made up my mind that professional baseball was what I wanted to do. If I signed, I was going to be on a plane in a few days, flying across the country to join my new team, or I could stay in my own backyard for the summer and play football and baseball at UCLA. So, I went back and forth about it. I'd just turned 18 or was in the last days of still being 17 and I'd never been away from my parents for any length of time. Leaving for several months if I signed was the sudden reality staring back at me. The Tigers wanted an answer, though.

Clearly, I had to come back with some reply. So I said it was a fair offer, but that I wasn't quite ready to make a decision. It's not what they wanted to hear. Maybe the Tigers thought I was holding out for more money, which was never my intention. So Jack, the scout at my house, immediately said, "This is all there is. This is all they have to offer you. There's nothing else."

I replied, "No, no, no, I'm not asking for more money. I just need time to consider all my options."

That's when my dad chimed in and wanted to have another conversation with me in the back room. When it was just the two of us, he said "$60,000? Do you know how much money that is, Lance?" He was ready to pull his hair out.

I told him he wasn't making the decision any easier for me because once my mind was made up either way it was going to affect my life in a huge way. So, I did not come out of that discussion with my father ready to sign. I still needed more time. But we agreed that Jack the scout should return in a couple of days, which gave me enough time to think it over, which I did. Well, the first thing he said when he came back to the house for the second visit was that the Tigers were ready to increase their offer to $67,500. *But I hadn't asked for more money!* I hadn't asked for anything else at all. It struck me as funny, so I just started laughing. By then, however, which Jack didn't know, I had made up my mind to sign with the Tigers, so I said, "Okay, great, I'm ready to go."

I had decided that my best opportunity as an athlete would be in professional baseball. But he probably thought the extra money had decided it. I've wondered from time to time how good I might have been in football if I had gone to UCLA. Obviously, there's no way of knowing, but working in my favor was that I enjoyed the conditioning required for football, and that I never doubted my talent as a football player. Plus, I always bought into what I thought was the benefit of making myself bigger and stronger. I believed in conditioning because how could it possibly hurt you?

I knew I wasn't going to be the fastest guy at whatever I did, but I damn well could be the strongest if I worked at it. In any case I signed when Jack came back to the house for that second visit and I remember thinking as he left, *Okay, let's see where this takes me.*

Chapter 5

A Scorching April

O ur season record was 3–0 on the first Saturday of April in Chicago when Jack Morris took to the mound at Comiskey Park. We were off to a good start but truthfully nothing more than that. The baseball world wouldn't really notice us for another week or so.

But our first two games in Minnesota had ended well, as had the first game of the series against the White Sox. Morris, Dan Petry, and Milt Wilcox all won their first starts. Now it was Jack's turn to pitch again—albeit on three days' rest. We had won the games against the Minnesota Twins by comfortable scores (8–1 and 7–3), but the Friday night game against the Sox wasn't easy. We scored three runs in the first inning off Rich Dotson, a 22-game winner in 1983, but he shut us down after that. Even so, we led 3–1 when Willie Hernandez took over. And after the Sox scored once in the eighth to climb to within a run, Willie retired the side in order in the ninth for our third win in a row as well as his first save as a Tiger. Not bad, considering he still was feeling the effects of the flu, including dizziness.

Jack set out to make it four straight victories for us in the next game. He'd been good in his first start—even better than good—allowing one run on five hits in Minnesota. What had been impressive about him in that outing was his control. He didn't allow a walk. That was a relatively rare occurrence for Morris. In just four of his 37 starts in 1983, he hadn't allowed a walk. So, his control was off to a good start. As was he. And with a 3–1 record in previous seasons, he generally had pitched well at Comiskey Park. But those stats would soon mean next to nothing.

Beginning the game efficiently, Jack retired the side in order in the first inning, striking out Carlton Fisk and Harold Baines. In the bottom of the second, he again retired the side in order, chalking up another strikeout. From all appearances Morris was on his game. Plus, it helped that Chet Lemon staked him to a 2–0 lead in the second inning with a home run off Floyd Bannister. Jack had an exceptional splitter that day. It was really biting. He mowed down three more in a row in the third inning. He now had four strikeouts without allowing a walk—or a hit. But his control wandered off in the fourth when he walked Rudy Law to begin the inning. Law then stole second. To make matters worse, Morris also walked Fisk and Baines to load the bases with Greg Luzinski coming up. That got a few people nervous. Morris would later say, though you couldn't tell it by how his plate appearances went, that Baines was the toughest hitter in the lineup for him. "If you look at the numbers, Harold probably got as many hits off me as anybody ever," Jack said. "He knew how to read all my pitches."

The record shows his recollection was nearly correct. Baines had 31 career hits off Morris. Robin Yount had 34. But anyway, the Sox now had the bases loaded with no outs—and even a double-play grounder to an infielder would have scored a run. But Luzinski hit a topper back to the mound instead. Jack tossed the ball to me to get Law at the plate for the first out, then I threw it to Barbaro Garbey at first to get Luzinski, completing the double play. To get out of that jam was amazing. Buoyed by the reprieve, Morris struck out Ron Kittle to end the fourth inning. That escape was the turning point, Jack said. From then on, he felt "so positive." Dave Duncan, one of Chicago's coaches, would later say that the fourth inning was the only chance for the Sox to break the game open, but Jack had made excellent pitches to get out of it. Indeed, he had.

We scored two more runs in the top of the fifth, stretching our lead to 4–0, and Jack got through a hitless bottom of the fifth despite another walk. His control was far from perfect that day, and to tell you the truth,

Campbell's Call

It wasn't long after the final out of Jack Morris' no-hitter against the White Sox in Chicago that Tigers president Jim Campbell called our clubhouse. The call went to Sparky Anderson's desk, but Sparky wasn't in his office at the time, so one of the clubhouse kids answered the phone. It was Campbell wanting to congratulate Jack.

However, the young man who answered the phone didn't know what Morris looked like. So, guessing incorrectly, he mistook me for Jack and came out to the players' area and said that Campbell was calling me. I, of course, reacted by saying, "No way!" But I took the call anyway.

I didn't say a whole lot, but Campbell did. He went on and on about the no-hitter and how there might be something extra for it in my next check. Thinking he must have really liked the game I called, I figured he was giving me some credit. It wasn't until the very end of the conversation when he said, "And when you struck out that last batter, I nearly fell off my chair," that I muttered "uh oh" to myself.

"Mr. Campbell, this isn't Jack," I informed him. "This is Lance."

At that point he started bellowing: "What the hell are you doing on the phone?"

And when I asked if I was still going to get something extra in my next check, that only made matters worse. "No, you're not the one I want," he yelled. "Go get Jack!"

I put the phone down at that point and walked away. But I was pissed. I never did go get Jack for him. I found out later, though, that Morris did get a bonus. I was happy about that because he deserved it. All I ever got for catching that game was an earful.

I had seen him have better stuff, but he was laser focused from the first pitch on. Kittle said Morris went after the Sox the entire game, challenging them in every at-bat That's not all Kittle had to say, though. After the game he commented humorously about Jack: "I'd rather have watched him bowl a 300 game."

When he retired the side in order in the sixth with two more strikeouts, Jack noticed on the scoreboard for the first time that he had not allowed a hit. Previously in his career, he had not been the type of pitcher to carry a no-hitter deep into a game. Even in 1980, when he one-hit the Twins for the low-hit game of his career, it had been Rob Wilfong, the second batter Morris faced, who had gotten the hit. At the same time Morris noticed he hadn't allowed a hit, a heckler behind our dugout started yelling at him, trying to jinx him with loud reminders that he was working on a no-hitter. Jack, at first, paid no attention to him. As a rule, he didn't let people like that bother him. But now that he was six innings into it with three to go, Jack started thinking seriously about a no-hitter. No Tigers pitcher since Jim Bunning in 1958 had thrown one.

After a leadoff walk to Luzinski to start the seventh for the Sox, Kittle flied out to right, but Tom Paciorek followed with a hard liner to first base, where Dave Bergman had just replaced Garbey. Initially, it looked like Paciorek's liner was headed for right field, but playing off the bag because Luzinski was slow, Bergman brought it down with a diving grab. When pinch-hitter Greg Walker followed with a grounder to first, there were six outs to go. Jack said, "I remember thinking, *This is meant to be because balls that typically would have been hits weren't becoming hits.*"

Pitch count was never an issue in the game for Morris. Just the opposite. It was always difficult to take the ball out of his hand anyway. He'd been known to pitch as many as 11 innings (1982 vs. the New York Yankees) if a game was on the line. This time, though, it wasn't only a game that was on the line; it was his quest for a spot in the history books.

As he came off the field after the bottom of the seventh, you could tell Jack's confidence was strong. You could even hear it in his voice. For instance, when the obnoxious heckler got on him again about still having a no-hitter in the works, Morris looked up at the would-be tormentor and said, "Yeah, I know, now watch me get the next six guys."

Take that, fella.

No wonder pitching coach Roger Craig said Jack had "a killer instinct" that day. Or as Morris said about his reply to the heckler, he wasn't defying superstition; he was just being cocky. But in that case, Jack's cockiness was a plus.

When the bottom of the eighth began, it was none other than Jerry Hairston coming up for the Sox, pinch hitting for Scott Fletcher. We all remembered Hairston ending Wilcox's bid for a perfect game with an out to go the year before; would he ruin Morris' hopes of throwing a no-hitter as well?

We quickly got our answer: no, he would not. Hairston hit a grounder to first for the first out. Bergman made a diving stop of the ball. "When you have to dive to save a no-hitter, you dive," he said. "I'm just glad it went into my glove."

I remember thinking that in most no-hitters, there probably had to be a couple of good defensive plays. We were seeing that happen in this game. After the second out, Law ended the inning with another grounder to first. Bergman had been busy at first base since entering the game. Four of the six outs had been hit to him. I wish we had been able to give Jack more time to rest between innings, but we rapidly went down in order in the top of the ninth. The pace of the game didn't present a problem, however. Morris marched right back out to the mound to finish the job. As he told us before the bottom of the ninth, "I've come this far, I have to do it."

Standing in his way was the heart of the White Sox lineup. Fisk had been unusually quiet with two strikeouts and a walk, but here was a chance for him to cause some trouble. He didn't, though. He grounded out to first instead. Fisk would later praise "the devastating change-up" Jack had that day.

I was pretty confident Morris would close out the no-hitter at that point. He hadn't lost any velocity and he looked just as strong as he'd been at the start. With two outs to go, he now had to face Baines. It had been cold and breezy all day, but Jack said the weather "invigorated" him. Apparently, that was still its effect. Baines dribbled a pitch back to the mound for a routine second out. With a *Game of the Week* television audience looking on and a shivering crowd of 24,616 at Comiskey Park now pulling for him, Morris faced Luzinski with one out to go. The big guy wanted to make up for his bases-loaded double-play in the fourth, no doubt, so he made sure to get a long look at all the pitches in this plate appearance.

Jack, meanwhile, was so focused on securing the final out that on one pitch he rushed himself and fell off the mound. But on a close 3–2 pitch to Luzinski, he walked him as the crowd groaned. I groaned, too. I thought home-plate umpire Durwood Merrill squeezed Jack. I mean here we were with a no-hitter on the line. Whether that pitch was a fraction of an inch out of the zone or a fraction within was clearly close. When I caught the ball, I even jumped up, thinking it was the last pitch of the game. To me, there was no way it wasn't a strike. Yet Durwood called it a ball. Morris was animated in his reaction to the call, wanting it so badly. "I jumped around and did some crazy things," he said. "I'll go to my grave knowing it was a strike."

Fortunately, Jack got past the call. With two outs and Luzinski now on first, that brought up Kittle, who was hitless in his first nine at-bats of the season at that point. Just hoping to make contact, he failed to do so. On Morris' 120th pitch of the game, Kittle struck out swinging—and Jack had his no-hitter. The crowd gave him a standing ovation, and we all rushed to the mound to congratulate him. What a wonderful moment it was, one to remember. With that we were 4–0 and feeling great about ourselves.

But April had just begun.

I shouldn't continue, however, without giving our victory on Opening Night in Minnesota the attention it deserves. What we enjoyed most about that game was Darrell Evans' excitement about hitting a home run in his first game as a Tiger—after failing to hit a home run for his new team the entire spring. Not one to conceal his feelings, Darrell said it was the most excited he's ever been about hitting a home run—and that it "meant as much to me as anything ever has." He added: "It's the best first week of baseball I've ever had…Everything is going right for me."

We were happy for Darrell. To hit a home run right away broke some of the tension he must have been feeling. I mean, as a newcomer, you want to contribute as fast as possible. He'd been brought in to hit home runs and—*boom*—he went deep in his first game. It was a good feeling for everyone actually. We were thinking, *Yeah, that's why we got this guy. That's why he's here.*

Speaking of newcomers contributing, it was Garbey's turn the next day in the last game before our home opener. Driving in three runs, including two on a pinch-hit double in the fifth inning, Barbaro was a big reason we were able to spoil Tom Seaver's American League debut.

Everything about Garbey was calm and cool, though, like a golfer with a smooth swing. He'd been through some tough times, having to leave his family in Cuba, but was always in a good mood. It didn't take long for him to fit right in. "I want his bat in there as much as possible," Sparky Anderson commented. "I said he was going to hit up here, and he is."

After that game it was time at long last for us to head home, where on a sunny day we didn't skip a beat in front of our own fans. With Evans hitting a three-run home run in the first inning off Dave Stewart—on his first swing at Tiger Stadium, in fact—we upped our record to 6–0 behind a complete-game, four-hitter from Petry. A welcoming Tiger Stadium crowd of 51,238 had a great time.

Not that he thought it was possible, but Morris' bid for consecutive no-hitters didn't last long in the next game. On his fifth pitch, he allowed a leadoff single in the first inning to Mickey Rivers of the Texas Rangers. But with the help of home runs from Alan Trammell and Lemon in the sixth, he won his third start in a row 9–4.

Meanwhile, I was hitting just .154 at that point, but not hurting us—thankfully. Then again, nothing was hurting us. We were 7–0. Sure enough, though, in the next game I hit my first home run in a 13–9 victory against the Boston Red Sox at Fenway Park. But the home run didn't get nearly as much attention in media coverage that day as the fact I dared to wear No. 13 (my usual number) on Friday, April 13—and that we sent 13 hitters to the plate in the top of the first, not to mention that the two teams combined for 13 runs in the first inning. I accounted for all three outs in our eight-run first inning with a strikeout and double-play grounder to short. But now that we had set a Tigers' team record with an 8–0 start, superstition wasn't exactly foremost on our minds.

We knew we'd eventually lose, of course, but we went into each game wanting to keep the winning streak alive as long as possible. Not every game was a breeze, mind you. Sometimes we needed a break—such as the one we received in Game Nine. After Jorge Orta's three-run home run on a mistake pitch off Morris in the eighth inning at home against the Kansas City Royals, we scored the winning run in the 10th on an error at second base by the usually reliable and sure-handed Frank White. "I screwed it up," White said after the game.

Meanwhile, about our start, Morris said it best. "I have a good feeling about this team, but it's hard not to when you're 9–0."

Our winning streak ended the next day. On April 19, in a weather make-up game, we lost rather flatly to Kansas City 5–2. I suppose you could say it wasn't even that close as Kirk Gibson's solo home run in the ninth accounted for our second run. "Nobody told me they were unbeatable," Royals pitcher Bret Saberhagen said about us after winning his first major league start.

The loss stopped us two triumphs short of tying an American League record, which was too bad, but as Petry said after the game about keeping it in perspective: "This team is too good to worry about one loss."

We wanted to bounce right back after the defeat, naturally, but falling behind 2–1 at home after six innings to the White Sox wasn't the most direct way of going about it. We dug deep to tie it on Larry Herndon's RBI single in the seventh, then won it on my disputed two-out single in the ninth with Lou Whitaker on third. Kittle claimed he caught the ball, but it was ruled a trap instead. With 10 hits in the last five games, though, I felt my swing might finally be emerging from its hibernation.

We got a great effort in the next game from Dave Rozema, who blanked the White Sox on two hits in six innings. Rosie hadn't won a game since July 31 of the 1983 season, but while downing the Sox 4–1, he got the better of reigning Cy Young Award winner LaMarr Hoyt, who entered the game with a 15–0 record in 16 starts since the previous July. "I'm trying to change my reputation," Rozema, whom Craig called a man-child, told the *Detroit Free Press*. "I was hurting my career by having too much fun. Who wants a player who goes out all the time, getting blasted? The only way I can stay out of gossip columns for doing things wrong is by doing things right. I've gotten over that stage of my life. My system is flushed out now. I'm going to bed early. I'm feeling good."

With that game we were squarely back on track after our first loss, feeling confident that we were a good, solid baseball team. On any given day, we could score a bunch of runs and beat your brains in or we could win a tight, low-scoring game. In other words, we could win in a lot of different ways.

Maybe if we'd been struggling instead of winning, we wouldn't have even played the scheduled game on April 22, Easter Sunday. The weather was terrible. With high winds and a temperature in the low 40s, everyone was miserable, especially during an 83-minute weather delay. But after a 9–1 victory, we ended up far less miserable than the White Sox. Juan Berenguer made his first start of the season in that game—his first appearance, in fact— and tossed seven shutout innings. A three-run home run from Gibson in the first got us off to a strong start, then five runs on seven hits in the eighth gave us a much more comfortable lead. With the Twins coming to town next, we were still rolling. "Long layoffs can really hurt a pitcher," Craig said of Berenguer having to wait until our 13th game before making his first appearance. "But Juan kept a good attitude. When it came time for him to pitch, he was determined to do well in rain, snow, or 110 degrees."

As it turned out far from 110 degrees, Berenguer pitched in rain and snow and had to get through that long weather delay, but nothing bothered him. During that incredible start, reminders of how difficult it was for opposing teams to entertain a sliver of a chance of beating us occurred from time to time—and one of those reminders helped us in the first game of a doubleheader at Tiger Stadium. We trailed the Twins 5–3, heading into the bottom of the ninth when Gibson's leadoff triple off Ron Davis steered us in the direction of a comeback. Then Whitaker's two-out single, driving Bergman in from second, finished it off. We won 6–5. After my three-run home run in the fifth off Frank Viola, we didn't need late heroics to win the second game that day against Minnesota, but three innings of shutout relief from Aurelio Lopez certainly helped. As Sparky said, "Whenever you win a doubleheader, it's something special."

When asked if we were a team of destiny, Gibson replied, "We think we are." Or as Craig noted: the fact we had come from behind was a sign of champions.

The shellshocked Twins couldn't believe what they'd just seen, however—two frustrating one-run losses in games they could have won. After the second game, an angry Davis barked at reporters, "Don't even talk to me!"

Incredibly enough, we were 14–1 as we headed to Texas. Among the many traits I liked about our team at that point was how we never took our foot off the pedal. If we had a team down, we rubbed their faces in it—figuratively, of course, like in the next game against the Rangers. My three-run home run off Stewart in the seventh stretched our lead from 3–2 to 6–2, but we didn't stop there. Garbey doubled in another run later that inning, and Tom Brookens singled in Garbey. Plus, after my home run, Gibson singled and stole both second and third. That's what I mean about keeping our foot on the pedal all the time. All three of our home runs in that game, by the way, were hit into a strong wind blowing in from center. Not even Mother Nature was stopping us. "This club is playing the best I've ever seen in my life," said Anderson, who had managed the Cincinnati Reds' Big Red Machine teams.

Keeping up the pressure, we began the next game in Texas with four runs in the first inning off Frank Tanana. And once again, Lopez slammed the door with two-and-two-thirds innings of shutout relief. The strength of our bullpen was really showing at that point. In our first 17 games, Lopez and Hernandez combined for three victories and four saves. "All we want," Wilcox said before we left Texas, "is for this to last another three or four months."

In the other dugout, Larry Parrish of the Rangers muttered about us that "these guys could fall out of a tree and land on a pillow."

So, we brought a 16–1 record home to play the Cleveland Indians but lost our first game back. We made them earn it, though. In a game that lasted nearly six hours—after we had arrived home at 6:00 AM from Texas—we lost 8–4 in 19 innings. Despite bouncing back with the tying run in the

10th inning, we had nothing left after allowing four runs on three errors in the 19th. Besides, it was almost 2:00 AM. No excuses, but we were exhausted. "I honestly think we were pooped," Sparky said. I went 1-for-8 in that game, catching all 19 innings."

So now we had two games remaining in April, and what would be a good way to finish the month? With a couple of pitching gems, of course, which we thought were possible, knowing that Morris and Petry would be starting. Jack was up first. Into his Saturday afternoon assignment against Cleveland at Tiger Stadium, he took a 4–0 record with a 1.98 ERA. But his excellent start only got better with a 6–2 complete-game victory, in which he allowed just three hits. No opposing runner advanced past first base against Morris that day after the fourth inning.

Then again, Jack pitched like the well-rested pitcher he was. He hadn't gone to Texas with us, so he'd been spared the 6:00 AM arrival back home on Friday morning. And in the 19-inning game we played Friday night, he was allowed to leave the ballpark in the 10th. By the time that ordeal ended he was fast asleep.

It would take quite a game to outshine Morris' performance, but Petry was equal to the task in our last game of April. With a one-hitter, he beat Cleveland 6–1—the one hit was George Vuckovich's two-out double in the eighth. That meant for the second time in the first month of the season, we'd been on a no-hitter watch.

When Brookens made a great play at third for the second out of the eighth inning, one of three outstanding plays he made that game—Petry thought, *It's my lucky day; go get it*—then Vuckovich lined a 2–1 fastball to the gap in left-center for his double. I remember feeling disappointed for Dan, but he took it in stride. And the crowd showed its appreciation by giving him a standing ovation. "I always said, 'I never wanted to lose a no-hitter on a bloop,'" he said. "At least he hit it good." With a no-hitter no longer in the works, Petry was relieved after the eighth but had pitched shutout ball. In fact, he called it "one of my greatest nights in baseball." The lone Cleveland run scored with two outs remaining in the ninth after Petry had left the game.

With that game, though, the best first month in Tigers' history was in the books. Talk about a fun time: we were in first place by six games with an 18–2 record. Trammell hit .403 for the month. Playing less, but making the most of his chances, Garbey hit .444. Both Trammell and Whitaker scored 21 runs, an unbelievable pace. "I said all along he would hit," Sparky said of Garbey, "but nobody could have expected this. I'd be happy with .270."

As for Tram, "he can take full credit for the ballplayer he's become," Anderson said. "I've never seen a more complete player."

Our starting pitchers were 12–1, and Morris' 5–0 record was the best. But to me it felt like they'd all done well. Craig was the unsung hero on that front in my opinion. He was an extremely good pitching coach who had great rapport with everyone. He pushed all the right buttons, keeping the pitchers upbeat, on top of their games. Craig had a tremendously positive influence on everybody. "I could drop dead tonight, and this club would never miss me," Sparky said. "But if we lost Roger, we'd be in big trouble. He makes the pitchers believe in themselves."

As far as production numbers were concerned, I led the way in April with five home runs and 17 RBIs. But Lemon was atop the team with 47 total bases. That month went pretty much the way the rest of the year unfolded for me at the plate. I ended up leading the team with 98 RBIs, which was fine, but I could have had 150, considering how often I came up with runners on base. I would have had a monster year if I had hit for higher average or come through in more situations with runners in scoring position. With April over, though, the question that faced us was this: how far would the magic carry into May?

Chapter 6

An Amazing May

Months before we won the World Series, the 1984 Detroit Tigers were destined to become best known—and best remembered—for our 35–5 start. To reach that point, after going 18–2 in April, we won 17 of our first 20 games in May. In other words, the incredible sensation of winning nearly every day continued. It wasn't until late May when we lost three games in a row in Seattle, after topping out at 35–5, that we had anything more than a few grains of sand kicked in our face.

Every season makes its own emotional impact on those going through it as a unit, of course. You hope to get off to a good start. Because if you do, it creates a cohesive impact right away. We bonded almost instantly in '84 because everything was so positive. Rusty Kuntz called it a 25-man brotherhood. Our 35–5 start was a great way for us to come together, to become a tight-knit group, and to create momentum as a team. "But nothing goes to our heads," Dave Bergman said. "We don't dwell on the good start, only on what we have to do tomorrow."

Good thing. Because then came our road series against the Seattle Mariners.

For an extended period of time in the first two months of the season, everything clicked for us. Then, for a short period of time, it somehow un-clicked. We jumped the track. I suppose it was bound to happen.

We had gone 17–3 in May ahead of that series. It truly had been a team effort. We were solid all the way through. At 35–5 we had seven .300 hitters on the team—some of them everyday players such as Alan Trammell at .340, Chet Lemon at .331, and Lou Whitaker at .317. Others were bit players such as Kuntz, Johnny Grubb, and Marty Castillo. The real surprise had been Barbaro Garbey. Down somewhat from his lofty .400-plus heights of April, he was still hitting .355 at the end of May. Whitaker had scored 31 runs, Trammell had scored 36, and three of us—Darrell Evans, Lemon, and I—were on a pace to knock in 100 runs for the year.

Our starting pitchers were 26–4. Our bullpen was 9–1 with 15 saves. Willie Hernandez and Aurelio Lopez had done their jobs almost flawlessly. But there were big contributors all the way through. Plus, you couldn't underestimate the importance of veteran newcomers like Evans and Bergman. It was almost as if they were two additional coaches, reminding us to stay focused on the little things that win ballgames. They helped shape the team into what we turned out to be.

Before Seattle the most games in a row we had lost were two, and both of those defeats were by one run. In other words, we'd won or had a chance to win nearly every game we had played. Only once in 40 games had we lost by more than three runs, and that loss (by four runs) occurred because of three errors we made in the 19th inning after arriving home from Texas at 6:00 AM. We prided ourselves, however, on how we played the game defensively. We had worked at it tirelessly in spring training. Reacting the right way to various game situations was drilled into our heads early on.

Despite the Toronto Blue Jays' excellent 27–14 start, we led the American League East by eight-and-a-half games. The third-place Baltimore Orioles at 23–20 were a distant 13½ games back. So, yes, it was a genuine 35–5 juggernaut, which headed to Seattle for that three-game series at the Kingdome against the Mariners. "I keep looking in the paper at our record, thinking it must be a misprint," Sparky Anderson said.

But as good as we were, we took nothing for granted. The next tempering encounter, in one form or another, was always just around the corner. Or so we conditioned ourselves to believe—even away from the field. During the series in Anaheim against the California Angels, for instance, before we traveled up the coast to Seattle, a man from Dayton, Ohio, greeted Sparky at the hotel and said he'd always been a fan of Sparky's Big Red Machine in Cincinnati. After praising Sparky and those powerful Reds' teams up one side and down the other, the man from Dayton ended his complimentary speech by saying, "By the way, Sparky, what are you doing now?"

Doing now? Huh? What kind of question was that for the manager of not just a first-place team, but of the team that was off to the most celebrated major league start in years? Sparky told us of the incident later that day, getting another laugh from it. We all got a good laugh. Apparently, our 35–5 record hadn't made an impression on everyone.

No doubt the game in May that best reflected our tenacity before we reached the pinnacle of 35–5 was played on May 8 in Kansas City. Despite being 23–4 at the time, we were trailing tough Royals pitcher Bud Black and his team 2–0 as the top of the seventh inning began. Except for scattered singles, we hadn't caused an ounce of trouble for Black. But we knew our team. We rarely went away quietly. And sure enough, Larry Herndon led off the seventh with a single—the first time we'd put our first batter on base. One hit led to another after that. Evans singled Herndon to third, and Lemon singled him in. Just like that, we'd cut the lead to 2–1 and still had two runners on base.

But Black wasn't ready to capitulate. He struck out Kirk Gibson and retired Tom Brookens on a pop to short. That swung the momentum back in the Royals' favor with two on and two out. When Black walked Whitaker to load the bases, however, the Royals replaced him with their bullpen ace, Dan Quisenberry. The bases were loaded, but Quisenberry had never allowed a grand slam. Typically, when Quisenberry was on the mound, you'd just pound his pitches into the ground. And our next hitter, Trammell, had seldom felt comfortable facing him. "I was looking for the sinker every pitch," Trammell said. "But that kind of approach hadn't helped me in previous at-bats against him. I'd worn out a lot of shortstops with ground balls while hitting against him."

A ground ball isn't what Tram hit this time, though. With his funky, submarine style of throwing, Quisenberry got ahead of him with a called strike on the first pitch. But the second pitch went into orbit. "He hit it to North Dakota!" Quisenberry later declared.

Not quite that far obviously, but Trammell's drive to deep left landed in our bullpen for a grand slam. "I thought it was at least off the wall when I hit it," Tram said.

Over the wall was more like it.

Jack Morris retired the last 12 batters he faced for his sixth victory in seven decisions, thanking Trammell after the game not only for the slam, but also for the fine play he made in the fourth inning that turned Don Slaught's would-be bases-loaded hit into a 6-4-3 double-play. "The best DP I've ever seen," Sparky called it.

The victory enabled us to tie the 1955 Brooklyn Dodgers for the best 28-game start (24–4) ever in the majors. It was also notable for Morris' post-game introspective admission that he occasionally would get "inexplicably perturbed" on the mound. To which Jack could predictably react immaturely. According to Roger Craig, whenever Morris was upset, as he'd been for some reason in this game, he acted like a little boy who's had his candy stolen. "I don't know what sets it off," Jack said. "Lance doesn't know how much he helped me today. I love the guy. I do. He's like a big brother to me but one with so much more class than I have."

It was my experience, however, that because they were only human, every pitcher would get irritated now and then. To help them through it, I probably got criticized for not going out to the mound enough. But I figured pitchers didn't want me talking to them all the time. They had enough on their minds. But thank you, Jack, for acknowledging that I did something which calmed you down. I always tried.

In any event, we had battled back for a 5–2 victory against a tough Royals team and two tough pitchers, Black and Quisenberry. As Quisenberry said about Tram's slam, "It was the longest ground ball I've ever given up." He also quipped, "The wind blowing in stopped just before that inning began. Sparky must have some pretty high connections."

Two weeks later, though, we would be stunned by what happened to us in Seattle. Heading into that series on top of the world at 35–5 and with 17 consecutive victories on the road, we were facing a Mariners' team that was 20–24 but not out of the running (just two-and-a-half games back) in the muddled American League West. Seattle was a team we had swept three straight from at Tiger Stadium earlier in the month, however. Not only that, the M's came into the series with a 2–8 record in their last 10 games—and had been shut out in their last two games. They were gasping for air, in other words.

The first starter we were scheduled to face in Seattle was lefty Ed VandeBerg, a converted relief pitcher. In Detroit we had scored five runs in the first five innings against him. Meanwhile, our opening starter in Seattle was Milt Wilcox, who had limited the M's to one run on four hits in six innings of an earlier matchup against them. The opposite of all that, however, is what took place in the first game at the Kingdome. As Sparky said, "we stunk up the place."

Not sharp at all, Wilcox allowed five earned runs on nine hits before exiting in the fifth, and VandeBerg held us to one run in seven innings. Go figure. The loss ended Milt's personal nine-game winning streak. Blanked on eight hits in the previous two games combined, Seattle's offense suddenly came alive with four extra-base hits, a pair of home runs and a pair of doubles while beating us 7–3.

After 17 consecutive wins on the road, we had finally suffered our first loss away from home. So…we were 35–6. It didn't seem to be an insurmountable setback because we would recover in the next game. Or so we intended.

But we didn't recover. "We were awful again," Sparky said.

One out into the bottom of the first, Juan Berenguer came apart with a walk, a wild pitch, and five consecutive singles. Doug Bair took over for him, but the Mariners would have a four-run lead after the first inning. Our offense, meanwhile, didn't wake up until the ninth when it was too late. We lost again 9–5. For the first time, we had lost two games in a row. But it would stop there, right? After all, we had scored five first-inning runs off Seattle's

Rusty Kuntz

Rusty Kuntz was the most unlikely Tiger in 1984. After a season for the Minnesota Twins in which he had hit .190—and five partial seasons with the Chicago White Sox before that—he'd been acquired during the winter meetings for pitcher Larry Pashnick, whose role for us in 1983 had been reduced to 12 games, six of them starts.

On the surface, it appeared to be a nothing-much-for-nothing-much sort of deal. It wasn't even certain in spring training that Rusty would make the team. But when we acquired Willie Hernandez from the Philadelphia Phillies at the end of spring training, it meant that two other left-handed hopefuls in the bullpen, John Martin and Howard Bailey, were no longer needed— and could be sent back down to the minors—so Kuntz made the team as defensive insurance, and Rod Allen made it because of his bat.

Kuntz was not expected to see a lot of action, though—and didn't, especially in the first month. He started only three games for us in April, all of them in right field, going 2-for-11.

There was no indication he would become the valuable player that he did in May. Not that he became a regular, but when he did play, Rusty contributed in a huge way. In 18 games in May, nine of them starts, Kuntz hit .539 (14-for-26.)

Additionally, he drove in 10 runs, scored 12, had five doubles, hit two home runs, and played fine defense, seeing action at all three outfield positions. He didn't have just a good month of May; he had an outstanding month, not only solidifying his roster spot, but also making him an immensely popular teammate because he also was selfless and affable. He always had a great attitude, a smile on his face, and a wonderful work ethic. It also helped that he was someone with a sharp baseball mind. Whatever role he was given, he accepted it, never complaining, always dedicating himself to whatever he was asked to do.

Plus, he made big contributions that often helped us win games. Rusty went on to start 38 games for us in 1984 as a reserve outfielder, hitting .292. He also proved to be a clutch hitter, batting .344 with runners in scoring position. So, he went from being one of the last players to earn a spot on the team to being a useful player to have around. In May alone he had a pair of two-hit games and also two three-hit games.

The inning after he hit his first home run as a Tiger, the crowd at Tiger Stadium began to chant his name "Rus-ty, Rus-ty" when he took his position. As hard as he worked for us, he deserved moments like that. "That kind of thing lifted me several inches off the ground," Kuntz said in appreciation of the fans' reaction to him. "Everybody is playing well on this team. I don't want to be the guy to mess it up."

Who said anything about messing it up? In fact, it was Rusty who drove in the go-ahead run in the fifth inning of Game Five against the San Diego Padres for our clinching victory of the World Series. The RBI came about on a pop-up to second base that Kirk Gibson turned into a sacrifice fly with aggressive base-running down the line at third, but Rusty triggered the play by getting his bat on the ball. He had often contributed in unexpected ways during the season. So why not in the World Series, too?

next scheduled starter, Matt Young, in a 10–1 victory at Tiger Stadium just a short time ago, and Dan Petry, our next starter, was 5–0 in his last six starts. The mound matchup heavily favored us on paper.

But just when you think there's something that looks probable in baseball, it becomes improbable. Seattle completed its sweep with a 6–1 victory. We were outscored 22–9 in the three-game series. Sparky chalked it up to inevitability: "Thank God we're leaving Seattle," he said. "But I'm not alarmed. When you play 162 games, you're going to lose some."

The jarring reality was that it had been a while since we'd "lost some." Suddenly, it was gut-check time for us. Making it worse, Toronto had won both ends of a doubleheader against the Cleveland Indians while we were spinning our wheels in Seattle, so we had our faces rubbed in it. In our three-game series against the Mariners, we had lost three-and-a-half games in the standings to the Blue Jays.

Even though we had played well for most of the first two months, I personally found there were times I was feeling like a million bucks at the plate, only to suddenly run out of gas for a few days. Maybe a few of us experienced that kind of tumble at the same time. But whatever the reason, that series against the Mariners caught us without any wind in our sails—as another boat gained on us. I remember having breakfast one morning at the hotel in Seattle, reading the paper and thinking, *Holy cow, Toronto's right behind us. They're right there!*

That was concerning. Suddenly our boat, though far from sinking, was rocking. We needed to get our act together soon. That meant a return to winning was urgently advisable as soon as we got to Oakland. So four runs in the first inning of the first game there was a welcome sight. A couple of walks helped against the Oakland A's, so did three singles, a sacrifice fly, and a bases-loaded pitch that hit Herndon. That gave Morris an early lead, which he protected by allowing only one earned run en route to a 6–2 victory, which gave him a 10–1 record. "Everyone was embarrassed about Seattle," Jack said. "We just wanted to get it out of our minds. Good pitchers rise to the occasion. This was an occasion. It's what they pay me for."

Because his record already was 8–1—compared to Denny McLain being 6–1 at the same point in 1968—we were already being asked if Jack could win 30 games. "It's not absurd to think he can do it," I told a reporter. "Personally, I think it's possible."

Jack dismissed such thoughts, though. "Thirty is a dream," he said. "It's too early to talk about dreams."

Our good feelings didn't last long. Handing us a reminder that it wouldn't be easy to shake Toronto, the A's roughed up Wilcox early the next night en route to an 8–5 victory. That meant we needed something good to happen in our last game of May if we were to head home happy from the West Coast. It was amazing: we'd gone 35–5, a major league record for 40 games, but we were well aware the battle was far from over. There could be no taking our foot off the pedal. We had to keep getting after it because Toronto was for real. They had some great offensive players on that team, some real boppers.

Still not ourselves at the plate, we struggled in the series finale against the A's—getting only five hits—but one of those, fortunately, was a long, one-out home run by Gibson in the ninth that proved to be the difference in a 2–1 decision. It also helped that Hernandez and Lopez combined for four-and-a-third innings of shutout relief. Having hit a strong .297 as a team for the month, we arrived home with a 37–9 record and a five-and-a-half game lead over the tenacious Blue Jays…who would soon be coming to Tiger Stadium.

Chapter 7

The Minors

Isigned with the Detroit Tigers in June of 1974. I had just turned 18. I hadn't taken the field yet, but with my signature on the dotted line, I was a professional baseball player. It was time to say goodbye to everything I'd known growing up in California. So, I got to Tampa on the redeye and caught a shuttle to Lakeland, Florida. The Tigers wanted me there as soon as possible for extended spring training.

I checked into the minor league dorm—Fetzer Hall they called it—named for the owner of the team at the time, John Fetzer. But no one was around except someone at the front desk who thankfully showed me to my room. I can honestly say I was fried. I was hot, sweaty, and hadn't slept a wink all night because I hadn't yet learned how to sleep on airplanes. I was a wreck. So, I threw my bags down, jumped into bed and fell asleep, figuring I'll find out later what the daily routine is. Well, the next thing I knew, the door to my room slammed opened with a loud—*BANG*—and there's a guy looking like he wants to tear my head off. "What the hell are you doing in bed?" he yelled at me. "Your team is over at the ballpark working out! You're supposed to be with them! Get your ass out of bed!"

It was Hoot Evers, the Tigers' director of player development, bellowing at me. I literally jumped up, put my clothes back on, and hurried over to the ballpark to get fitted for a uniform. Then they put me at third base because I'd been drafted as a third baseman and they hit about 1,000 grounders to me in the humidity and heat of a blistering hot day in Florida. I mean I was sweating my brains out because I'd never known such humidity. I thought I was going to pass out. After infield work, of course, I took batting practice and, while that was going on, I began to think, *Man, I don't know if I made the right decision. This is insane.*

That was my introduction to being a Tiger: a redeye, getting yelled at for not knowing what I was supposed to do or where I was supposed to be, taking a ton of ground balls followed by batting practice. I slept well that night, I can assure you.

Fortunately, Hoot wasn't always that way with me. He wasn't someone you messed with, though. He intimidated many players, but I gained a lot of respect for him later, finding out more about him and his years as a player with the Tigers. In fact, I'm happy to say I ended up thinking he was the best, a great guy.

But it was a rough way to break in with him.

My becoming a third baseman in the minors was a matter that had been discussed from the moment Tigers scout Jack Deutsch came over to my house in Diamond Bar to sign me. I remember looking at my dad kind of puzzled about it. I thought I could do it, but I had been a pitcher and a catcher my whole career until that point—except for filling in at third my senior year in high school. When the Tigers threw that third-base change of pace at me, I just kind of shrugged and thought, *Fine, do what you want.*

Somehow, despite all the errors I made, I ended up as the All-Star third baseman of the Appalachian League in rookie ball. Once the pitchers in that league found out I was a sucker for breaking balls, though, I got a steady diet of them. I felt I was progressing at third, but before I had a chance to follow through on my improvement, they pulled the plug on me. They moved me to catcher full time the next year (1975) at Lakeland.

Those first two years seemed like one big change after another. Playing third my first year was followed by the Tigers trying to make a switch-hitter out of me my second year. The entire experience was one of "let's try this, let's try that," then on to something different. I didn't really get to settle into

First Purchase

Once I signed, it wasn't as if I suddenly had a lot of money to spend. I went off to join the Bristol team at extended spring training, and the check I received for signing must have gone straight to our house in Diamond Bar. I never saw it. No one told me when it arrived, so I guess it was simply a matter of my parents depositing it for me. It's not like I had a lot of reasons to spend it or a lot to things I could think to spend it on, but after my rookie season in the Appalachian League, I went to the instructional league in Florida, where I needed transportation because I didn't have any.

So, that was the first purchase I made with my signing bonus: a way to get around. But it wasn't a car. Many of the guys at instructional ball had motorcycles, so I called my dad and told him I was going to buy a motorcycle. I remember he quickly asked me if I'd ever driven one. I admitted I hadn't but that "it can't be that tough."

I was wrong. It turned out to be an educational process.

For one thing, I didn't know how to shift gears. I had to have someone teach me, which was kind of scary—and sort of embarrassing. It took me a while to figure it out. I had that motorcycle for I'd say a year, starting in Florida. But I did get it home to California for a while. Luckily, a teammate from Southern California, Bob Adams, was towing a U-Haul trailer back home and he agreed to take it with him. But I never did feel safe riding my motorcycle in California.

To this day, my problem wasn't that I didn't get the hang of operating it—because after a while I did—but I learned that very few automobile drivers pay attention to motorcycles. It's like they don't even see you half the time. At least, that's what I encountered. On that motorcycle I had several close calls of being run off the road or drivers pulling abruptly in front of me when there wasn't room for them to do so. I got tired of all the near-misses I was having, feeling that eventually something worse was going to happen.

When I got home that winter, I also helped my parents with some bills. I was happy to do that. It felt like money well spent, but it's not as if I ever treated my signing bonus like I'd come into a sudden fortune. Eventually, I sold the motorcycle and bought a van—a vehicle other drivers paid attention to.

anything my first couple of years. The weird thing is at Lakeland, when they tried to turn me into a switch-hitter, I didn't have a hitting coach. *There wasn't a hitting coach on the team!* That was kind of crazy. We had a pitching coach but no hitting coach. So I had no one to give me any instruction or feedback on how I was doing with a new style. I've had player development directors tell me in the years since that they would lose their job for doing something like that now with a first-round draft choice—or with any draft choice—for that matter.

The Tigers went ahead with it, though, thinking that if I could hit left-handed, I'd eventually be able to reach the short porch in right at Tiger Stadium with my power. But I never had switch-hit before, I had never done anything left-handed, so I was as surprised at what they were asking me to do as I would have been if they had suddenly said, "We want you to start throwing left-handed."

I think I said something like "Are you kidding me?" But I gave it my best shot.

Without knowing how to go about it, I never learned how to pull the ball as a left-handed hitter, let alone hit any home runs. I don't think I ever did hit a home run left-handed. I mean, you can't hit home runs when you don't feel comfortable turning on the ball. It wasn't until the end of the season that I started feeling a little more relaxed on that side of the plate, but that's when they told me the experiment was over. Just like that, they didn't want me switch-hitting anymore. I think it was Les Moss who told me it was over. The way he put it was: "You have too much power right-handed to be screwing around left-handed. This isn't working."

Les went on to be my manager at Double A Montgomery in '76, then at Triple A Evansville in '77, and was also my manager briefly for the Tigers in 1979. He became a very important person in my career.

Meanwhile, back in Lakeland in 1975, I liked the move from third base to behind the plate full time because I liked catching. I had always liked catching. But this would be the first time I'd ever caught that many games in a season. I mean, I had caught in high school, but you only play a handful of games in high school.

This was my first full year as a professional catcher, and I still was getting accustomed to the humidity of a summer in Florida. It felt like it was 100 degrees every day. My catching gear was soaking wet the whole year. I could never dry it out, no matter how much I tried and no matter where I would hang it. It smelled bad. It was nasty. It just never seemed to dry out. I remember my hands would be wet by the third inning of most games in Florida because of the humidity, but there was nowhere on my body, or on my equipment, that I could dry them off. So, the entire 1975 season was one adjustment after another: from playing third to catching, from not ever having been a switch-hitter to switch-hitting.

It wasn't until 1976 when I was at Montgomery that I finally settled in and started developing the tools, which would help me get to the major league level. That was the year in my opinion I started to become a ballplayer.

But the season didn't start well.

I will admit I was not very good the first half of my Double A season. I think I was hitting .180 halfway through the year. I remember Hoot getting on my case again, asking me if I was out running around at night. I told him, "No, Hoot, I'm not. I'm just struggling. That's all."

He replied very directly that I needed to get my act together, or adjustments would be made. That's when Les took it upon himself to start having me come to the ballpark for early morning workouts. The plan was this: I would work on my hitting while the team was at home and on my defense on the road.

My hitting definitely needed some help. I was a big lunger at breaking balls, jumping out in front of them all the time. So I had to learn how to stay back on anything that broke. It was Les' mission to teach me how to become a hitter. We started with me hitting off the curveball machine, and it felt like that's all I did the rest of the season. His message was very basic: my job was to hit the ball up the middle. Not to left field, not to right field, just up the middle. But in the beginning, I couldn't even do that. I was swinging and missing, fouling balls back, or pulling them. Other guys came in for early work from time to time. They could set their own schedule, but I was always on the mandatory attendance list.

The Bird

For my year in Lakeland, Florida, in 1975, I was Mark Fidrych's catcher. It was the season before he burst upon the major league scene as a phenom with 19 wins. But he went only 5–9 for Lakeland. There was no huge hint of what was to come. He didn't have a very good year for Lakeland, but to be honest with you, I don't know that anybody did. And there really was no explanation why.

I specifically remember Mark, though, because he was such an intense guy when he was pitching. It was a different story when he wasn't. He was as fun-loving and happy-go-lucky as anybody on the planet, but put him in a game, and something changed. He was very focused, starting with how he'd come out of the bullpen with his fists clenched. It was kind of weird actually. He would cultivate the dirt on the mound even back then. That was Mark from Day One, patting the dirt down. We all learned what his routine was like. It was one quirky thing after another. That was just Bird. That's what he did.

People always thought he was talking to the ball, but he was really talking to himself, reaffirming out loud things he wanted to accomplish. It was fun to watch, entertaining to say the least. But he was effective as well. Regardless of his record that year for Lakeland, he showed enough improvement to those in charge. He made consistent pitches and had good enough stuff that they felt it was warranted to move him all the way up from A ball to the majors. The Detroit Tigers obviously thought he could handle it, which he did. He figured out how to pitch and stuck with it.

But the guy I always thought was going to be the phenom was lefty Bob Sykes. When we were in rookie ball, he went 11–0 with a 1.07 ERA. He just dominated the entire season, leaving me saying "holy mackerel" to what I'd just seen. He was in the Tigers' organization a few years, and I watched his progression, but I think he eventually ran into arm issues. Sykesy was one of those guys who could never throw enough. He was like a hitter who wanted to take batting practice all day long. He'd go out after his workouts and throw over and over again against a cement wall at Tigertown. I kept thinking, *Man, you're going to throw your arm out.*

From the Tigers' organization, he got traded to the St. Louis Cardinals as part of the deal for Aurelio Lopez, which turned out great for us, and from St. Louis to the New York Yankees in the trade for Willie McGee, which turned out great for the Cardinals. So he figured in some heavy-duty deals that benefited the teams trading him. In fact, I've read that the McGee trade has been judged by some as one of the worst the Yankees ever made.

What I felt about Sykes as a pitcher, I also felt about Tim Corcoran as a hitter. Not that he was going to be a phenom, but that he was going to have a very successful major league career based on how consistently he hit in the minors. But it just never panned out for him. When the bus was going to leave for the airport on the very last day of spring training one year, there was one more roster decision to make. Darrell Brown made it over Corky—but only after Tim's girlfriend had taken off in their car for Detroit with all their stuff. To me it seemed like a cold-hearted way to do business. Sometimes, though—with so many players grappling for so few spots—that was the way it was in the minors.

The work never involved changing my stance, however, or how I held my hands. Nothing mechanical, just hitting the ball up the middle. That was the requirement for staying in the cage. If I did anything else with a pitch, I had to give way to the next guy and wait for my turn to come around again. In the beginning, of course, I'd take one swing and be out of the cage. Then someone else, like Tim Corcoran, who knew what he was doing, would step in and hit 15 balls in a row the correct way. He'd stay in the cage forever by earning it. Me? I was out of the cage instantly because I never hit the ball where I wanted to hit it.

It was very embarrassing because I just couldn't do it. Eventually, out of desperation, I figured out how to cut down on my swing and just steer the ball up the middle to stay in the cage. That seemed to work. From that point on, I progressed to swinging harder. I advanced to hitting hard ground balls up the middle, then line drives. Before it was all done, I was hitting home runs to center field. But I had started with baby steps. Throughout the second half of that 1976 season, I began to show progress and, I'm happy to say, so did my team. We ended up as Southern League champions that year. It wasn't until the next season at the Triple A level, though, that I finally broke out and had a pretty good year.

The other half of improving as a player involved concentrating on my defense. Les had been a catcher, too, so he worked with me on blocking balls, game calling, communicating with the pitcher, everything that went into being able to play a solid game. After the season I went again to instructional ball in Florida, where Les supervised my workouts. At one point he had me and the other catchers blocking 90-mile-an-hour sliders off the machine. At the beginning of one of the workouts, he told us to leave our gloves outside the cage. That was a stunner. We all replied, "What? No gloves? You can't be serious." But he was.

He replied, "This is blocking practice, gentlemen, not catching practice. You're going to learn how to get your body in front of a pitch without relying on your glove."

Well, the first three pitches coming off the machine, all of them nasty sliders, hit me on my forearms. Alan Trammell was watching the workout from the end of the bench, and every time I'd take one off my arms, he'd laugh out loud. So, out of sheer self-preservation, I began to laser in on the ball. I wanted it to hit me in the chest protector, not anywhere else. In that sense Les accomplished his mission. I had issues with blocking the ball throughout my career, but I think I got pretty good at it. Even so, when a pitch would get by me and I'd be chasing it down, it was like I could always hear Mossy's voice in my head, saying, "Catch that ball. Block that ball!"

I know I'm fairly high on the all-time list of passed balls in the majors (48th) so I also had issues with that from time to time. There were reasons. Some of them are sour grapes, but I always counter the passed ball criticism I hear by saying I never made a double-digit number of errors in any season of my career. I always looked at that as something to be proud of—along with the three Gold Gloves (1983–1985) I won.

But I need to say something about Les. I know he had some shortcomings about not being the most talkative guy. When it came to on-field instruction and teaching us what we needed to learn, though, he was outstanding. In my eyes he was a great instructor and a great baseball man. He just wasn't a world-class conversationalist. In 1995 I was in my final year with the Toronto Blue Jays, and Danny Darwin was a teammate of mine.

He'd been with the Houston Astros with guys like Mike Scott and Nolan Ryan and he said, "All the guys there loved Mossy," who was the Astros' pitching coach from 1983 to 1989.

In 1977 I was in Evansville at Triple A, and a lot of the good things I learned during the second half of my Double A season carried over. Plus, Les moved up as my manager and he continued to work with me. I still focused on driving the ball up the middle because that made me a better hitter. It enabled me, for instance, to hit off-speed pitches better. Plus, now I had the confidence I could hit home runs to all fields. I got off to a pretty good start at Triple A, and it carried through the season. I had a productive year. After a rude awakening earlier in the minors because of all the new pitching styles I'd been exposed to—styles that wore me out—I finally felt like I knew what I was doing, like I finally knew how to hit.

Les was the guy who opened my eyes to making the adjustments I needed to make. That made all the difference in the world to me. In my mind, had it not been for Les, I would not have made it to the major leagues. He changed everything about who I was, everything about the confidence I needed as a ballplayer. The first couple of years, I'd been lost. I was confused most of the time, but once I hooked up with Les, my development stabilized. I finally began to take steps in a positive direction.

I clearly remember the day in 1977 when I was told I was going to be a September call-up to the majors. Obviously, I was excited about it, but looking back, my comfort about it was what really helped me. I'd been going to spring training for a long time with a lot of the guys I'd soon be joining. I was familiar with just about everyone on Detroit's major league team because it felt like I'd played with them all somewhere. But just the experience of knowing I was headed to the big leagues was exciting. I was pumped. We were in Evansville when I was told, so I had to jump into the car and make the 450-mile drive to Detroit. Quite possibly, I drove over the speed limit on my way there. I was known to do that from time to time. But like my journey up the ladder in the minors, I got there safely.

Chapter 8

A Challenging June

The month of June was memorable for us—not to mention pivotal—because of several individual performances—and for one important team reason. After losing four of six games to begin the month and seeing our lead in the American League East dwindle to three-and-a-half games after it had been as high as eight and a half in May, we corrected our course. We started winning again. In fact, we began to win so steadily that we went 16–8 the rest of June after stumbling through the first week. In doing so, we built our lead up to 10 games by the end of the month.

Looking back, June was every bit as much proof as April and May in why we won the American League pennant because it was the month in which we learned how to respond to adversity. Collectively, though we believed in ourselves as a team, we knew we'd have to come down to Earth from our early pace and that the season would eventually become more of a challenge. But if I do say so myself, we responded rather well with a solid team effort.

Outstanding individual performances had a lot to do with that, of course. Thankfully, there were many of them, including Dave Bergman's dramatic home run off Toronto Blue Jays pitcher Roy Lee Jackson. There also was Ruppert Jones getting called up from Evansville after we signed him as a free agent in April, then hitting the third deck in right at Tiger

Stadium with his first home run and—better yet—clearing the roof in right with another home run later in June. A lot of us were stunned after the season began that Jones was still available for any team to sign. But it was entirely to our general manager Bill Lajoie's credit that we were the team which landed him.

June was also the month in which Tom Brookens emerged from his slumber, and we were so happy for him that he did. Brookie was one of our most popular teammates, but at the end of May, he was hitting just .156 before busting loose with a .366 surge in June. On a scale of one to 10 personality-wise, Tom was a 10. I think everybody on the team felt that way. With his quick wit and his work ethic, we loved him. He would do some crazy things and say some crazy things that endeared him to everyone on the team. So, we were hoping he would get back on track not only to help the team, but also for his own sanity. Numbers like he had for a while eventually wear on you. It was great to see him bust out in June, solidifying his spot on the team for the rest of the year,

Another player we were happy for was Howard Johnson, who hadn't been used much in April and May but would get more plate appearances in June than in those first two months combined. He responded with increased production, hitting .305 with four home runs for the month. In my eyes Howard was a very good player. But he was young, and Sparky Anderson didn't trust young players right away. He was tough that way, sometimes unfair. They had to prove their worth. Johnson just needed to play, though. I was glad he eventually was given a chance.

And one more thing—one more huge thing, in fact—June was the month in which we began to fully realize what a treasure we had acquired from the Philadelphia Phillies in Willie Hernandez. After winning a game and saving five in relief for us in May, Willie won two and saved seven in June. By the end of the month, his ERA for his last 25 games was an astounding 1.35. As the season progressed, he just got better and better. His consistency, the hallmark of a great player, was simply amazing. I, for one, marveled at it. "We wouldn't be in first place without him," Sparky said. "It's that simple. I could use him in 80 games, and he'd ask me for more."

So, I think it's fair to say we felt even better about ourselves and our direction by the time June ended than we did on the final day of May. The month began auspiciously with a 14–2 victory against the Baltimore Orioles before a welcome-back crowd of more than 47,000 at Tiger Stadium—and tons of national media. "When you're interviewed for one-and-a-half hours before a game," Sparky said of the media attention, "it's hard to concentrate."

We led 9–0 after the third inning and 13–0 by the fifth, making short work of Scott McGregor, who had previously pitched well (a 7–2 record) in Detroit. Alan Trammell, Chet Lemon, and I hit home runs while Dan Petry improved his record to 8–2. Our fans were totally behind us by this time—with crowds of more than 40,000 often in attendance. To tell you the truth, I don't remember anything other than the ballpark being full that season. It was electric. Our fans were absolutely awesome the entire year. No sooner had we treated them to a blowout, however, than we disappointed them, scoring only one more run while losing the next two games of the Baltimore series. Storm Davis shut us down on three hits in one of those games. In the other contest the Orioles scored the winning run on a bases-loaded walk.

With our lead over the Blue Jays now down to a precarious four-and-a-half games, we needed to begin a showdown series against them at Tiger Stadium on the right foot after the Orioles left town. The early returns weren't encouraging, however. We trailed 3–0 against Dave Stieb after six innings of the Toronto opener when the tide began to turn. In the bottom of the seventh, Lemon was hit by a pitch with one out, and Bergman singled him to second. Johnson hadn't hit a home run at Tiger Stadium all year, but with two on, he connected, glancing a high drive off the top of the foul pole in right, tying the score. Johnson had hit a long foul on the previous pitch and was confidently thinking he could handle anything Stieb threw at him. His positive attitude had led to a positive result.

With Hernandez on the mound, we survived a runner-on-third threat with no outs in the eighth but stranded runners at second and third to waste a scoring chance of our own in the bottom of the ninth. Both teams, of course, were well aware of the game's importance. The Jays knew that after our 35–5 start they had climbed to within striking distance of first place. However, we had no intention of stepping aside. We were 38–11 when the series against the Jays began. They were 34–16. But as Hernandez succinctly put it: "We needed this one."

The game was in the bottom of the 10th when my single off Jimmy Key began the inning. This was Key's first year in the majors, and prior to his considerable success as a starter over the course of the next decade for the Jays and New York Yankees, he was being used exclusively as a relief pitcher by Toronto in his rookie season. Darrell Evans bunted me to second, which led to Roy Lee Jackson taking over for Key. Jackson retired Rusty Kuntz on a topper back to the mound for the second out, but he walked Lemon.

That brought up Bergman with runners at first and second, setting the stage for one of the great at-bats of the entire season—baseball in its "purest and simplest form" as Roger Craig called it. Not known for his power, Bergie hadn't hit a home run since a walk-off blast for the San Francisco Giants in his only plate appearance of a 5–4 victory on September 21 of the 1983 season. In his first 88 at-bats as a Tiger, he was homerless—and even in this at-bat he said he got "some real good pitches to hit out" but only fouled them off. His duel against Jackson began with five consecutive foul balls, most of which were a matter of Bergie stubbornly fighting off pitches, one after another. The sixth pitch was high for a ball, but the seventh—on a 1–2 count— was tantalizingly close to the outside corner. Bergman took it. But he said, "I knew it was close."

It could have gone either way, but luckily it went our way. Umpire Terry Cooney called the close pitch a ball. *Phew.* I was on second base, so I had a good look at the 1–2 pitch. Yes, it was very close. A break, Dave correctly called it. But there were other pitches in that at-bat I don't know how he got even a piece of. Bergman fouled off the next pitch, then took a ball low and inside. The count was now full, but the battle continued to rage. "He was up there for a full seven minutes," Sparky said. "It seemed like a whole season."

Bergie fouled off the next pitch, a breaking ball—and the pitch after that as well, a fastball. The Jays were trying everything they could, but 11 pitches into the at-bat, nothing had been resolved. Nor did it end with the 12th pitch, as Bergman spoiled that one, too, for foul ball No. 9. Oddly enough, he hadn't missed any of the pitches he'd swung at yet. And the only three he took were out of the strike zone. On the 13th pitch, Jackson came back with yet another slider just inches off the ground, one of his best of the entire at-bat.

Bergman nailed it. Reaching down for it, he golfed the low pitch into the upper deck in right for the game-winning home run, a no-doubter as soon as he connected—truly one of the season's great moments. Instead of prancing around the bases, though, Bergie's home run trot wasn't the least bit celebratory. "I'm not much of an emotional person," he said. "It makes my wife angry, but that's the way I am."

Amazed, but with a smile on my face, I scored ahead of him, as did Lemon, and with one dramatic swing of Bergie's bat, we had won the first game of the Toronto series 6–3 in 10 innings. "I felt if the pitch was hittable, I was going to hit it," Bergman said. "It was only six inches off the ground, probably a ball, but I happened to hit it right on the button."

Many of us had marveled at the tense showdown. Craig even called it "the best battle I've ever seen between a pitcher and hitter." Added coach Dick Tracewski: "Without a doubt the best at-bat I've ever seen."

There are at-bats, and there are big at-bats, but to me that was one of the greatest I'd ever seen. I mean, the showdown ended the way you would script it for a book. But it had played out in real life. Jackson refused to talk after the game, but Jays catcher Buck Martinez praised Bergman "for hanging in there. The pitch he hit was a slider, down and in. He did a good job of getting his bat beneath it."

Brookens, of course, embraced the moment with his unique sense of humor. Hitting .159 but waiting on deck with Bergman batting, Tom said, "Yeah, they saw me there. But they didn't want to face me. So you knew they were going to go hard after Bergie."

That was Brookens for you, always keeping us loose with a laugh.

The Addition of Ruppert

Who was Ruppert Jones, where had he come from, and how was he suddenly in our lineup as of June 6 hitting long home runs while contributing on a regular basis? The answers were relatively easy.

Many of the questions—such as why Jones was still available for us to sign as a free agent after the start of the 1984 season—were far more complex. Ruppert was no rookie when he joined us. He was a 29-year-old, eight-year veteran, who had been the first selection of the Seattle Mariners in the expansion draft of 1976. That's how highly the Mariners thought of his future when they chose him.

Jones responded by becoming the expansion team's first All-Star in 1977, a season in which he was the M's starting center fielder, played in all but two of their games, hit 24 home runs—which remained a career high—and established himself as a solid major leaguer. The best season of his three with Seattle was probably 1979, when he hit .267 with 21 home runs and 78 RBIs while playing in all 162 games. He was traded to the New York Yankees after that season and then to the San Diego Padres in 1981. While playing for the Padres in 1982, he earned All-Star status for the second time.

Becoming a free agent after the 1983 season, Jones eventually signed with Pittsburgh and had a good spring for the Pirates in 1984, but he was the odd man out in their final roster cuts. "I could have been crushed," he said, "but I wasn't. All good things happen for a reason. I had faith someone would call."

And sure enough, someone did call. We wisely signed him on April 10. If anyone thought Ruppert's best years were behind him, he did a thorough job of changing their minds. Needing to play himself back into shape, however, Jones spent the first two months at Triple A Evansville before being summoned to play his first game for us. The intention was for him to help at all three outfield positions but mostly to platoon in left with Larry Herndon, who was off to a slow start.

Jones became a building block of our club. Instantly, he made an impact. Becoming a fan favorite for the impressive distance (and height) of his home runs, "Rooftop Ruppert" quickly made himself at home in our batting order. Herndon had averaged .297 with 21 home runs and 90 RBIs for us in the previous two seasons, but he was homerless with only 13 RBIs when Jones made his Tigers' debut. Both players responded well to the platoon plan. In almost the same number of at-bats—237 for Jones, 235 for Herndon—after it was put into place, Ruppert hit .284 with 12 home runs and 37 RBIs, including a .345 batting average in July when the rest of our offense sagged. Herndon, meanwhile, responded with a .306 average, seven home runs, and 30 RBIs. Between the two of them, left field became a productive position for us again.

Ruppert blended right in. He had a great personality, was very upbeat, everybody liked him, plus he had a lot left in the tank. He was still a very good ballplayer. And that was evident throughout the rest of the season. When we didn't keep him around after 1984, I was surprised.

The victory allowed us to feel good but only temporarily because we lost the next two games of the series. And, yikes, that dropped our lead down to three-and-a-half games, the slimmest in more than six weeks. More than once, because we were in a constant dogfight with the Blue Jays, I kept thinking—like Butch Cassidy looking back at the posse chasing him—*Who are those guys? If we don't step it up, we'll find our butts in second place one of these days.*

As thrilling as Bergman's home run had been, the reality was that it served as only a one-game boost. Having lost eight of 12 games by the end of the Toronto series, we needed more of a permanent pick-me-up than that. Bill McGraw of the *Detroit Free Press* even wrote that "the party might be over" for Sparky and Our Gang as a play on words for Spanky and Our Gang, a singing group of the day. "Nothing upsets me more than someone saying the pressure is beginning to build," Anderson replied. "I also don't like it when they say the honeymoon is over."

But we needed help. Fortunately, it came from a hitter in his first week of being a Detroit Tiger. Jones might have been new to us, but he wasn't new to the majors. Heck, in 1979, he had played in all 162 games for the Seattle Mariners. And in 1981 he finished second in the National League with 34 doubles for the San Diego Padres. He knew his way around the big leagues and how to connect off major league pitching. After spending a few weeks at Triple A, he doubled and scored a run in his debut for us on June 6, but it was too late for us to avert a 6–3 loss to the Blue Jays.

Jones was back in the lineup the next day, batting seventh and starting in center, though there wasn't anything wrong with Lemon that a couple of days rest wouldn't fix. Jones had been a center fielder for much of his career, though. It was home to him. He was a capable outfielder, to be sure, and whatever he contributed at the plate would be a bonus. Not taking long, this was the bonus he provided for us in his second game as a Tiger: a three-run home run off the facade of the third deck at Tiger Stadium to break a 1–1 tie against Toronto's Jim Clancy en route to a 5–3 victory that enabled us to split the series against the Jays. When Ruppert returned from rounding the bases, the crowd summoned him out of the dugout for a curtain call, the first of his career. "I don't even know what kind of pitch I hit," Jones said. "My mind was blank. My adrenalin was pumping."

The net effect was that we had minimized the damage the Jays could have inflicted after taking two in a row from us at Tiger Stadium. "Until we get it back together and get hot again, which we're going to do," Trammell said, "we've held on."

What we clearly needed at that point was to string together some victories, which we hadn't done immediately after Bergman's home run began the Toronto series. It would not be easy to achieve, though.

After all, we were heading to Baltimore, where we would face Davis and Mike Flanagan in the first two games, the same pitchers who limited us to one run in the two games they had recently started at Tiger Stadium. Fortunately, we got a break in the first game against the Orioles when right fielder Jim Dwyer misplayed Johnson's double to the corner with one out and Bergman on first in the seventh. With us trailing 2–1 at the time in nearly 100-degree weather, Bergman's run tied it, and HoJo ended up at third.

That knocked Davis out of the game. Tippy Martinez replaced him but without his best stuff. He walked Lou Whitaker, then came in with a hittable pitch that Trammell drove to left for the go-ahead sacrifice fly. Doug Bair pitched a scoreless bottom of the inning, and Hernandez finished it with his first save in two weeks. Then again, we hadn't won back-to-back games in two weeks. "This was a very big win for us," Lemon said, "maybe the biggest one yet."

Or as Sparky added, "landing the first punch was very important."

If nothing else, the comeback effort helped offset the gem that Flanagan tossed against us the next day in a 4–0 Orioles victory. We were at a crossroads now. Would we continue to be the inconsistent 6–9 Tigers of the last few weeks or would we begin to assert ourselves again, which we needed to do with two more games in Baltimore, followed by three in Toronto?

What we hoped was the definitive answer to that question showed up the next day against the Orioles—when the top third of our batting order became a wrecking crew in a doubleheader.

Whitaker, Trammell, and Kirk Gibson combined for 14 hits, 11 RBIs, and nine runs while we outscored the Orioles 18–4 in the two games. Having scored more than five runs just three times in our last 20 games, the sudden splurge was warmly welcomed. "This has to be one of the greatest days in Tigers' history," Anderson said.

We also won the first night in Toronto, holding on for a 5–4 triumph with the help of Hernandez's third save in the last five games. "I wouldn't be waiting for a collapse from this team," Sparky said. "Somebody might catch us, but we're not going to collapse."

Still hoping to be the team to catch us, the Blue Jays dominated the next two games, 12–3 and 7–3, trimming our lead to six games after what the Toronto newspapers labeled "the June World Series." It was still cat and mouse, though, between the Jays and us. In the first 13 days of June, we had increased our margin over Toronto by a mere half game. As Sparky observed, "We could have blown the lid off everything simply by playing well."

At this point with another city to visit, our trip was getting extremely long. Heading to Milwaukee, we were still on the road after leaving Toronto, while the Jays stayed home against the Boston Red Sox. The Sox were in the initial throes of an eight-game losing streak. Meanwhile, not exactly setting the world afire, our next opponents, the Milwaukee Brewers, had lost 10 of their last 14. With our opposing teams struggling, neither us nor the Jays would stumble. We swept the Brewers; the Jays swept the Sox. Talk about being in lockstep with each other: the Jays were desperately trying to creep closer to us while we were still doing our best to fend them off.

Baltimore was a distant third, 11½ games out of first. But we couldn't afford to lose our focus.

As good as it felt to be back home, returning from our three-city trip didn't help us right away. The Yankees' Phil Niekro handcuffed us on three hits in a 2–1 Yankees' victory while Toronto had the day off. We all agreed that Niekro had pitched a terrific game.

The next night we needed something good to happen while trailing 4–3 in the eighth—and it did. With one out and the bases empty against Ron Guidry, we sandwiched four singles around a walk. The runs of that rally enabled us to withstand a rare rocky ninth inning from Aurelio Lopez en route to a 7–6 victory against the Yankees. Toronto, meanwhile, lost by a run at home to Milwaukee.

When we won the next night on Johnson's walk-off home run in the 13th inning—another big blast from HoJo—after the Jays had lost again by a run at home to the Brewers, it felt like the team chasing us so tenaciously had finally blinked. Until that point, the Jays hadn't lost consecutive games by a run at home all year. As for Johnson he was just happy to contribute. As a bonus his parents and in-laws were in the crowd of almost 44,000. "Sparky told me I'd get a fastball and I did," HoJo said. "But whenever I hit a home run, it's an accident."

We liked his accidents, though. In fact, we hoped he'd soon have many more of them.

Our big surge of the month didn't begin until two days later during the second game of a four-game series at home against Milwaukee. We scored five runs on five hits and three walks in the first inning of that June 22 game, a cushion Dave Rozema protected long enough for an eventual 7–3 victory. After not winning since April, it was Rosie's third victory in his last three starts. With his best game since May 1, Milt Wilcox pitched us to a 5–1 victory in the next game—and after missing two starts because of a hyperextended elbow—Jack Morris limited the Brewers to one hit in six innings of a 7–1 triumph the following day. With that, we had won three in a row.

In the game Morris pitched, Jones again lifted a mammoth home run to right. This one bounced on the roof, then cleared it, and dented a Buick on Trumbull Avenue when the ball finally landed. "That's the hardest I've ever pulled the ball," Jones said about his blast that soared over the roof while barely staying fair.

"Ruppert gives us another dimension," Anderson said.

I don't want anyone thinking that we were suddenly on another April-May spree, but we did go 11–5 in the last 16 games of June while the Jays suddenly stumbled to a 4–9 finish. By the end of the month, we were in front by 10 games. Through thick and thin—and there'd been measures of both, to be sure—we had weathered the season's initial storm.

But just to prove we were still winning games dramatically at the end of the month—as Bergman's 13-pitch home run had done earlier in June—my two-run home run in the 10th inning against the Yankees handed us a 9–7 victory on June 26, and Gibson's walk-off blast beat the Minnesota Twins 7–5 on June 29. "Kirk is an amazing player when the chips are down," Sparky said.

In the final game of the month—in less dramatic fashion, but equally welcome—we scored the tying run in the seventh inning on Jones' sacrifice fly followed by the eventual winning run against the Twins in the eighth on a wild pitch by Ron Davis.

As we headed into July, Whitaker, Trammell, and Lemon all were hitting .309. Morris was 12–4, Petry was 11–3, and Hernandez was 4–0 with 14 saves. Of Willie's saves, Sparky said, "That's why we got him, but I never dreamed it would be nothing like this."

Above all, though, we still felt good about ourselves. There were many reasons to be smiling…until July began.

Chapter 9

Trouble in July?

J uly began with a thud, actually. A loss on the first day of the month was followed by another, and another, and another. After three blowouts the first week, we didn't win until the fifth game we played. Then we won just once in the next four games. *What the heck was going on? Was the season falling apart?* "No amount of perfume could help the ugly way we've played recently. But it might be a blessing it's all happening at once," Sparky Anderson said of what went wrong during the slump, hinting with hope that it couldn't possibly all go sour for an extended amount of time.

But it wasn't going well, that's for sure. After we went 2–7 in the first nine games of July, our lead was back to where it had been in mid-June. Just like that, in other words, our 10-game advantage was back down to seven, which meant the Toronto Blue Jays were uncomfortably close again in our rearview mirror. Not only that, but we also were worried about Alan Trammell, who had a bum shoulder—and also about Jack Morris, whose season suddenly had gone off the rails.

Then again, we should have known from the first day of the month that July looked like trouble. We had easily won the opening games of April, May, and June, outscoring our opponents 33–5. But when we lost 9–0 at home to the Minnesota Twins on July 1, something was definitely different. Making matters worse, we didn't lose any of the next three games by fewer than four runs, so it wasn't until we salvaged a victory in Texas with a six-run ninth inning that we finally got a glimpse of some pennant-race sunshine in July. "If this wasn't a miracle," Sparky said of how we finally were able to win a game, "then my hair isn't white."

But even that rally against the Texas Rangers required a trio of two-out hits for us to avoid another loss. The big blow of the inning was a three-run home run from Kirk Gibson that finally put us in front. "That game was in the grave with grass growing on it," Anderson said of how unlikely it had looked like we would win. "But a victory like this is better than anything. If you tried to invent something to get us out of our spin, you would invent a game like this."

Then, of course, we promptly lost the next three of four leading up to the All-Star break. Even Sparky was depressed after those defeats. What helped is that while we were spinning our wheels, the Jays didn't take full advantage of the opportunity to gain substantial ground. In a nine-game stretch before and after the All-Star break, we maintained a seven-game lead. By the time we snapped out of it, the Jays had wasted their chance. "But we still have to kick ourselves in the rear," Anderson said.

So, we kicked ourselves in the rear. We went 14–5 the rest of July and led by 12 games when the month ended.

During the All-Star break, I'm happy to say that six of us didn't get much of a break. That's because we were chosen to participate in the game on July 10 in San Francisco. The National League beat us 3–1, but the Detroit Tigers were well represented. Sparky coached third base, Lou Whitaker doubled and singled in three at-bats, Morris worked two scoreless innings, Chet Lemon singled in one of his two at-bats, Willie Hernandez pitched an inning of relief (in which he gave up a solo home run to Dale Murphy), but I, well, I didn't have the best of games, striking out twice and dropping a throw for an error that cost us a run.

Making matters worse, on the play on which I made an error, I got blasted in the mouth at the plate. In the first inning, Dave Winfield made a throw from left field that was wide of the plate. I tried to reach across to grab it, then come back to the plate quickly, but the runner, Steve Garvey, gave me a forearm shiver right to the mouth. When that happened, I dropped the ball.

The odd thing is that I was chewing gum on that play, which I had never done before—and certainly never did again—and when Garvey hit me in the mouth, I bit my tongue badly because I'd been chewing. In fact, I bit a big chunk out of my tongue. Dave Stieb was pitching at the time, and when I told him, "Man, it feels like I just bit my tongue in half," he checked it out.

But as I stuck my tongue out at him, he yelped, saying, "Lance! There's a big ol' hole in your tongue!" Plus, there was a lot of blood. Then I looked down at my wristband, and the chunk of my tongue was on it! Step by step, this was getting grizzlier. I stayed in the game, though. My tongue was hurting, but that didn't affect my ability to play. That's my big memory of that game, though: I didn't leave my heart in San Francisco, as the song goes. I left my tongue. After getting sewed up, I couldn't talk very well for a while.

I was hoping to somehow get even with Garvey someday but never got the opportunity. And to be fair, he didn't know he had caused a problem. It was my fault. I had put myself in a position to get run over. But even with all that, it was an honor to be an All-Star, representing a first-place team. Seriously, that's the way I looked at it. I felt it was important for the Tigers to be well represented because we had played so well through the first half. It was great we had as many players chosen as we did, though I felt Dan Petry got snubbed. Alan Trammell also would have been there had it not been for his shoulder situation. Petry, meanwhile, reacted to not being named by saying, "I'll make it next year."

When the regular season resumed, two of the biggest wins we had all year took place on July 13 and July 14 in Minnesota—the first time (and only time in 1984) that we won two consecutive extra-inning games. And since we had lost seven of nine at that point, they could not have occurred at a better time.

We won the first game 5–3 in 11 innings on Whitaker's inside-the-park home run after a hit almost as rare: Tom Brookens' two-out triple. Brookens ended up at third when his liner eluded Kirby Puckett in center, though Brookens briefly thought about going all the way for home. "I'm glad I was held up at third," he said. "I would have been out by a mile."

Whitaker followed with a drive to left that eluded outfielder Darrell Brown, a former Tiger. This time there was no stopping at third. Lou made it all the way around with an inside-the-park home run. Hernandez and Aurelio Lopez teamed for the win and save, respectively. On that same day, however, we learned that we'd be facing extended time without Trammell, who went on the disabled list with tendinitis in his right shoulder.

The next night Dave Bergman's solo shot off Ron Davis in the ninth inning tied the game, almost matching the drama of his home run off Toronto's Roy Lee Jackson in June.

Then we broke the 4–4 tie when Gibson scored from second on a single in the 12th by Lemon. The Twins howled at the call at the plate by umpire Vic Voltaggio, but when the dust cleared (literally)—after a collision at home between Gibson and catcher Dave Engle—we were in front by a run.

The controversy wasn't about the collision, actually, because as Voltaggio explained later there'd been no tag on the play. But Gibson also hadn't touched the plate, so Vic didn't make a call right away. He declared Gibson safe only after Kirk went back and touched home while eluding Engle after the collision. Well, the Twins weren't buying it. "I tagged him," Engle insisted. "You all saw it. He was out."

"Ray Charles could have made that call," fumed Minnesota manager Billy Gardner.

About whether he was tagged, Gibson said, "I don't know if I was or not."

Gibby being involved in a collision was nothing new, though. He was always a very aggressive runner. I thought he would hurt himself someday sliding violently into second base because he slid so late. I even warned him once to start sliding sooner, but that's just the way he played. The ground would shake when he ran. You could hear him coming.

In any case, we led the Twins by a run at that point but would need another. I had been walked intentionally after Gibson's one-out double in the 12ᵗʰ and took third on Lemon's run-scoring single. I was still at third when the Twins elected also to walk Darrell Evans intentionally and pitch to Bergman, setting up a possible double play. Instead of complying with a ground ball, Bergman crossed up the Twins by hitting a fly ball to center for a sacrifice fly. Our lead was now two runs—enough to withstand the solo home run Minnesota countered with in the bottom of the 12ᵗʰ.

We closed out the series with a 6–2 victory the next day—our third win in what would eventually become a five-game winning streak. After a solitary defeat, we followed one winning streak with another, a six-gamer, which meant that July had turned from being problematic into a plus for us with a stretch of 11 wins in 12 games.

The only storm clouds at that point were Trammell's sore shoulder and a bad stretch for Morris, in which he went 0–3 in four starts. As he struggled he also stopped talking to the media.

After being 10–1 in the first two months of the season, Jack was 3–6 with a 5.40 ERA in June/July, a reversal that irked him. When Morris visibly lost his temper between innings of one of his July starts, pitching coach Roger Craig commented that he "still has a lot of growing up to do, as we all saw tonight. He's acting like a little baby, and it's upsetting the entire club."

Sparky preferred to focus on the silver lining of Morris' struggles, though. "If I worried about every player who got upset, I'd go stark raving mad," he said. "The good thing is he doesn't have a sore arm. He's just in a slump."

But a slump that was taking a toll.

Thankfully, Jack seemed more like himself when he blanked the Cleveland Indians on five hits in six innings of his next start, a 4–1 victory. Sparky wasn't satisfied, though. "He threw hard. That was good," he said, "but his pitches were all over the place."

Having witnessed it more than once, I remember Jack's temper. Sure, I do. He was high-strung. I think we all wished at times he would get more control of himself. He could be very emotional. I told him once that when he acted that way, the other team fed off it, thinking they had him on the

White Sox Skirmishes

In 1980 Al Cowens, one of our outfielders, charged the mound in Chicago instead of running to first base after hitting a grounder to short. Al was still fairly new to our team when it took place. We had acquired him just a month before from the California Angels for Jason Thompson, and this was the first time we had faced the White Sox since the trade. Or more accurately: it was the first time we had faced the Sox with Ed Farmer pitching for them. As we would soon find out, Al was eager to get even with Farmer for breaking his jaw and several teeth with a pitch the year before. This was his chance.

So, with Farmer on the mound in the 11th inning of a 3–3 game on June 20, Al hit a grounder to short but ran to the mound instead to start swinging at Farmer. A brawl ensued, of course. I was on deck when Al charged. It was the craziest thing I'd ever seen. I didn't really know what was going on. I sort of hesitated wondering, *What just happened? Did I miss something?*

Then I went out to the mound to break it up. Soon we were all out there, and there I was at the bottom of the pile, holding onto Farmer beneath a bunch of bodies. All I could hear was Tony La Russa yelling at me, "Don't hurt him, don't hurt him."

I answered back, "Don't hurt him? I don't even know what's going on!"

Al got ejected, of course, (and eventually suspended), but the Sox—probably because it was the 11th inning, and they might have been short of pitchers—left Farmer in the game. I was the first one up when play resumed and walked. John Wockenfuss then drove me in from first with a double. We scored another run that inning after Farmer was out of the game and beat the Sox 5–3. But it had not been a routine game.

In 1984 a situation with Britt Burns of the White Sox occurred. Glenn Abbott was on the mound for us—we didn't have Glenn very long, just about a year—and what we didn't know was that this game would his best of the season, as well as his last major league victory. In the second inning, however, Glenn hit Carlton Fisk with a curveball. Well, La Russa—Chicago's manager—made a big deal out of it with a bunch of yelling and I'm thinking, *C'mon, Tony, he got hit with a breaking ball for crying out loud.*

Sure enough, though, when I came up later, Burns drilled me with a fastball. But I knew Tony had told him to hit me. As I headed to first base, I stopped part way and yelled something to Britt along the lines of: "I should come out there right now and kick your ass!" Then I turned around and yelled at Tony, "But I know you're the one who told him to do it!"

That ignited Tony, of course. As soon as I pointed at him, he came flying out of the dugout, waving his arms, and yelling. I was so tempted to drop him right then and there and I told him so, but he had Ron Kittle and Greg Luzinski, a couple of big ol' dudes, nearby, and it clearly would have started an all-out brawl. Not that the presence of those guys swayed me, but I wasn't the type of player who just hauled off and punched somebody anyway. We kept exchanging words, however, back and forth, back and forth, and I kept saying to Tony, "If we had hit Fisk on purpose, we would have done it with a fastball."

But then I heard Kirk Gibson behind me in the scrum chirping, "Punch him, punch him!"

Cooler heads needed to prevail soon, or else everyone on both teams would have gotten involved.

"I'll be by the batting cage tomorrow if you want to find me," Tony called out to me, getting in the last word.

It all kind of died down after that somehow, and I went to first base. But it was so typical of our games with the White Sox. We were always getting into fights with them because it seemed like Tony's approach was that: if you hit one of ours, we'll hit two of yours. "I don't think I've ever liked La Russa," I said after that incident. "They ought to throw him out of baseball. He tells pitchers to throw at people—like he's some sort of tough guy."

Wow, tough words…but no one was immune to the heat of the battle.

ropes. I summarized his struggles at the time by saying, "Jack fights himself a lot—himself and the umpires." And sometimes the media. But Jack was Jack. Getting emotional was the way he was back then.

Trammell's temper wasn't a problem, of course, but his arm was. Not only was he suffering from tendinitis in his right shoulder, but he also had an inflamed nerve in his elbow.

"The shoulder problem caused the nerve issue," he said. "I'm not concerned with that. The good thing is there's nothing else wrong."

In other words, he was expecting to be back after a few weeks of rest. "We haven't been playing well," Tram said when he first started feeling discomfort in his shoulder, "but that includes while I was in the lineup. Good teams, and we're a good team, overcome these things."

Losing Trammell for any length of time would be a challenge, though. He would miss more than three weeks of games in July, not returning—even as a designated hitter—until the second game of a doubleheader on the 31st. It wouldn't be until August 17, however, that he was able to play shortstop again. What helped is that in 22 games as our DH, he hit .333.

Fortunately, our season didn't fall apart without Trammell at short. Far from it, in fact. We went 14–5 in the games he missed, then lost eight of 10 when he came back. Doug Baker hit only .157 in 21 games as Trammell's replacement in July, but he made only two errors. After Baker was returned to the minors, Brookens served as Tram's defensive replacement at short for more than two weeks of August. I don't think anybody panicked when we lost Tram. He was a big part of what was going on, sure, but we all felt we could keep things together until he got back. The key was defense. As long as Baker and Brookie played solid defense, which they did, we felt we could pick up the slack offensively.

It certainly didn't come from me, though. I had my own problems, hitting just .191 in July, but as consolation I led the team with 18 RBIs and in runs scored with 16. Production was the name of the game, however—and also the name of my game whenever I was hitting with power. That's what Sparky often talked to me about. He never was concerned about my batting average; he just wanted me to put balls in the seats. So, when I wasn't hitting for average but still knocking in runs, you bet it was considerable consolation because I was helping the team. I was contributing.

With Trammell out, much of the offense came from Ruppert Jones, who hit .345 in July; from Lemon, who hit .313; and from Whitaker, who tied Gibson for the team lead in total bases with 44. Whitaker and Jones each had a four-hit game in July. Both performances highlighted a victory. For Lou it was his second four-hit game of the season.

Pitching-wise, Petry had an exceptional month, going 3–1 with a 2.35 ERA in five starts. In his last three starts of July, all of them victories, Dan allowed only three earned runs. So, he was especially strong the second half of the month when we started stringing some wins together again. "It wouldn't surprise me," Sparky said, "to see him get a lot of Cy Young votes."

Petry dismissed such talk, saying he'd rather just win as many games as Jack. Overall, we pitched better in July than in June. The best games came from Petry and Milt Wilcox in the last 10 days. Petry blanked the Rangers on four singles for eight-and-two-thirds innings on July 22 at Tiger Stadium, getting final out help from Hernandez. Sparky was booed for making a pitching change with just one out to go, but Willie needed only one pitch to retire Pete O'Brien on a pop-up as a pinch-hitter. "I can't worry about what the fans were doing," Anderson said after the game. "They can't shoot me. But if O'Brien had done some damage against Dan, I wouldn't have been able to sleep."

Petry didn't mind the move. Later he admitted he was "bushed" with one out to go after thinking throughout the game that he hadn't been sharp. "But maybe I had good stuff and just didn't know it," he said.

In that game Bergman was used as our leadoff hitter for the first time all year and responded with a first-inning home run off Charlie Hough, who limited us to two hits the rest of the way. Bergman also scored our second run on a wild pitch in the third. "I knew he would make Hough throw strikes," Anderson said of the unusual move to bat Bergman first against the knuckleballer. "He was the only batter we had with any semblance of a strike zone against that guy."

Wilcox followed a week later with a three-hit gem against the Boston Red Sox, another game of nothing but singles for the opposing team. Dennis "Oil Can" Boyd was tough on us that day, striking out 10, but we got all the runs we needed in the second inning on an error at third base by Wade Boggs, followed by Baker's RBI single. Our third run in the 3–0 victory scored on a sacrifice fly in the eighth. Wilcox, meanwhile, was ahead in the count the entire game against the Red Sox. "Maybe the best example all year of one of our pitchers dominating the other team," Anderson said.

"It makes a big difference when a hitter is 0–2 instead of 2–0," Wilcox said. "They were chasing pitches all day long."

The secret to Milt's success in July was his renewed control. After walking seven in a wobbly start to begin the month, he issued only one walk (on a disputed pitch, he claimed) in his next four starts combined, winning three of them. "He can be something of a nibbler," Craig said of Wilcox, "but lately he's been doing a great job of challenging hitters."

To me, Milt was always a guy who worked the corners. That was his bread and butter. Pitchers like that, however, would sometimes miss the corners more than they hit them, leading to some walks. But I gave Roger credit for saying what he said. My respect for Roger was always very high. In my opinion he was a genius. He was beginning to say he might retire after the season, though, that 35 years of buses, trains, and planes were enough. No one liked hearing that, of course. *Roger retiring?* We were hoping he'd change his mind.

Anyway, by the end of July, we had a 71–33 record and were in first place by 12 games. We'd also gone 36–28 since the end of our famously fast start. In the same amount of time, second-place Toronto was 33–33, so in the standings—where it counted most—we were still playing better baseball than the Jays. "I don't care about Toronto, I care about us," I said at the time. "This is make-or-break time for our attitude. We need to maintain a killer instinct. So far, I think we have."

But our most challenging month was just around the corner.

Chapter 10

Major League Debut

I made my major league debut with the Detroit Tigers in 1977 as a September call-up. I was 21 years old. But the major development of my first three years as a Tiger was the hiring of Sparky Anderson as manager in 1979.

Ralph Houk was the manager when I got to the majors. He remained in that position through the 1978 season. Then, my minor league mentor, the man who had been so instrumental in the development of my skills, Les Moss, was named the Tigers' manager for the start of the 1979 season. I was thrilled about that. But Les lasted only 53 games.

Sparky was just too much of a proven winner, and too much of an available personality, for the Tigers to let some other team hire him. So, they swooped in and—in a bold move—hired him themselves. We had just come off a West Coast trip when the announcement was made. I suspected something was taking place that day, but my wife was expecting our first child at any moment. So I told the higher-ups I was headed to the hospital. David, our son, was born on June 13. *Welcome, David. Welcome, Sparky.* What a whirlwind time it was.

Sparky managed his first game for the Tigers on June 14. Frankly, I wasn't quite sure what the situation would be when I got back to the team and whether Dick Tracewski would still be in charge as the interim boss or if Sparky would already be there. I had put baseball out of my mind for a bit during the excitement of the baby being born.

As it turned out, the day I came back coincided with Sparky's first game. When he came on board, his primary objective—other than to shape and mold us into a championship team—was to change the culture of the clubhouse. The Tigers were in the process of ushering out the old and bringing in the new. We were a young team. And Sparky was not shy about laying down the law. One of the first things he said, for instance, was that there would be no facial hair allowed. There were some guys who had mustaches, but the one who most comes to mind was Aurelio Rodriguez, our third baseman. His big, bushy mustache was his trademark. When Sparky said he would allow no facial hair, it was almost like Aurelio was going to cry. But holding his ground, Sparky looked right at him and said, "No exceptions!"

I read in Sparky's book, *Bless You Boys*, that he called home about 10 days later, telling his wife he'd made "the gravest mistake of my life" taking the Tigers' job because he considered us so "unprofessional." He called us "a bunch of frauds" who were happy with fifth or sixth place. That's why he was so committed to "changing the culture."

Within a month Tom Brookens was recalled from Evansville and started sharing time at third with Aurelio, who was sent to the San Diego Padres the following offseason.

Les had been key to the progress of my career. So I was a little frustrated that they let him go, but I never got to say anything like "thanks for all the help" to him before he left. We were told it had happened, that the switch had taken place, and he was gone. I never did see him. It wasn't as if I was an emotional wreck about it, though. I mean that didn't bring on the sudden tailspin I went into after the switch. It was just one of those badly-timed slumps. Then again, there's no such thing as a well-timed slump, is there? Besides, Sparky and I went on to have a great relationship.

My first major league game was on September 5, 1977, in the second game of a doubleheader against the Baltimore Orioles at Tiger Stadium. Rudy May, a pretty good lefty, started for the Orioles. Steve Grilli was on the mound for us. His son, Jason, eventually had quite a career as a relief

Lucky No. 13

Why did I wear No. 13? People have always asked me that. I wore it in the big leagues basically because I had always worn it. Going back to Little League, No. 13 was given to me. I didn't ask for it. It was just the number on one of the bigger uniforms, and I was one of the bigger kids. That's where it all started: Little League.

From then on, as I moved up in team sports and got the chance to pick a number, I always picked No. 13 because I began to identify with it. Even as the years went by in pro ball, I asked for it whenever it was available. The guy, who tried the hardest to talk me out of it, back in the day, strangely enough, was Jim Campbell, my first general manager on the Detroit Tigers. He called me on the phone when I was coming to the big leagues—I was surprised to hear from him at the time—but during that call, he asked me what number I wanted to wear. When I told him No. 13, he sounded startled and said, "Any number but that one! Aren't you superstitious?"

I said, "No, Mr. Campbell, I'm not. That's the number I want."

We went back and forth about it for a while. He put up the biggest argument, but I stood my ground. Eventually he caved in, but I must say it was a fight to get it. He definitely tried to talk me out of it—because he couldn't imagine why anyone would want to wear No. 13. I always thought it was strange that the general manager was calling me about a uniform number. Usually, it was the clubhouse manager.

As the years went on, the media kept asking me about the number. One time in Boston, we were scheduled to play a game on Friday, April 13, so I got a lot of questions about it that day—but more after the game than before because everything about the game added up to 13.

For instance, we scored eight runs in the first inning, and the Red Sox countered with five. We sent 13 batters to the plate in the first, and a lot of them did something productive, but wearing No. 13, I accounted for all three outs of that eight-run first by striking out and hitting into a double play. It was really odd. The media had a lot of fun that day with my choice of a uniform number, which wasn't surprising. It was always an attention-getter.

pitcher. I had made the seven-hour drive from Evansville the day before and got in late but was excited to play in my first game. Al Bumbry, the Orioles' leadoff hitter, began the game with a single and, as soon as he could, took off for second on a steal attempt. Bumbry was a pretty good runner—he twice stole more than 40 bases in his career—but with an accurate throw to our shortstop Tom Veryzer, I got him.

Pat Kelly, another speedster who would eventually steal 250 bases in his career, walked in the first and he, too, took off for second. This time I didn't get him. Bumbry later tried to steal third, so it was clear the Orioles wanted to challenge me right away, but after getting him at second in the first inning, I also threw out Bumbry at third in the fourth.

We lost the game 5–0, but the key to me was that I hadn't been intimidated. In fact, the Orioles were playing right into my wheelhouse because I felt at the time that nobody could throw better than I could. I had that kind of confidence. I wanted teams to run on me because I enjoyed the chance to show what I could do. If I hadn't thrown someone out that day, I would have been upset. But I just remember going into that first game thinking that I should be able to throw anybody out who was going to try.

I was excited about playing in my first major league game but not nervous. My parents had come to Detroit for the series, so they were in the stands. I remember thinking what a big day it was. I grounded out to second base in my first at-bat, walked in my second, flied out to center in my third, then walked again in my fourth. I wasn't normally a hitter who walked much. I didn't walk twice in the same game again until the following July, in fact. Go figure. Walking twice in my first game was one of the early achievements of my career.

So I went 0-for-2 in my debut, but in my second game, I was more productive. I had three hits, scored four runs, and knocked in four in a 12–5 victory against Baltimore. It was one of the best offensive games of my entire career. Among the highlights: I had a bases-loaded double, hit my first home run, and scored a run on a Mickey Stanley single. Yes, in 1977 Stanley was still playing for the Tigers—and playing well. I got my first hit in my second at-bat of my second game. It came off Ed Farmer, who jammed the crap out of me. The pitch almost hit me in the hands, but I managed to put the ball in play off the handle of my bat.

For a moment, though, it seemed like everything was suddenly happening in slow motion. My hands were still vibrating from getting jammed, but I had to take off for first base with the ball in play. I had hit a soft liner over the pitcher's head. Farmer tried to jump up and catch it, but it went just over his glove. The ball landed in the grass between the mound and second base—and just stuck there. I beat it out because nobody could get to it in time. Of course, time was called, and the ball was thrown to our dugout as the first souvenir of my career. I still have it somewhere. When I got back to the dugout, the guys handed me the ball, but by that time, they had put Band-Aids all over it, jokingly indicating how hard I hadn't hit it. Everybody got a big laugh out of that.

I'd already scored twice when I came up in the fourth inning with the bases loaded. That's when I doubled in all three runners—Tito Fuentes, Rusty Staub, and Jason Thompson. When I later scored on a single by Stanley, it meant that a player from the eventual 1984 champions had been driven in by a player from the 1968 champions, a link between the generations of great Tigers teams. Stanley was an amazing athlete, though. I well remember playing with him and being his teammate. There was the day, for instance, when we were taking batting practice at Tiger Stadium, and he grabbed a ball that was lying on the ground. He must have been 35 or 36 at the time, but that didn't matter. "How much would you give me," he asked, "if I could hit this ball into the upper deck in right with one hand?"

We didn't bet on it, but I said to him, "No way!" I then challenged him to do it.

Well, he flipped the ball up in the air and freakin' smoked it into the upper deck with a one-handed swing of the bat. I couldn't believe it. I think all I could say was "Oh, my God!" Mickey had called his shot. But that's the kind of guy he was, fun to be around. I loved playing with him.

I hit my first home run off a lefty reliever, Earl Stephenson. It went into the lower deck in right at Tiger Stadium, but hitting it to right was par for the course for me. Spraying the ball to the opposite field was the way I'd

Japan

At the end of the 1979 season, I was invited to play with a major league All-Star team on a trip to Japan. I was excited about that because it marked the first time I'd been part of any All-Star experience at the major league level. The Japanese were great hosts. Everything about the trip was top shelf, but the pitchers over there drove me crazy. They all threw sidearm! Still, I managed to hit two home runs in Japan.

Arlyne didn't like leaving our baby (David) for so long, but she went with me on the trip. At some point, though, she said, "I have to leave. I must get back." She was still a new mom, you see, so she jumped on a flight by herself and flew back to California. A few days before we left, though, we were in the lobby of the team hotel, waiting to go on whatever the next excursion was, and across the lobby, I saw Tommy Lasorda talking with Chuck Tanner. Lasorda was the manager representing the National League. Chuck was one of his coaches. But Tommy kept looking at me and laughing. Eventually, I went over to him and said, "What's so funny?'

In no uncertain terms, he told me, "The next time I have to negotiate my contract, I want you representing me because if you could talk that beautiful girl into marrying you, you have to be the greatest negotiator on the planet."

Arlyne was a former Miss Hollywood and had been a runner-up at one point in the Miss California beauty pageant. So, I laughed at Tommy's comment. We both did.

been swinging the bat all year at Triple A before the Tigers called me up. Moss, my manager that year at Evansville, had been working with me about hitting the ball up the middle or hitting it the other way, so I had hit many of my 25 home runs at Triple A that year to right.

I felt really good when I first came up to the big leagues and I did well in the games I played in initially, but as the month progressed, my playing time became more sporadic, which prompts me now to truly tip my cap to those guys like Gates Brown, who played sparingly and still could be productive, because it was not easy for me to do. As the month went on, I got worse and worse. After my first five games that first year, I went 2-for-27, but both hits were home runs, so at least I was staying in touch with my power. One of the two was off Boston Red Sox pitcher Bill Lee and went to center field at Tiger Stadium. The other was off Baltimore's May, who had held me hitless in my first game. That home run was to left field in the old ballpark, Memorial Stadium, in Baltimore for my first home run on the road.

Defensively, I fared better, throwing out five of seven runners and not making an error. I had always considered throwing one of my biggest strengths, if not the biggest.

In 1978 I was platooned with Milt May, but I understood going into the season that I would be. I faced the left-handers; he faced most of the righties, which meant, of course, that I didn't see many right-handers and when I did—like for the second game of a doubleheader or a day game after night game—it wasn't very pretty. They just hammered me with breaking balls.

I hit .161 for the year against right-handers and a better, but not enormously so, .235 against lefties. Thirteen of my 14 home runs were hit off left-handers. I'm sure Milt didn't like the arrangement either. But I imagine he could see the writing on the wall, that they were trying to work me in. May probably thought that he'd eventually be squeezed out. That's exactly the way it worked out—but in 1979, not in 1978. I just wasn't ready in '78. I got off to a slow start, hitting .194 in April and just .235—but with four home runs—in May.

One of the highlights of my season came later when I hit a home run off Wilbur Wood, the knuckleballer for the Chicago White Sox. What I remember about that home run is that he had just thrown a knuckleball that I hit about nine miles foul. *Dang it*, I thought, because I'd at last nailed one of his knucklers but swung too early. I didn't ever have much success against anyone who could throw a knuckleball. It was a big mystery pitch to me. But then he threw me another, and I hit it just as far—but fair this time into the upper deck in left. I couldn't believe I had hit a ball that far twice in a row. Usually after hitting a long foul ball, you end up doing nothing.

So, hitting that home run was a big thrill for me, and it carried over to the next day when I hit two more home runs off Britt Burns. I remember reading a comment from Britt the next day that he would never let me do that again. To which I just thought, *Okay, whatever.* I got to know Britt a little bit after our playing careers when both of us were coaching. We had a shared interest in hunting that we talked about, so we hit it off.

Those home runs weren't the only highlights of the year. I had a six-RBI game in Minnesota that featured a two-run triple—just my second triple—and my first grand slam. I remember hitting the slam because it came after the hitter in front of me was walked intentionally, the first time I'd experienced having the batter in front of me walked to load the bases. The Minnesota Twins walked Staub after Ron LeFlore stole second, then I hit a bomb to left. I always regarded an intentional walk to the batter in front of me as a personal insult, but I wasn't always able to capitalize like that.

There were times I thought the season was getting better for me near the end. For instance, I had my first four-hit game as a big leaguer in Cleveland on September 16, but even with that boost, my batting average climbed to only .229 before settling back down to .219.

On the downside, I also made my first error that year—but at the beginning of the season, not the end. In the first game I played in 1978, Tommy Hutton of the Toronto Blue Jays stole second, then went to third when my throw to second skipped away for an error. The good thing is that Hutton got greedy after that, and with Jim Slaton on the mound for us, we nailed him attempting to steal home.

We got off to a fine start as a team in 1978 and thought we might be headed for a good season. As late as May 21, we were in first place with a 23–12 record, but when we went 12–23 in the next 35 games, our balloon burst. The problem was our offense. We went 2–9 in late May because we didn't score more than three runs in any of the 11 games. With that slump we fell from being in a tie for first to third place, seven games out. Eventually, we finished in fifth place, 13½ games out. Thompson and Staub combined to hit 50 home runs with 217 RBIs, but neither of those guys would be around when 1984 arrived. Slaton led the team with 17 wins but was not re-signed after the season.

When 1979 rolled around, it still didn't look like a future championship team was in the works. We had a strong core up the middle with Alan Trammell and Lou Whitaker at short and second, and Jack Morris seemed poised to have his first good year in the majors, which he did with 17 wins, but we were still many moves away from being the team we would become a few years later. We were a work in progress at many positions, but fortunately for me, the situation behind the plate had become clearer.

I was the starting catcher from the get-go in 1979 and while April, when I hit .265, went better for me than any month the year before, it wasn't until the second month of the season that I felt like I finally made any kind of impact as a big league hitter. In May of '79, I hit .365 with 20 runs scored and a .563 slugging percentage. I was excited about that because as a young player you always wonder how long they're going to stick with you if you're not producing. So, putting a pretty good month behind me and showing that at least I was capable of being the player they wanted me to be—and needed me to be—was a big confidence boost.

Another boost, I must say, was that the Tigers traded May, my competition for the catching job, to the White Sox on May 27. I took that as an indication of their commitment to me. I responded by going 15-for-26 in the first seven games after the trade, raising my batting to .336. In those seven games, I drove in seven runs and scored eight. But even then I attributed a lot of the success I was having to Moss, who always seemed to push the right buttons where I was concerned. He helped me stay focused. He helped me adjust.

A little more than two weeks after the departure of Milt, however—and while I was still sizzling at the plate—Moss was dismissed as the Tigers' manager. The Sparky Anderson era was about to begin. And so was one of my prolonged slumps—much to my bewilderment. I should have been able to figure things out, which I did off and on, but I never was the consistent hitter that I would have liked to be. I had spurts when I was really good, but there were other times when I fell off the cliff for a while. Bottom line: there was no rhyme or reason to the way I hit. I just wish I'd been able to solve it. What took place in 1979 was a clear example of my ups and downs. With my batting average at .336 on June 2, I hit only .213 the next two months. It wasn't until August 10 that the boat stopped rocking. From that point on, I hit .312 for the rest of the season. Don't ask me how or why, however.

We played some crazy games in 1979. One of my hits that year was a double that put us ahead of Boston in the 14th inning—but more specifically, it put us ahead in the six-run, 14th inning. With four RBIs and three hits, including that double and a home run, it was one of my better offensive games. Plus, I also threw out two runners. I was pleased with how I was playing late in the year. After being so close to Les, I really wanted to show Sparky what I could do. Liking how things were going, but not thumping my chest about it, I felt I had done enough to establish myself in the majors and solidify my spot on the team. I was just hoping to show Sparky enough to be his guy for a while. As far as the team was concerned in 1979, we never looked like contenders. Steve Kemp had a big year, but it wasn't until July 25th, with a 49–48 record, that we remained over .500 en route to a second consecutive fifth-place finish.

Chapter 11

Cusp of Contention

The only time we had a contending chance at the postseason before 1984 was in 1981, and I must say we made a heck of a run at it. It was a weird, work-stoppage season, however. Starting in June, there was no baseball for two months because of a labor dispute, and when it finally ended, Major League Baseball decided the best way to generate interest was to crown a second-half champion. Each league would have a first-half and second-half champion who would play against each other in a postseason series to determine which team would go to the World Series. The New York Yankees were the first-half champion with a 34–22 record, so they were headed to the playoffs already. But there were a few teams—us among them—thinking they could win the second half.

I wasn't much help at the plate when play resumed in August. I hadn't done anything baseball-wise on a consistent basis during the two months we didn't play. So when we came back, I was a mess. It took me a long time to get going. As late as September 8, for instance, I was hitting .219. But the team was doing well. We had finished the first half with an 8–1 streak, so we felt we were getting our act together when the work stoppage intervened. And when the second half began, we picked up where we had left off, going 10–3. Suddenly, instead of spinning our wheels in sixth place, which had been the case for much of the first half, we were in first place. For much of the second half, in fact, we were in and out of first, never leading by much or trailing by much.

Plus, we got a big boost from our bench players, who called themselves "The Riders of the Lonesome Pine" that year—guys like Mick Kelleher, Lynn Jones, Stan Papi, and Rick Leach.

The Stolen Base King

I always felt good about being able to throw out runners. I was accurate, had a strong arm, and enjoyed what I considered to be steady success. The big challenge for any catcher of my era, of course, was Rickey Henderson. I was fortunate enough to throw him out 17 times, the most of any catcher, but it took 53 attempts for me to do it.

My percentage wasn't the best. That belonged to Bob Boone, who threw him out 15 times in 34 attempts. Bob was a close friend. I'm glad he was successful at throwing out such a great runner.

I took a lot of pride in my throwing, though. As far as I was concerned, I could throw anybody out, but I changed my entire style when Rickey was on first base. It seemed no matter what I did, he always beat my throws. I would put the ball right on the money, but he often slid in just ahead of the tag. It used to drive me crazy. I kept asking myself, *What more can I do to get this guy?*

So, I eventually got to thinking that when Rickey was on first, I would drop my right foot back a little bit because the only way I'd be able to take any time off my throws was to not move my back foot. Plus, I made some adjustments angling my body, trying to cheat as much as I could. I did that in a game at Tiger Stadium and I finally threw him out. But I also remember he once stole four bases in a game against us.

Sometimes Rickey didn't even have to be running on us to score. There was a game in which he walked, was bunted to second base, went to third on a wild pitch, and scored on another wild pitch. We made it easy for him. But he rarely made it easy for us. Rickey was a great base stealer, the king, and a true challenge for me my whole career. I tip my cap to him. Thankfully, I ended up getting him a time or two (or 17), but most of the time, it was the other way around.

"The Pine Brothers have been more instrumental in this streak than the regulars," outfielder Steve Kemp said of our second-half surge.

The entire playoff picture came down to our final series in Milwaukee. We went into those games trailing the Milwaukee Brewers by a game, but we felt good about our chances. The first game did not go well—or as we needed it to go, let's say. The Brewers grabbed an early lead, added some later runs, and soundly beat us 8–2.

That left us two back with two to go, but we weren't out of it going into the second game of the series, which we clearly needed to win. And as late as the eighth inning, it looked like we were going to. Jack Morris took a 1–0 lead into the bottom of the eighth. Going head-to-head with Brewers ace Pete Vuckovich, Jack had been on his game that day, blanking the Brewers on six hits without a walk for the first seven innings. But he walked Paul Molitor to start the eighth, losing him on a 3–1 call that I questioned. Then we screwed up Robin Yount's sacrifice attempt, allowing both runners to be safe. What's worse: we also botched Cecil Cooper's bunt attempt to the third-base side of the mound after that, loading the bases. Without getting the ball out of the infield, the Brewers had manufactured a threat, which they made the most of. On Ted Simmons' grounder to short, Molitor scored the tying run, and after an intentional walk to Ben Ogilvie, Gorman Thomas drove in Yount with a sacrifice fly to right. Then we were staring down the throat of being eliminated from our playoff hopes, and Rollie Fingers, in true future Hall of Famer fashion, retired the side in order in the ninth to put us away in the 2–1 Brewers' victory.

We won the next day, but it was too late to matter. Milwaukee won the second half but was eliminated in its postseason series by the Yankees. I remember that everyone had been excited and upbeat going into that weekend against the Brewers, and it would have been nice to take that next step into the playoffs, but it wasn't meant to be. That was the highlight of the 1980–82 years. At least, it was the team highlight. Those seasons were full of personal ups and downs, however.

In 1980, his first full year of managing us, Sparky Anderson decided to experiment with me at first base and in the outfield. It was his way, it turned out, of sparing me the everyday wear and tear of catching, but the plan didn't get off to a good start. In spring training that year, I was playing first base against the Montreal Expos, and Ron LeFlore—whom we had traded to the Expos—was on first. On a wide pickoff attempt, I reached awkwardly for the ball as Ron came back to the bag feet first. His knee hit my elbow, hyperextending it. I remember thinking, *Oh great, here I am at first base and I'm going to end up with a broken arm.* Fortunately, it felt a lot worse than it actually turned out to be and, except for missing a chunk of spring training, the injury didn't set me back. In fact, the opposite was true. I hit .362 for April.

The team didn't start as hot, however. We fell to 9–16 before turning things around in May. But when we turned it around, we really turned it around. By July 4 we were in second place with a 41–32 record. Not able to sustain that caliber of play, we slipped to 84–78 for the year, a lackluster 19 games out of first. On a personal front, I was gratified when John Hiller said that the pitchers weren't "shaking Lance off as much as they used to. He calls an excellent game now."

My whole philosophy of calling a game was to pay attention to the hitter, which dictated what I called. For the most part, I went with the pitcher's strength, but he could shake me off whenever he wanted. What told me how I was calling a game was if the pitcher didn't often shake me off. That told me he might be thinking, *This guy knows what he's doing.*

My temper and Morris' stubbornness also surfaced in 1980—in the same game actually.

On May 3 in Oakland, with Billy Martin managing the A's, the eventual meltdown began when Wayne Gross stole home on us. As everybody knows, who watched him—especially back then—when Jack pitched from a windup, it was very slow and deliberate with a pretty high leg kick. Well, the A's obviously knew that, and when Gross got to third in the second inning, Jack continued to pitch from his windup, as was his choice. What happened, though, is that as soon as he began his windup, Gross took off from third. Jack saw him, but when he tried to speed things up, he got a little ahead of himself and ended up firing the ball into the ground in front of the plate. Consequently, Gross was safe with an easy steal of home. Now, allowing a steal of home is an embarrassing thing to happen to a team. Meanwhile, the A's were pretty charged up about it.

An inning later, when Dwayne Murphy was on third for Oakland, our pitching coach, Roger Craig, went to the mound to tell Jack to pitch from the stretch. But Jack refused. Roger insisted, but Jack replied that he felt more comfortable pitching from a windup. He said, though, that he would make sure Murphy didn't steal home on him. Roger tried once more, but Jack absolutely refused. So, Roger walked back to the dugout, and I walked back to the plate. On the next pitch, though—sure enough—here came Murphy. And the same thing happened. Trying to compensate for the runner racing down the line from third, Jack sped up his delivery and fired the ball into the ground again. I couldn't get a glove on it, so the ball went back to the backstop as Murphy scored. What a fiasco. I was running after the ball, the crowd was laughing, the A's were celebrating, and everybody's going crazy. I thought, *This is humiliating. We're getting our asses kicked because Jack had to prove a point that didn't work.*

When the inning ended, I was still pissed. Mitchell Page had tried to make it three steals of home on us also in the third inning, but we finally executed the play correctly. Still, the damage had been done. I got to the dugout but was still frustrated while taking off my glove. I went to throw it against the back wall of the dugout, but the moment I did, I could see it was headed for trouble. There was a thin little water pipe on the back wall with a spigot at the end of it—about knee high. My glove hit that spigot squarely, snapping it off. Water started spraying out of that pipe like a broken fire hydrant. And there was no way to turn it off. Suddenly, there was pandemonium in the dugout with everyone scrambling because of all the water.

Watching this, the A's were over in their dugout, getting a big kick out of it because we looked like a bunch of clowns. It was just a miserable game all the way around, and when it was over, Sparky made us all sit down in the clubhouse and aired everybody out, one guy at a time.

When his eyes shifted over to me, I knew it was my turn. "And you!" he bellowed at me, "I'm fining you $500 because I'll be damned if I have to go swimming in my own dugout!"

Going for the Cycle

I counted them up one time: I had 14 four-hit games in my career. But the only game in which I ever had an at-bat with a chance for me to hit for the cycle was on August 22, 1980, at the old Metropolitan Stadium in Minnesota. I came up with one out in the top of the 12th, needing a triple to complete the cycle and I got a hit, but it was another double.

The thing is that I could easily have tried for third on the play, and I regretted it later that I didn't. Instead, I shut it down at second base. I don't know what I was thinking except I didn't really have hitting for the cycle on my mind. So when I was running the bases, it just seemed wise when I got to second base to just stop there. But I should have at least tried to go for it and would have if I'd been mindful of what was on the line. I remember thinking later that I could have made it because the double went deep into the right-field corner.

Later I thought, *Gosh, dang it, I might never get another chance like that.* And, sure enough, I never did. To make matters worse, Al Cowens was the next batter, but all he did was top a ball in front of the plate on which the Twins threw me out at third. So, on what could have been—and maybe should have been—a triple to complete the cycle, I didn't even score. And we ended up losing by a run the next inning.

It had been an eventful day, to be sure.

Later that year, also in Oakland, I hit the only pinch-hit home run of my career. Batting for Champ Summers with two on, which I'm sure pissed Champ off, I connected off (future Detroit Tigers pitching coach) Jeff Jones. Jonesy became a good friend of mine later in our careers, but I also hit a walk-off grand slam off him that I never let him forget. For instance, as coaches we were at a stop one year on the annual Tigers' preseason tour when someone asked me what had been the most memorable moment of my career. With Jonesy sitting next to me, I started to mention the grand slam, but I couldn't even get it out of my mouth before he jumped off his chair and started beating on me, saying, "Don't say it! Don't say it!" But, as I said, I've never let him forget it.

I also made my first All-Star Game appearance in 1980. What a thrill it was because it took place at Dodger Stadium, and Arlyne and my parents sat in the stands. But I struck out against Bruce Sutter, an at-bat I've relived a million times. He hung me one of his infamous forkballs that—I don't know how—I swung through. It had "hit me" written all over it, but I still somehow missed it.

The experiment of me playing other positions continued into May that year, but on May 8, when the Seattle Mariners beat us with four runs in the ninth, the winning run scored on my error at first base. I started only two more games at first after that. So it was the beginning of the end of using me at different spots. I started in right field a few times after that, but all the fooling around at other positions was thankfully over for me by June 1. I can't say I was ever comfortable at first base, but my entire time there and in the outfield had come out of the blue. It wasn't as if I had ever worked out at those positions on a regular basis. The only experience in pro ball I'd had in the outfield was shagging during batting practice when there's no pressure on you.

It wasn't a totally lost cause for us as a team, however, in 1980. Starting the next day after that May 8 game, which I cost us with my error at first base, we went 32–16 and were in second place by the Fourth of July, seven-and-a-half games out. But we never got closer than that the rest of the way. Still, to play that well for that long felt good to a bunch of us young guys.

At some point in 1981, Roger, our pitching coach, decided he should start calling the pitches. At first, I took that very personally. Sparky was actually the one to lay down the law, saying Roger would be calling the pitches and that no one would be allowed to shake him off. My first thought was, *Oh man, this isn't going to go over well.*

Some guys liked the crutch of Roger calling the pitches, but Jack and Milt Wilcox weren't big fans of it. They wanted to throw whatever they wanted to throw whenever they wanted to throw it. As for me, I didn't know why we were suddenly doing it. Because of the pitchers or because of me? I remember reading a comment Sparky made that, "Either we have the dumbest pitchers in the league, or there's another problem."

I thought what other problem could he be talking about if it isn't the pitchers' fault? So, with that comment in mind, I went right into his office asking, "What does this mean? Explain it to me because it sure sounds like you're pointing the finger at me."

Sparky replied, "Well, I'm not. Sit down and let me explain. We have a lot of young pitchers on this staff, and they can shake you off whenever they want to. But there's a pattern developing here. They must understand that if they're going to be successful at this level, they can't always come back with a fastball when they get behind in the count. This is what the new strategy is all about. They need to learn how to throw their other pitches. So, we decided that by saying they couldn't shake off Roger, they had to learn to throw their off-speed pitches when they get behind. They'll become accustomed to it that way and hopefully develop some confidence in throwing those pitches."

I saw the logic in that. It made sense to me, but at first when I entered Sparky's office, I was ready to go toe to toe with him. Roger called the pitches for quite some time after that, and I think they were pleased with the results. Eventually, though, Sparky loosened the reins.

After settling my differences in spring training with Sparky about weight training—he wanted me to report at 220 pounds, but I reported at 245—the 1982 season began in a painful way for me when I strained some ligaments in my left hand while checking my swing in the second game of the season. It was so painful that after I came back for good 16 games later, I changed my way of holding the bat for the first time in my career. I dropped two fingers off the knob to take some pressure off my hand. Fortunately, it worked out because I hit a home run against the Minnesota Twins in my first game back and batted .309 in my first 21 games. But it took a while before the injury completely healed.

Things were going well for the team, too. In 1982 we were in first place as late as June 12 with a 36–19 record, but then we lost 14 of 15 and never fully recovered. We were four games over .500 when our tailspin ended and still only four games over at the end of the season. What really hurt us is that with a 36–45 record we couldn't win away from home. In fact, we became the worst road team I'd been on as a Tiger. But it was simply and easily explained: we didn't hit well on the road, we didn't pitch well on the road, and we suffered 13 walk-off losses on the road. At one point, we encountered walk-off losses in three of four games and soon after that in four of five games. I felt sorry for the pitchers in those situations, good guys like Dave Tobik.

Things went better for me individually. With 32 home runs, I set an American League record for catchers and, at the All-Star Game in Montreal, I set another record by throwing out three runners: Steve Sax, Ozzie Smith, and Al Oliver. Plus, I helped to erase that disappointing All-Star Game strikeout against Sutter, which had been in my mind since 1980, with a double off Mario Soto. What was bad about that double, though, is that I had forgotten to bring my batting helmet to Montreal and had to wear a Cleveland Indians helmet. So, there I was, standing at second base after hitting a double in the All-Star Game, wearing an Indians' helmet instead of one from the Tigers. I didn't throw out all the runners who tried to steal a base on me in that game. Tony Pena stole second, but it soothed my wounded pride that when we were leaving the field after that inning, Frank White came over to me and said, "You got him, Lance. He was out."

As for setting the home run record for American League catchers, which had been shared since the 1950s by Yogi Berra and Gus Triandos, I was excited about it, of course, and when I got home for the offseason, I received a telegram from Yogi congratulating me. For him to take the time to do that was pretty cool.

Late in the 1982 season, we were in Oakland when Rickey Henderson was close to breaking Lou Brock's record of 118 stolen bases. He came into our two-game series with 114, and I really wanted to be the one to prevent him from getting it. In the first game of that series on a Monday night, he got me once, and I got him once. So then he was at 115 with one game of the series remaining.

But after that first game, Arlyne called to say that if I didn't get back to Michigan right away, I was going to miss the birth of our second child. We'd made a pact that I would be on hand for the birth of all our children, so I went to tell Sparky that I had to leave. He tried to talk me out of it at first, saying he hadn't attended the births of any of his three children—"They're still going to get born," he insisted—but I told him, "Save it. I'm going," and he finally relented.

But that meant Bill Fahey would take over behind the plate in my absence with Rickey still in search of the record. And sure enough, Rickey was determined to test him. He needed three stolen bases to tie Brock and intended to get them that very day. It didn't take long for the hunt to resume. Rickey walked to lead off the bottom of the first and stole second. Then he stole third to give him 117 stolen bases, one short of tying Brock.

He didn't get on again until the eighth inning, but at that point, the stage was set. With one out Rickey took off from first base. But Pooch—that was Fahey's nickname—threw him out! Rickey was stopped short of tying the record, let alone breaking it. I had so wanted to be the guy in that situation, but I couldn't be because our son Matthew was being born.

I thought it was awesome, though, for Bill. When I rejoined the team two days later, we high-fived. Everybody was fired up for Pooch. As for Rickey it was merely a temporary setback. He tied the record in the next game—but against Milwaukee, not us. Then he broke the record the following night against the Brewers by stealing four bases. He was such a great talent.

This was also the year we had the mother of all brawls with the Twins. We fought twice in the same game at Tiger Stadium on May 14 actually, but the bigger, more violent brawl took place in the bottom of the 11th after Enos Cabell was brushed back by Minnesota's Ron Davis.

That pitch was the last straw in an angry game, which had become a tinderbox when Chet Lemon was hit by a Pete Redfern pitch in the fourth. Chet charged the mound, and, of course, all hell broke loose.

The wilder fight that took place in the 11th is remembered for Dave Rozema's kung fu kick on which he injured a knee so badly that he missed

Shake It Off

Which pitcher shook me off the most over the years? This might surprise you, but on the Tigers, it was Milt Wilcox. I had a hard time getting into his head. It almost felt that at times it didn't matter what I called with Milt on the mound. He was going to throw something different because he didn't want to throw what I called.

Jack Morris and Dan Petry didn't shake me off as much—even Jack. He was a three-pitch pitcher—fastball, slider, split—who monkeyed around for a while with a change-up, but it wasn't very good. And he never wanted to throw his splitter to start off a hitter. So, I knew not to call for it early in the count. It was more often his strikeout pitch.

Petry was a dominant sinker/slider guy. We might have mixed in some other stuff now and then, but those two pitches were his bread and butter. Milt, though, was different. He was a good pitcher who had some great games, but I never did quite figure him out.

the rest of the season. It's also remembered for finding out that we would always want Larry Herndon on our side in a brawl. I don't think we've seen such crushing haymakers before or since, which was surprising because most of the time Hondo was the most mild-mannered guy you could ever meet. But he changed from Dr. Jekyll into Mr. Hyde in that brawl. Rozema, oddly enough, turned out to be the winning pitcher in the game for throwing three innings of shutout relief. It was a home run by Kirk Gibson, two batters after the brawl subsided, that handed Rozema the victory.

I was in the bullpen when the second outbreak began, so we all ran across the field to reach the action. I remember jumping into the middle of the pile, grabbing a couple of guys to pull them off. I wasn't a player to just start throwing punches. There was enough of that going on, so someone had to be a peacekeeper. Usually, these things are mostly about shouting and shoving, but this one escalated. I remember Sparky getting thrown around and rolling on the grass while trying to break it up. I also remember

Rosie flying in with his infamous kick. It wasn't the leg he kicked with that he hurt. It was his landing leg. He twisted it, injuring his knee. He was the big casualty of the day, which was unfortunate because he was pitching very well that year.

At some point in 1982, I was quoted as saying, "We're always a couple of players short because the team is looking for ways to save money. What we're going through gets old after a while." I don't remember making those comments, but I also never remember being misquoted. So if those comments were attributed to me, I said them. But I probably was speaking out of frustration over what appeared to be another so-so record in the works for the team. I tried to keep my mouth shut as a player most of the time, but on occasion, being human, I vented. There were times I'd just had it. I kept it inside most of the time, but if there was something I felt that had to be said, I didn't back down from saying it. I'm just glad I didn't have to do it often.

Besides, we'd begun to take shape as a team in 1982 despite going only 83–79. We had added Lemon and Herndon as offseason acquisitions. Plus, Dan Petry and Lou Whitaker matured into being players who would become major contributors in 1984. Lou hadn't hit for any kind of power or production until 1982, and Peaches went from 22 starts to a full workload of 35 in 1982. At the same time, he jumped from 10 wins to 15. We weren't a championship team yet. There was more work to be done, but the pieces were coming together.

Chapter 12

Bumps, Not Bruises in August

I wish I could tell you that as soon as August began we identified an unobstructed path between us and the finish line of the season. And that the division championship was clearly ours for the taking. But I can't.

We still were in the driver's seat, leading by 12 games when the month began, but two weeks later, four-and-a-half games of that lead had disappeared. One moment we were cruising—or relatively so—and the next thing we knew there was a second-place team honking at us to pull over. So, we weren't out of the woods yet.

That's because the season could be summarized in this fashion: combining our record of the first 40 games with our record of the final 40, we were a dominant 60–20 team. The best record any other team put together, using the same criteria, was the Toronto Blue Jays' 46–34—good, but clearly not close. For the 82 games in between the first 40 and the last 40, however, our record was 44–38. There were times we struggled; there were times we didn't. There were times we took charge; there were times we got pushed around. That explains why even as late as August, we weren't sure if we were going to be a playoff team or not.

The unrealistic portion of our entire season was the 35–5 record we put together at the start. That was beyond anyone's comprehension. But we could not maintain that pace, so from then on it became like any other season—with us doing whatever we could to win. I wouldn't characterize the middle stretch of the season as being difficult, but it was a grind—because a 162-game season is a grind. We started great, we finished strong, but in between it was a battle.

During the up times, of course, it was a wildly fun year. But during our crazy swings of momentum, we wondered how such an enjoyable season could at times be so difficult. And I can tell you: the first two weeks of August saw some of those difficult times. "We're drab. We're tired. We're not hungry," Kirk Gibson said, "but we better get hungry soon."

Faced with a heavy schedule of doubleheaders, we went 6–10 and suddenly had reverted to a mid-July kind of margin over the Blue Jays. When the California Angels swept us 6–4 and 12–1 in a doubleheader on August 14, the Jays were sweeping two from the Cleveland Indians the same day. That dropped our lead to seven-and-a-half games. It was easy for the casual observer to think, *Hey, no problem, it's still seven-and-a-half games*, but when you're in the middle of it, swatting at the bees buzzing around you, it's an entirely different feeling.

The staggering number of make-up doubleheaders we were facing heavily weighed on our minds as an upcoming challenge. At one point—confronted with a first for any Detroit Tigers team since 1945—we played three doubleheaders in three days followed by another a week later. Try keeping a pitching staff in some kind of order when you're grappling with a schedule like that. During one stretch in mid-August, we played 18 games in 15 days. "The doubleheaders aren't going away, no matter how much you think about them," Sparky Anderson said. "So, you might as well just bear down and get through them."

It was an endurance test for us all—but a good one to have behind us when it was over. "I've never played so much baseball in all my life," Chet Lemon said. "It was exhausting."

"But no one cares if you're tired," Sparky insisted. "If you want to win, you have to overcome all obstacles."

At one point Gibson even thanked Anderson for the opportunity to play in all the games. "I mean it," he said. "I'll never forget playing six games in three days."

We went 7–11 over that stretch of 18 games and came out of it dazed. For one thing our pitching, which had been sturdy all season, suddenly had become shaky. From a respectable 3.35 team ERA in our July games, we climbed to 4.57 in August. The only pitchers who could point to their stats with any kind of pride in August were our bullpen stalwarts: Willie Hernandez and Aurelio Lopez, plus starter Juan Berenguer, who bounced back from a tough July. "But they all have to get with it," Anderson said of the entire staff. "Willie and Lopey can't do it by themselves."

I marveled at those two, though. They were the best 1–2 punch in baseball. To me the one who didn't get as much credit as he deserved was Aurelio. "I've never known a pitcher who can come back as fast and for as long as Lopey," said pitching coach Roger Craig. "Without him I don't know what would have happened."

But the pitchers weren't the only ones who needed to rebound. Our team on-base percentage had steadily declined from month to month as had our slugging average, and our run production also slipped. The net effect was fewer games in which we provided ourselves with a comfortable cushion. For instance, we went 69 games between scoring a double-digit number of runs after reaching that level six times in our first 56 games. Deep into the summer, we all too often had to scratch and claw. "Left-handers are stopping us cold," Sparky said at one point, "and we can't let that happen. Of all the problems I thought this team might have, hitting wasn't one of them."

Neither was scoring. But in our first 16 games of August, we scored fewer than three runs six times. We still felt good about ourselves and about our playoff chances—there was no doubt in our minds that we were the best team in the division—but we had to return soon to taking charge—and staying in charge. "It ain't April, May, June, or July no more," Sparky said.

Castillo

Marty Castillo had been with us the entire season. But when finally called upon, he had to be dusted off. That's because he had not played even close to regularly until August. In April, for instance, he started one game. Over the course of the next three months, he started only 22 more—17 of them as my backup behind the plate. The other five were at third base. Marty was a very good third baseman, in my opinion. He had excellent hands and a great arm. But when they asked him back in spring training if he would also consider catching to enhance his value to the club—and spend more time in the big leagues—he agreed to do it.

I know that I, as well as Bill Freehan, who was frequently at the ballpark, shared a few tips with him, which might have been helpful. But as it turned out, Marty was more than adequate behind the plate. He did a good job. I remember him being very solid defensively. It hadn't helped his cause, however, that he hit only .118 in June, then .177 in July. By the time August rolled around, his batting average was .195. That had dropped to .179 before some timely reminders were provided of how useful Marty could be.

In a 4–3 victory against the Seattle Mariners, he doubled, walked, and put down a sacrifice bunt. The next night he drove in the only run against Mark Langston—granted with a bases-loaded walk—but with only four hits off Langston, we weren't mustering anything else.

Langston was tough on us both times we faced him during his rookie season in 1984. He beat us twice, allowing only six hits in 17 1/3 innings.

Marty didn't start for another few days after that, but in an 11–4 triumph on the road against the Oakland A's, he contributed an RBI single and a two-run triple. Both hits came off left-handers. And because Sparky Anderson was thinking that Howard Johnson no longer was producing enough as a switch-hitter against lefties, he quickly noticed the sudden life in Castillo's bat. It wasn't much later, in fact, that Anderson announced he would be using Castillo instead of Johnson for a while against left-handers as Darrell Evans' platoon partner at third base. That led to Marty getting more hits, RBIs, and runs in the last two months of the season than he did in the first four combined. He also hit four home runs for us down the stretch after hitting none until August.

In other words, he became a surprise contributor, hitting .281 in the last two months after having that .195 batting average at the end of July.

Sparky had said of Marty, "I never dreamed he would straighten himself out at the plate."

But he did.

And like others, who chipped in along the way as role players, it was one of our feel-good stories. In essence, as the 1984 regular season wound down, Castillo experienced the most memorable moments of his career, which ended as a Tiger the following season. He also hit .294 in the postseason—complete with a home run in Game Three of the World Series against the San Diego Padres.

A popular teammate, Castillo was known for his quick wit. When he was asked, for instance, if his World Series home run might lead to some commercial opportunities, he replied by saying "I'm not going to worry about it, but my new phone number is…"He also got a lot of laughs when he said he had an attendance clause in his contract "that kicks in when the team draws its two billionth fan."

Marty was one of a kind. I'm just glad we didn't let him gather dust the entire season.

Sparky rallied everyone simply by reminding us of how far we'd come. It was no time to let down our guard, he kept saying. We had to kick it in gear. He did a wonderful job of cracking the whip late in the season, saying we really needed to stay focused. Little did we know, however, as the second half of August began that better days weren't far off. Or as I put it back then, "Sooner or later we were bound to rebound."

Our attitude was still good. That was a plus. We'd had some ups and downs, but all of us were trying to keep a positive attitude. Some of the fans' impatience surprised us, though. Their grumbling had become audible. This was the situation as of August 15: we led by seven-and-a-half games but had gone 9–14 in the last three weeks. "It would be nice to have it be easy for us the rest of the way," Darrell Evans said, "but that's hardly ever the case. It's going to be a dogfight."

Were we ready for the challenge? We felt we were. "You can't even allow yourself to feel crummy," Dave Bergman said. "There's no time for excuses now."

We won a big, big game on August 16, scoring twice in the eighth inning to tie the score against the Angels, then winning the game in the 12th on Barbaro Garbey's pinch-hit RBI double.

It was the kind of game that demonstrated our toughness. But we'd been showing that characteristic all year. I mean, we went 11–2 in extra-inning games in 1984 and were 25–11 in one-run games. Both were proof of us being a tough team. "We don't lead in any department," Sparky said, "except one: we win the close games, the crucial ones."

We took a lot of pride in '84 in thinking we could rise to any occasion. When the heat was on, we had many players who simply dialed up their game another notch—so we had a lot of success in close outcomes.

The other good news in August was that Alan Trammell said he was ready to play shortstop again. He'd been serving as our DH while taking care of a sore shoulder and did a fine job in that role but hadn't played short since July 8. However, his tendinitis had sufficiently improved for him to give it a try. "I'm not a DH. I'm a shortstop," Tram said. "You can adjust to not playing your position for just so long."

His return also gave us more flexibility. "At this time of year," Sparky said, "you need all the people you can get. I can make a lot more lineup moves with Trammell playing short."

Four days after downing the Angels in extra innings, we beat the Oakland A's 14–1 with 20 hits, a splurge we warmly welcomed. It got so bad for Oakland that even our former teammate, infielder Mark Wagner, had to pitch for them. I, for one, needed the reassurance of a home run in my first at-bat after a stretch of five consecutive strikeouts. Heck, I'd begun to hear some boos, which I felt at the time I didn't deserve. But looking back, I may have deserved them. Fans have a right to feel what they feel.

And then after three bad starts in which he had allowed 20 earned runs in 13 2/3 innings, Jack Morris had his best start in a while because of renewed life in his slider. We hoped it was a sign of better days to come for Jack. What he needed most, however, was to follow one good start with another because he hadn't won consecutive starts since May.

The series against the A's, which began with the 14–1 rout on August 20, turned out to be pivotal for us because we followed that game with two more offensive explosions in which we won 12–6 and 11–4. This was the kind of performance we needed to show that our offense hadn't gone into permanent hibernation. We couldn't expect to do it all the time, but winning by a large margin was always a good feeling—and a confidence boost. Even Sparky dared to say after those three splurges, "We're in great shape."

It was the first time all season we had scored in double digits in two consecutive games—let alone in three. And because Toronto had encountered a rough stretch of losing six of eight games with its bullpen struggling, our divisional lead was suddenly up to 12½ games with 34 remaining. "We can taste it," Lemon said. "We want to be the kind of team people talk about for a long time."

It was a good feeling to have that kind of lead again—and to have the Jays become "dots on the horizon" as Craig said—but we weren't in the clear yet. After so many bumps since May, though, hopefully there weren't many more to come. And initially there weren't. But we'd long since grown accustomed to seeing our division lead fluctuate like a crazy stock market.

The good news is that we won three of the next four and that Jack, finally, won a second consecutive game with a 5–1 decision against the Angels in Anaheim. Not only that, but also for the first time in five weeks, he spoke to the media. That wasn't a reason to stop the presses, so to speak, but it was an indication Morris might be emerging from multiple funks at the same time. "I couldn't breathe," Morris said of the reason for his prolonged silence. "I couldn't be me. I've read so much about my temper, it's literally nauseating."

I don't think what Jack went through affected the team at all. I mean, even while he wasn't talking to the media, he was talking to us. Plus, we always thought he was giving us his best effort on the mound. But I did worry occasionally it would affect him emotionally. Whatever demons he was dealing with, though, he was able to overcome.

While we were on a month-ending trip to the West Coast, we made two moves designed to help us the rest of the season. First, we acquired left-handed reliever Bill Scherrer from the Cincinnati Reds (for pitcher Carl Willis). Bill wasn't brought on board to take any of the load off Hernandez, but we did have a need for a lefty in short situations. Sparky was pleased with the trade. "An inside guy I know with the Reds told me we got a real good lefty in this deal," he said. "He's going to be great for getting tough left-handers out in certain spots."

And after seeing him pitch, we were all pleased. Other than hitting Bergman with a batting practice pitch his first time on the mound for us, which put Bergie out for eight games, Scherrer was a huge help the entire time he pitched for us in 1984, becoming a big part of our success. However, I attributed that to general manager Bill Lajoie, who had a knack for finding just the right piece to improve the team.

The other move was Sparky's decision to give Marty Castillo more playing time at third base. Switch-hitting Howard Johnson had been strug-gling against left-handed pitching, so when Marty suddenly chipped in with a strong stretch of games, he was handed the platoon role at third with Evans. "We'll go this way for a while and see what happens," Anderson said.

What happened was that Marty came through for us big time, making us stronger while earning more playing time for himself. The month ended in sour fashion, though. After Morris and his counterpart Jim Beattie had both tossed shutout ball through the seventh in Seattle on August 30, the Mariners scored twice in the eighth. We countered with only one run in the ninth, so despite being held to just four hits, Seattle won the game 2–1.

There was a weird finish in that game: the Mariners scored twice on a bunt single. With a runner on first, Seattle's Jack Perconte put down a sac-rifice attempt, and after falling to his knees while fielding the ball, Morris threw wildly (and angrily) past first base, allowing a run to score. Then as the play continued—and without Jack backing up the play at home—Perconte scored on a wild throw from right.

We answered in the ninth with a run on a bases-loaded walk to Trammell, the third walk of the inning, but with the bases still loaded, the game ended on a grounder to second. We all felt we'd given this one away. "Yeah, all wrapped up with a ribbon on it," was how Sparky put it.

The plus we took away from the loss was that it represented the third consecutive strong appearance for Morris, whose eight strikeouts were his most since May 28—a stretch of 16 starts. The last game of the month was also a bummer, one in which we allowed the tying run in the ninth in Oakland, and eventually lost 7–6 in the 13th. But the way we lost—on a two-out wild pitch—was just as frustrating as the two-error game in Seattle. It was our first extra-inning loss since April 27 and our only walk-off defeat of the year. We had won our last eight extra-inning games, however, so it was clearly a case of having the tables turned on us. "Talk about gifts," Sparky said.

After the game everybody was down because it was a tough way to lose, but I said we couldn't afford to stay that way for long. We had to bounce back. I wasn't the most vocal guy. But there were times I felt the need to pull everyone together. This was one of those times. We needed to stay focused on what we still had to do. More than anything, though, Sparky had ingrained in us that we needed to be a team, which didn't beat itself. And to lose two games in that fashion was uncharacteristic.

So, we addressed it, eventually worked through it, and got back on track. With that, August was a wrap. There were players who had performed well during the month, of course: Trammell hit .339, Gibson .322, and with fewer at-bats, Larry Herndon hit .355, pumping life back into his season. HoJo at .187 no doubt wanted to move past August—as Lemon probably did at .196. Gibson led the team with 71 total bases followed by Trammell with 67. I finished atop the production number categories with eight home runs and 22 RBIs. That was my job, however: knocking in runs.

Gibson's team-leading on-base percentage of .420 accounted in part for the 27 runs he scored in August—the most any Tiger had scored in a single month the entire season. No wonder Sparky was beginning to think out loud that Gibby might garner some MVP votes. That's not all he said about him, though. "When Kirk walks into the clubhouse," Anderson commented, "everyone knows it. He's a king right now—a guy who comes to play and is ready to fight down and dirty day after day."

The praise was warranted because Gibby had put together a dang good year. He became quite the catalyst for our club, doing a lot extremely well. Blossoming as a player, he came up huge the entire season. On the pitching side, there weren't as many standouts in August. But once again the tandem of Hernandez and Lopez stood tall. The two relief pitchers combined for a 5–2 record and six saves.

With a 16–15 record, August had been our most challenging month. But we were in first place by nine-and-a-half games with 27 to go when it ended. At that point, we were concentrating on was getting into the play-offs. Only a complete collapse could shatter our dreams.

Chapter 13

Clinching in September

S eptember was going to be a great month for us. That was more than a gut feeling. We could sense it. We had worked hard for it. But despite the good vibes, September couldn't become a time to deceive ourselves. So, we tried our best not to. *Keep focused. Don't let up. There were many more tough games to play.* Those thoughts had to be our mindset. But as Sparky Anderson said, he could "see the boys getting concerned."

I think that was probably right. We weren't beating the heck out of people, by any means. The season was still a challenge. But the final month had just begun, and we enjoyed a big lead in the American League East. However, we knew the difference between having a big lead and having an insurmountable lead. At nine-and-a-half games but with us not playing our best as September got under way, we didn't view our margin as being rock solid. One bad week and it could have been slashed in half. If we kept struggling for longer than that, who knows what damage could be done? No matter what, said Sparky, knowing we had some tough teams on the schedule ahead of us, "It's going to be a long September."

We either were going to be celebrating when it was over or kicking ourselves. Four days into the month, we still weren't sure which of the two it was going to be. That's because we lost three of the first four games in September, and our lead shrunk to seven-and-a-half games—the same size it had been on May 9. In fact, because this was the 12th time during the season we had led by seven-and-a-half games, it kind of felt like we'd been in front the entire way by that margin. To us, it was—let's say—an uncomfortably comfortable lead, one you couldn't take for granted. There were worse situations, of course, such as trailing by seven-and-a-half games, which was the predicament for the Toronto Blue Jays. But we still had to seal the deal. In our favor was the diminishing number of remaining games. There were only 23 to play.

The calendar was ticking down slowly. It would have been nice to have our lead increasing instead of decreasing. We could definitely use a well-pitched game. And, thankfully, that happened with a beautiful 1–0 gem from Juan Berenguer against the Baltimore Orioles on September 5—our first 1–0 victory in more than two years—and "perhaps the best single game of the season," as Sparky called it.

Juan pitched some very strong games for us. He was no slouch, by any means. I felt confident every time he was on the mound. I don't want to be so bold as to call it *the* game that finally pointed us in the right direction, but I don't know what else to call it because everything changed after that 1–0 game. Everything fell into place.

In any case, it was all you could expect of a tense, pivotal game. We scored our run in the first inning on Cal Ripken's throwing error—allowing Alan Trammell to come around from second base—then we held on while Berenguer did a masterful job of outpitching Mike Flanagan, a nemesis of ours that entire season. In four starts against us in 1984, Flanagan had an 0.51 ERA, allowing only two earned runs in 35 innings. Berenguer, meanwhile, had lost his only previous start against the Orioles (and Flanagan) that year. But this was Juan at possibly his all-time best, blanking the Birds on two hits through seven-and-one-third innings. Eddie Murray got our attention with a leadoff double in the second inning, but by striking out two of the next three batters, Berenguer rendered that extra-base hit harmless. "He's no dummy," Sparky said of Juan. "He knew what he had to do."

The only other hit Berenguer allowed was a one-out single in the fifth that caused no trouble. And of the three walks he issued, only a leadoff pass to Rich Dauer in the third was a possible troublemaker, but Rick Dempsey's liner to second, on which Dauer was doubled up, negated that chance. "This is a game Juan will always remember," Anderson said. "And so will I."

Berenguer might even remember that the scoreboard flashed "Juan-derful" when his day was done.

At the plate, however, we couldn't add to our one-run lead. Flanagan blanked us on four hits the rest of the game after the first inning. The biggest Orioles' threat occurred in the eighth after Willie Hernandez replaced Berenguer with a runner on first and one out. Willie hit pinch-hitter Gary Roenicke with a pitch, then he threw a wild pitch that moved the runners to second and third. As usual, though, Hernandez was equal to the challenge, striking out Benny Ayala, then retiring Mike Young on a fly ball to right. Willie also encountered first-and-third trouble with two outs in the ninth but secured the final out on Lenn Sakata's fly ball to left. "Was I nervous?" Hernandez said after the game, repeating a question. "If I had been, I would have told Sparky to put someone else in. So, the answer is: no, I wasn't nervous."

Then again, if Willie was *ever* nervous, I couldn't sense it. Nothing ever fazed him. He was always out there like a bulldog, coming right at people. He had all the confidence in the world.

Better yet, with Toronto losing in 10 innings to the New York Yankees on Don Baylor's home run off Roy Lee Jackson, we had managed to reverse our direction and bump our divisional lead to eight-and-a-half games. With us heading to Toronto next, it had been a truly important day—a momentum boost before a crucial series. We hadn't faced the Jays since June, but we were ready for them—if for no other reason than we had to be.

The first game in Toronto didn't initially look like we were ready, however. After seven innings we trailed 4–0 because Doyle Alexander had blanked us on four hits. That changed in the eighth. As Kirk Gibson said, "The thing about our team all year is that 4–0 meant nothing."

And it didn't mean anything this time either. With two on and two out, Gibson hit a three-run home run to cut the Jays' lead to a run. But we weren't done yet. When I followed with a walk, Jimmy Key replaced Alexander on the mound. Barbaro Garbey singled, then Jackson replaced Key. Roy Lee didn't give up any dramatic home runs in this game, but he did help our cause by walking the only two batters—Larry Herndon and Chet Lemon—he faced to tie the score.

In the 10th inning, Dave Bergman, who had just returned from a sore back, came through with a three-run home run (his fourth hit of the game) off Ron Musselman to give us a 7–4 lead. That proved to be the final score when Hernandez shut down the Jays in the 10th. After the game Sparky said, "Damn, that's what pennant fights are all about."

Willie improved his record to 9–2 with the victory and once again (for the 15th time that season) pitched three innings. What a remarkable year he was having. As Anderson would say, "Harry Houdini was never this good." Underscoring the importance of the series, Sparky also said, "I wanted this game more than any I've ever managed."

We took a while to get rolling the next night but eventually did with a six-run seventh, breaking open a game that was tied at two after six innings. Jack Morris had to exit in the fifth because of a stiff shoulder so Bill Scherrer picked up his first win in relief. Johnny Grubb, a player I haven't mentioned much but one who helped us all year long, hit two home runs in this victory. I appreciated Johnny so much. Oh my gosh, he wasn't just a stabilizing force in our clubhouse. At times he could do some really serious damage at the plate. He always seemed to come through with clutch hits.

In three nights, our lead over the Jays had increased from seven-and-a-half games to 10½. What's more: we had only 20 games remaining. We weren't giddy about our situation yet. As Craig pointed out, this was the time "to control our emotions," but we definitely were encouraged.

And when Gibson's three-run home run in the seventh inning the next night spurred us to a 7–2 victory, capping a sweep over the Jays, we felt even better. "They'll have to do something extraordinary now to catch us," winning pitcher Milt Wilcox said, "or we'll have to fall on our face. I don't think that will happen."

I'm in the middle of our Little League parade in 1966.

I stand by our family tree on Christmas morning of 1965.

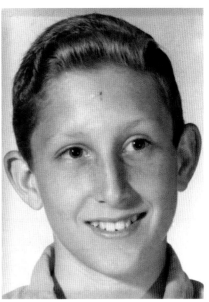

This is my sixth-grade picture from 1967.

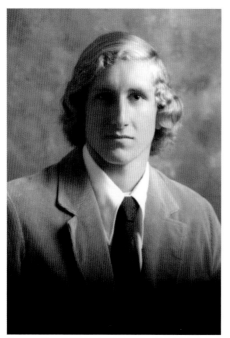

I pose for my senior picture in 1974, the same year the Detroit Tigers drafted me.

That's quite a mane I'm sporting in 1975.

Wearing my longtime No. 13, I sling it down for the field as Walnut High's quarterback in 1973.

I sign with the Detroit Tigers in June of 1974. I had just turned 18.

I stand next to Les Moss, my minor league mentor, in 1976. The man, who had been so instrumental in the development of my skills, was named the Detroit Tigers' manager for the start of the 1979 season, but it was a short-lived tenure.

I catch the first pitch from Tom Selleck, who was known for wearing a Detroit Tigers hat on *Magnum, P.I.*, in 1982.

I hang out with Arlyne and David during a break in the 1981 spring training.

Arlyne holds Baby Ashley, who was born during our 1984 postseason run.

My family, including newborn Ashley, joins me for the 1984 World Series parade.

Family Day at Tiger Stadium, including this one in 1983, was always a fun event.

I like to call this image from the dugout in 1984: "Big Wheel and the little wheels."

I shake hands with Detroit fans in Anaheim, California, after the May 24, 1984 game, in which we defeated the California Angels to set a new American League record of 17 straight games won on the road. That victory gave us a 35–5 record. *(AP Images)*

Kirk Gibson and I slap hands at home plate after Gibson hit a home run against the California Angels. *(AP Images)*

In my 18 World Series at-bats, I had five hits, including a home run. *(AP Images)*

I tag out Alan Wiggins at home plate in the first inning of Game Five of the 1984 World Series. *(AP Images)*

Kirk Gibson runs the bases in the eighth inning of Game Five after hitting his second home run in the 8–4 win. *(AP Images)*

Willie Hernandez and I embrace after defeating the San Diego Padres in Game Five of the 1984 World Series. *(AP Images)*

Kirk Gibson pours champagne over me in the celebratory postgame locker room. *(AP Images)*

Reportedly, some of the Jays even said, "It's going to take a miracle now. These were must games."

We had gone into Toronto and had done exactly what we needed to do: we swept the three-game series from the Blue Jays, leaving them demoralized. This was the series, which put us in good shape. We couldn't waltz to the division championship yet, but it was getting close…just beyond our fingertips.

With a 15–6 record in their last 21 games, the always-tough Orioles were next on our schedule, and, sure enough, the series in Baltimore would begin with us having to face Flanagan again. As his counterpart in the opener, Berenguer pitched well, but the Orioles' left-hander prevailed 3–1. Flanagan and Bret Saberhagen of the Kansas City Royals were the only pitchers to beat us three times in 1984. The good news was that Toronto lost again, so our magic number clicked down to eight.

We whacked out 16 hits the next night in a 9–2 triumph. Darrell Evans had four of the hits, and Gibson and Herndon had three each. Herndon had a wonderful second half of the season, hitting .331. Dan Petry improved his record to 17–8 with the victory but said, "When you don't have good stuff, you need to find other ways to win. My way tonight was to get a lot of runs."

Before heading home the next day for our final homestand of the regular season, we lost 3–1. But we were taking a 10½-game lead with us back to Tiger Stadium—with only 16 games remaining. By this time our big lead had become a commanding lead. With our next nine games at home, it looked like—knock on wood—we'd be clinching the division in front of our fans. At that point, we were pretty confident about getting into the playoffs.

But it wouldn't be happening for a while if our first game was any indication. Mustering only singles—and just seven of those—we lost 7–2 to the Blue Jays in our first game back home.

"I have to kick us into gear," Sparky said. "For some reason we just went through the motions."

As it turned out, the loss wasn't a sign of a downturn. With great games from Wilcox and Ruppert Jones the next night, we got back on track. Wilcox limited the Jays to one hit (George Bell's solo home run) through seven

Coaching Staff

All the coaches were pivotal to our success, encouraging us, guiding us, helping us to maintain our focus. They were former players who knew what a grind the season could be. And I liked them all to varying degrees.

Hitting coach Gates Brown—I loved him. He always had the right thing to say, motivating us when we needed it. He would talk to us as equals, not as coach to player. If you asked him a question, you knew you'd get a straight answer. But he never tried to remake your swing or make massive changes. It was always a little tweak here, a little tweak there. Gator helped people simply by reminding them what their abilities were. He always believed wholeheartedly in the hitters to whom he was speaking, allowing us to work ourselves out of slumps without wholesale changes. And most of the time, his method worked. When I went to other teams after I played for the Tigers, I had hitting coaches who tried to re-create my entire swing. Eventually, I'd forget what I had been doing wrong or right to begin with. I'd be totally lost. Gates always simplified the process. Everything was positive with him.

Bench coach Billy Consolo—He was the comic relief of our club. Nobody knew who he was when he came over with Sparky Anderson. A former bonus baby, he'd been out of baseball for a while, but he had a way of endearing himself to everyone on the team with his sense of humor. Billy always had a joke to make us chuckle, but he was serious about his job and in helping the team in any way he could. It was his quirky personality that everyone grew to enjoy. He kept us loose. That might have been his biggest contribution. Not all our coaches could throw batting practice, but Billy at least tried—and failed. He threw so slowly that he screwed everyone up. So, we kind of ran him off the mound. He always seemed able to break the tension, though, if there was any way to do it—and to put a smile on our faces. He was great to have on the club.

Pitching coach Roger Craig—What more can I say about Roger? He was the wizard behind the curtain, operating the levers and making it all work. He had considerable influence on Sparky, as well as on many of the decisions that were made. I wouldn't ever take anything away from Sparky, but Roger didn't get the credit he deserved. He was a positive factor in a lot that went on. In my opinion, he had the perfect demeanor as a pitching coach, just enough sarcasm—which was needed at times, especially with Jack—but he was also very intelligent and an excellent teacher.

I also marveled at his amazing sixth sense for calling pitchouts. I couldn't believe how adept he was at choosing just the right moment, which made my job easier, for sure. I can't honestly think of anyone on our pitching staff who didn't enjoy working with Roger. Everyone learned from him and we all respected him. It was like having a comanager on the bench.

Third-base coach Alex Grammas—He was a tougher guy for me to get close to. At times Alex could be difficult to deal with. He had a negativity about him that occasionally rubbed me the wrong way. When things were going badly for us as a team—and I'm not just talking about 1984—he had a way of making comments that would piss you off. I didn't appreciate that and I know some of the other players didn't either. He'd blurt things out at times that almost seemed demeaning, and I'd go, "What the hell?" I didn't think it was helpful for him to do that.

But all things considered, Alex did a really good job coaching third base. I never questioned his judgment. If I got thrown out at home, most of the time it was my fault because I didn't run fast enough. Plus, there were times his negativity faded away, and you'd have a great conversation with him. That's when you would say, "Wow, he really is a good guy." But he'd drive me nuts other times. All in all, though, I'd say he made some positive contributions.

First-base coach Dick Tracewski—He was like a relative in the clubhouse and very easy to talk to. A great communicator with everyone on the team, he had a little way of poking fun at guys with that laugh of his, but he was a great help to our ballclub because for one thing he was the only coach who could consistently throw batting practice. Plus, he always seemed to be the most organized of our coaches. He, for instance, even set the schedules. He maintained the order of everything we did. Plus, he was our infield instructor. He had a great rapport with all our infielders. They all really liked him. They all respected him. He did his job and did it very well.

innings en route to becoming the third 17-game winner in our starting rotation—along, of course, with Morris and Petry. Craig, however, backed out of his spring training promise to buy Milt a Jeep if he won that many games. Besides, Wilcox wouldn't have been in line for the victory if it hadn't been for Jones.

Ruppert led off the bottom of the fourth with a home run off Dave Stieb that put us in front by a run. He then preserved the lead in the eighth by stealing a home run away from pinch-hitter Cliff Johnson with a catch above the wall in left. On friendly terms with Ruppert, Johnson was so impressed with the catch that he came to our clubhouse after the game to congratulate him—but also to kiddingly ask him, "Why do you want to do that stuff to me, man? Don't ever let me catch you in a dark alley."

On the mound at the time, Hernandez weathered the scare—plus first-and-third trouble in the ninth—for his 29th save in 29 save situations.

Our magic number was down to four at this point. The division title was going to be ours. It was only a matter of when and who our next hero would be. There were several of them the next night as we grabbed a 7–0 lead by the third inning against the Jays en route to an 8–3 victory. With eight extra-base hits, we pounded the ball, and Marty Castillo led the way with a home run and triple. For the first time, the feeling in our clubhouse after the game was truly triumphant. After all, we had climbed to within a night of clinching the division. "The champagne is getting good and cold," announced Tom Brookens, who had hit a two-run home run.

"I feel like a little kid," Castillo exclaimed.

"The more I talk about it, the more I get excited about it," Trammell added.

In an odd twist, because of rotation issues involving Morris and Petry, it looked like a rookie would be on the mound for us in what could be the clinching game against the Milwaukee Brewers because our scheduled starters for the next two nights were Roger Mason and Randy O'Neal. But I don't think anyone gave that a second thought. They were rookies, sure, but we had confidence in those guys—and in ourselves. Regardless of who was on the mound, we just felt we'd find a way to get it done.

For Mason it would be his second start. He had pitched well five games ago but lost 3–1 to Baltimore. For O'Neal it would be his first major league start. Both rookies were looking forward to starting such possibly huge games. With four-and-a-half cases of champagne on ice—I remember it being ready—we were all poised to have it happen with Mason pitching. He did his part, allowing two runs in six innings of a 7–3 victory against the Brewers and—as I said—for "keeping his composure while everyone was screaming."

Lou Whitaker also did his part by hitting his first career grand slam in the sixth inning, but the Blue Jays had come back to beat the Boston Red Sox in Toronto, so we didn't clinch. The magic number was one. Was it a letdown? Sort of—especially after getting a false report that the Jays had lost. "It would have been beautiful, but it wasn't meant to be," Trammell said.

Sparky expressed the other way of looking at it: "I was kind of glad that Toronto came back to win it," he said. "It's going to be more fun for everyone if we win this thing ourselves."

That made sense to me. A little more patience would be required. Or as Evans put it, "I've been waiting this long. I can wait one more night."

On September 18, that night finally arrived.

The pitching matchup was this: O'Neal, a right-hander making his first major league start after being 9–10 with a 3.57 ERA at Evansville, for us against lefty Bob McClure of the Brewers. I'd always thought O'Neal was a talented guy. McClure was a relief pitcher for much of the season but had been converted to starting full time in August. We had faced him twice in June and won both games.

The game got off to a good start for O'Neal, who struck out Robin Yount, the first batter he faced, on a high fastball. "Robin kind of helped me out on that pitch," Randy said, "and it settled me in."

From there, he got through a clean first inning. McClure, however, walked Whitaker and gave up a double to Trammell. It hadn't taken us long to put a scoring chance together, and we took advantage of it on my run-scoring grounder to short. That's how matters stood through the fifth inning—with us leading 1–0.

O'Neal did an outstanding job of protecting the lead by blanking the Brewers on four hits through the sixth. He put down the biggest scare by retiring Doug Loman on a bases-loaded fly ball to end the top of the third. We finally stretched the lead to 2–0 in the sixth on my single that drove in Trammell, who had doubled again. We loaded the bases with one out later in the sixth but didn't add to our lead. So we were up by two runs with our clinching game still in the capable hands of O'Neal, who promptly retired the side in order in the seventh. By this time, the Tiger Stadium crowd of 48,810 was in quite a frenzy—and even more so when Brookens led off the bottom of the seventh with a home run.

It didn't matter what Toronto was doing—or even that the Jays would get trounced 10–3 at home by Boston. Our destiny was totally up to us. If we beat Milwaukee, we'd be division champions. And, with extra police security on horseback at the ballpark now visible, we were two innings away from that becoming a reality.

Hernandez took over for O'Neal in the eighth. He allowed a one-out single but otherwise worked through the inning unscathed. We were three outs away from clinching. And as he had in the eighth, Hernandez also allowed a one-out single in the ninth. Willie was on a mission, though. He retired pinch-hitter Mark Brouhard on a fly ball to Herndon in left, then struck out Jim Sundberg to end the game.

It's still vivid in my mind because I remember what had just happened. *Wow*—we had done it. We had won the division. Wire to wire.

Of course, our fans wanted to flood the field, which they did, but they didn't get out of control. Besides, it was just the irresistible urge to show their joy. We felt the same way but saved most of it until we were back in our clubhouse. It was a fun evening obviously. But as we got louder—and louder—Sparky sat quietly in his office. "I've never been one to party," he said. "My idea of celebrating is to watch TV, but seriously this is the most satisfied I've ever felt in my life. Since I got fired [by the Cincinnati Reds], it's been burning inside me. I've wanted to prove it was wrong. But good people make good things happen, and I'll tell you this [as he looked around], these are good people."

Meanwhile, the rest of us were partying. "Hopefully, we can redo '68 for our fans," said Trammell, dripping with champagne. But someone, and I don't remember who, yelled, "To hell with '68. We're the '84 Tigers!"

"I haven't had one drink, but I'm as drunk as any of these guys," said owner Tom Monaghan, whom Gibson and I drenched with ice water. Not one to favor the present over the past, I also doused our former owner John Fetzer. But I pretty much sprayed everyone because everybody was fair game that night.

I'm not exactly sure how we did it, but we also won the next night—not that it mattered anymore in the standings. It mattered to a lot of our rookies, though, including Scotty Earl, who started at second base; Nelson Simmons, who started in right; Mike Laga, who was our starting designated hitter; Doug Baker, who started at short; and it mattered to Dwight Lowry, our catcher. With Morris getting his 18th win and Simmons getting three hits, we beat Milwaukee 4–2 for our 98th victory. Not only had we clinched the division, it now looked like we were going to win 100 games. I know we wanted to. We wanted to be a part of something really big.

Two days later we won our 99th game 6–0 behind Petry's complete-game four-hitter against the Yankees. It would be Morris' honor to start the next day—and to win our 100th victory—making us just the fifth Tigers' team ever to win that many games. Jack blanked the Yankees on two hits through the six innings he pitched, his best outing since the All-Star break.

After the game, the crowd called one of us out of the clubhouse for a curtain call, but it wasn't a player. Their call was for Sparky, who had just become the first manager ever to win 100 games for two different teams. In the National League, he had won 100 games three times with Cincinnati. "I thought you were kidding me," Anderson said when we told him the fans were chanting his name. "But I'd be lying if I said it didn't feel great."

We also signed a game ball for him.

Sparky always had an interesting relationship with the fans. If they weren't happy with him and were letting him noisily know it, he'd hesitate as he headed out to the mound to let each of the paying customers give him a little extra verbal blast. That's just the way he was.

Even this late in the season with the division clinched and with us leading by 14½ games, we kept pushing—as if we had something to prove every day. There were seven games remaining, and we wanted to win as many as we could. The Tigers' record for wins was 103—set by the 1968 club. Sparky wanted to set a new mark. So did the rest of us. "We're going to take a shot at it," Anderson said with a week left. "These kids deserve it."

As it turned out, we won four of our last seven games to give us a final record of 104–58. We had set a new Tigers' record for victories. Among the winning pitchers in those four games was O'Neal, following up on his clinching triumph, and two for Berenguer. Jack fell short of winning 20 games by losing his final start, but he was okay with that. Craig said Jack was "disappointed, but not annoyed."

"I can't complain," Morris said. "The last two starts have probably been my best of the second half."

With three games left, we won our 103rd game on Whitaker's two-run home run in the 12th inning against the Yankees. We also set our three-man rotation for the postseason that day, as Sparky announced that Berenguer would only be used in long relief. "If we use him, you'll know we're in trouble," Anderson said.

We also learned that we would face Kansas City, the champions of the American League West, in the playoffs. The Royals finished strongly, going 28–18 down the stretch while fending off the Minnesota Twins. Five teams in the American League East ended up winning more games than the Royals, however. It hadn't been like we kicked their butt every time we had played the Royals, but to no one's surprise, we'd be heavily favored heading into the playoffs. "Get your rest," Lemon announced in the clubhouse. "Only two days to the postseason!"

We won our record 104th game in the next-to-last game of the regular season. Scoring five runs in the sixth and another five in the ninth, we pummeled the Yankees 11–3 on 16 hits at Yankee Stadium with a mixed lineup of veterans and kids. It was another of those feel-good games in which it seemed everyone contributed.

Our power was on full display that final week. Wanting to finish on a personally positive note, I hit three of our last nine home runs as the season wound down. Some of my other stats might not have been impressive—for instance, my .237 batting average was my lowest of any season from 1979 through 1987—but my 33 home runs were a career high.

I was happy with everything but my batting average that year. I would have loved to contribute more in that regard. But as Sparky had made clear on numerous occasions, I was paid for my power.

I never was disrespectful of him in any way, but I admit there were times I was critical of Sparky during the season. In the end, though, our intrepid manager—who I grew to love—deserved every bit of the credit he received. It had worked out great. In the clubhouse after we clinched, there was no handshake—nor hug—that felt better than his.

Chapter 14

The Pennant Chase

Farewell, regular season. Hello, American League Championship Series.

Our playoff opponent, the Kansas City Royals, was a scary team. I know we were heavily favored going into the ALCS against the Royals, but they had some serious weapons. After all, they had swept us in a four-game series (August 3–5 at Tiger Stadium). So, it wasn't as if we had kicked their butts each time we played them. They often gave us all we could handle.

They also had Bret Saberhagen, whom I could never hit, as one of their starters. Though only 20, he was as nasty as anyone we faced the entire year. I don't know for sure how many at-bats I had against him during the regular season, but I didn't get a hit off him. I know that. So my first thought when it turned out to be the Royals we'd be facing in the playoffs was: *Dang, now I have to figure out how to hit this guy.*

Overall, the Royals had a pretty good pitching staff and a solid lineup. I didn't take them for granted. Neither did anyone else I know of. When you get to the postseason, everything starts over anyway. As Sparky Anderson put it at the time: "Baseball fans know we were the best team in baseball this year. But that don't mean nothing now."

The challenge facing us? To fire it back up, of course, against a formidable foe. "Willie Wilson is their spark plug, and George Brett is their big threat," Jack Morris said. "You have to contain those two guys, but you can't let up on anyone else in the lineup."

The first game began the way we could only dream it would—with a couple of runs for us in the first inning. Lou Whitaker singled off Bud Black, Alan Trammell tripled, and with one out, I hit a fly ball to deep right-center for a sacrifice fly. Just like that, we led 2–0. Those runs energized us. They were proof we had indeed come to play—and that we were ready for the limelight. "Runs in the first inning, that's all I had to see," said Morris, who was sharp throughout.

At 97 miles per hour, in fact, his fastball was the liveliest it had been all year. I don't want to say he cruised, but he pitched a very good game. Jack didn't allow a base runner until the third inning when the Royals loaded the bases with two outs. They left them loaded, though, when Brett flew out to right. With a good play on that hard-hit ball, a sinking line drive that required every ounce of his concentration, Kirk Gibson was able to make the catch. "Had I not," he said, "that ball would have rolled and rolled. I love the drama of a big hit, but you can keep the drama of a big catch."

Sparky got a playful dig in on Kirk, while complimenting his improved defense at the same time, saying that, "A year ago Brett would have been running for a while."

The good news, though, was that Kirk got it done. He had worked very hard on his defense, and it became evident throughout the season it had improved. That was a huge play.

Momentum being a big factor, especially that early, if the ball had gotten past Gibby and all those runs had scored, it could have made all the difference. Gibson's catch was the start of 10 Royals going down in order against Jack. By the time Jorge Orta led off the seventh with a triple, we had upped our lead to 5–0 and had knocked Black out of the game. In seven career starts, he still was winless against us.

The additional runs we scored were the products of solo home runs from Trammell and Larry Herndon. And in the seventh, a two-base error in right by Pat Sheridan was followed by Tram's third hit, a line single to right, of the game. The Royals scored their only run in the bottom of the seventh, but we tacked on three more in the final two innings. Darrell Evans and Marty Castillo chipped in with RBI hits in the eighth, and I capped the scoring with a leadoff home run in the ninth. Jack didn't pitch a complete game but would have if it hadn't been for a nagging blister on his finger. He dismissed the severity of it later, saying, "It's one I've had hundreds of times."

"But I didn't want to take any chances," Sparky explained.

Willie Hernandez finished with two scoreless innings of relief in the 8–1 victory. We outhit the Royals 14–5. It was a perfect way to resume our journey, picking up where the regular season left off. Trammell had all the elements of a cycle except a double. Plus, four others in our lineup had two hits each. As confident as I was initially, and I believe all the other guys were, this was our first chance in the postseason to live up to what we thought of ourselves as a team. Our mindset was that if we didn't win it all, the season would have been for nothing—and no one would remember us, even though we'd started 35–5.

As pleased as we were after the game, we couldn't know at the time it would be our most lopsided victory of the entire postseason. The game had been umpired by replacements because of a strike by the regular umps, but there were no controversies. Bill Deegan worked the plate, as he would the entire series, but as a former major league umpire, he proved to be more than capable. Everyone was skeptical at first about replacements, but I thought they did extremely well. I remembered Deegan from earlier years and I had no problems with him in Game One—or the entire series for that matter. It was all good, as the caliber of our play merely picked up where it had left off. "It gives us a lot of momentum when we score early like that," Tram said. "Our pitcher—in this case, Jack—can start challenging hitters right away."

With two quick runs, momentum didn't take long to show up in the second game either. This time it wasn't a single, triple, sacrifice fly sequence getting the job done in the first inning, as it had been in the playoff opener. It was an error, double, double combo, but the result was the same. We scored twice in the first.

The game began with Royals' shortstop Onix Concepcion making an error on Lou Whitaker's leadoff grounder. Whitaker took second on Trammell's fly ball to deep center, then scored on Gibson's double to right. Despite the trouble I'd had against Saberhagen during the regular season, I doubled on a 2–1 pitch this time, knocking in Gibson. It was never easy facing Saberhagen. I hit only .178 against him in my career. So I considered myself fortunate to get an extra-base hit.

We quickly provided Dan Petry with the same early cushion we had given Morris the night before. And he did a fine job of protecting it, retiring the first 10 batters he faced. By the time Petry walked Sheridan with one out in the fourth inning, we had added another run on Gibson's home run off Saberhagen in the third. That walk to Sheridan, however, led to the Royals' first run of the game when Brett singled him to third, and Orta's grounder to second knocked him in.

Saberhagen, meanwhile, was in the process of settling down against us, reeling off a string of five shutout innings in which he held us to two hits. "He may be young in age," Ruppert Jones said of the 20-year-old, "but in heart and soul, he's a veteran. He had me in his pocket all night."

The Royals cut our lead to a run by adding a second run off Petry in the seventh. A wrong decision by Trammell, of all people, set up the run. With Frank White at first and two outs, Trammell tried but failed to outrace White to second base after fielding Don Slaught's soft one-hopper to short—instead of throwing the ball to first to get Slaught, the slower runner. "He sort of drew a blank," Sparky said of Tram. "He knows what the right play was."

The Royals capitalized when Dane Iorg singled to right, knocking in White. Even so, Petry exited the game after the seventh with a 3–2 lead.

Sparky was the one who made the next mistake. As Petry's replacement he brought in Hernandez to pitch the last two innings. Ordinarily, that would have been the correct move, but Willie had strep throat, and Sparky knew it. Or at least he knew Willie was ailing. Hernandez wasn't sharp, allowing the Royals to tie the score in the bottom of the eighth on Lynn Jones' leadoff single and Hal McRae's double. Both were pinch-hits.

Willie regrouped in time to get out of the inning without allowing another run, but it would be Aurelio Lopez taking over from that point on. "I made a terrible mistake," Anderson said. "I did what I didn't want to do. I tried to force-feed Willie. It was my fault."

Hernandez claimed he nearly fainted after leaving the mound and that the Royals' doctor advised him not to pitch another inning. Meanwhile, the Royals' three pinch-hits—by Iorg, Jones, and McRae—set a championship series record. It was their bench that tied the score. The Royals had proven their toughness, but the outcome of the game was still undecided. Whichever team scored next was no doubt going to win.

We were moving forward without Hernandez, but the Royals had Dan Quisenberry on hand to face us in the ninth. Quiz had been 44 for 44 in save situations and—although this was a game to be won or lost, not a save situation—he was a formidable pitcher to be facing. Jones led off the ninth with a walk and took second on Johnny Grubb's sacrifice but was stranded there.

The Royals answered with a two-out walk by speedy Wilson off Lopez. I was hoping Wilson would try to steal second because my arm was feeling great and I always enjoyed the biggest challenges—I thought I could throw anybody out if the pitcher gave me a chance timewise—but what helped is that this was one of those uncanny times that Roger Craig called for a pitchout on the precise pitch Wilson took off from first base. I have no idea how Roger detected it, but it made my job easy. We nailed Wilson at second, and the game was headed for extra innings.

Quisenberry retired us 1-2-3 in the 10th, including a strikeout of Trammell who had hit a dramatic grand slam off him in May. Both Brett and Darryl Motley singled off Lopez in the bottom of the 10th, giving K.C. a first-and-second opportunity with two outs. Big Steve Balboni then cranked one to center that initially looked like trouble. I didn't think he had gotten it all, though, and I was right. Chet Lemon was easily able to haul it down.

So, it was on to the 11th inning, where we hoped Quisenberry might begin to weaken. He had occasionally shown some vulnerability after

Without a Ring

As I look back on the American League playoffs, the weird thing was that we had a full complement of players there, including replacements to be used only if someone else got hurt.

They weren't players on the postseason roster but standbys who could be promoted in case of emergency.

One of those players was pitcher Randy O'Neal, who had won our division-clinching game in his first major league start. Randy went everywhere the team went during the postseason. That meant he not only was with us in Kansas City, but also in San Diego for the World Series. He was even in our postseason parade.

Know what though? The Tigers never gave him a World Series ring as a reward for his contributions. That was penny-pinching Jim Campbell for you. He's the one who made those decisions, like awarding rings of differing values. I remember Bill Scherrer took his ring to a jeweler to have it appraised after it turned his finger green—only to be told there was no gold in it. So, Bill had clearly received a ring of lesser value than most of the other players.

The rookies who had joined us in September—including O'Neal, who won another game in addition to the clincher—didn't receive any ring at all. I didn't know that then, but I know it now—and I find it appalling. I've talked to Randy about it, and he doesn't want to speak badly of the Tigers' organization. But he has offered over the years to pay for the ring himself because he says it's embarrassing when people, who know he was on the Tigers, come up to him and want to see his 1984 ring—only to have to tell them, "They didn't give me one."

He has a ring from 1987 when he was on the St. Louis Cardinals, for whom he started just once (the second-to-last game of the regular season) but had no won-lost record. Because Randy wasn't married yet, the Cardinals even offered to give one to his mother but sent her a ring made into a pendant instead. Even so, they were generous—or as O'Neal put it "a classy organization."

Randy was proud to be a Tiger and happy to help us win. But he said he's done the research and has learned that he and the other September call-ups are the only players in the last 40 years not to receive a ring as part of the world championship team for which they played.

Every team since 1984 has rewarded a ring to their entire 40-man roster, athletic trainers, their minor league coaching staff, scouts, announcers, and front-office personnel. He said he was the only player in our postseason celebration parade who didn't receive a ring. "Rest his soul, but Jim Campbell was never one to spend money on anything he didn't have to," Tom Brookens said years later. "If he could cut a corner, he would cut it. Whatever was right in the 1950s was still right in the 1980s. We used to call him Big Chief Save-a-Buck."

This isn't just a commentary on the years Campbell was the boss, however. Randy has contacted Tigers' executives since JC's time and hasn't been able to get anywhere—despite offering to pay for the ring. I would like to see this rectified—maybe on a future September 18th, which is the anniversary of his clinching game. Randy deserves a ring—plain and simple. It would be right. It would be appropriate. Just because Campbell was thrifty (to a fault) doesn't mean the situation can't be rectified generations later. C'mon, Tigers, the guy won the division-clinching game for us in 1984. Do it.

working a couple of innings. I led off with a single to left on a 2–2 pitch, the ball glancing off the glove of Greg Pryor at third base. After going 0-for-4 against Quiz with two strikeouts during the regular season, I was happy just to be on base. With differing degrees of success, Evans and Jones attempted sacrifice bunts after that. The net effect was that we had runners at second and third with one out. Grubb would be hitting next.

It was a matchup we liked, of course, runners in scoring position and a left-handed hitter facing a side-arming right-hander. But Quisenberry got ahead of Johnny with a 1–2 count. No matter. Grubb belted the next pitch to deep center. We initially liked the looks of it, but the ball was hit high enough for the speedy Wilson to have a chance of catching up to it. This was a tense moment for both teams because we weren't sure if Wilson would get there or not. "I held my breath," Grubb said.

"Willie ran forever," Rusty Kuntz said. "We all kept still. But when he didn't catch it, you can imagine what happened."

"A sinker," Quisenberry said of the pitch, "but I don't think it sunk very well."

Our dugout exploded with joy. "I bought someone a Cadillac today," said Dave Bergman, who'd been robbed of all the money he had set aside for tickets earlier, "but what the heck, we were back in front."

About all the attention he'd get, the mild-mannered Grubb would say, "I've never been the guy in the spotlight like this. I'll remember it a long time."

Johnny came through for us the whole season. But it couldn't get much bigger than that double. Despite the lead we weren't home free. The Royals put together a pair of singles in the bottom of the 11th against Lopez, including Wilson's infield hit on a 1–2 pitch that extended the inning for a few more agonizing minutes. Lopez retired Lynn Jones on a liner to right, however, to end the game.

This was a huge victory for us—and a big blow for the Royals, who had put up a great fight. They were down now and they knew it. "It's hard for me to feel confident after a loss like this," said their manager Dick Howser. "We now have to win three in a row at Tiger Stadium, but we've done it before."

Indeed, they had—as recently as August. We couldn't forget that. But with an off day between games, we weren't about to. I had a personal matter to attend to on the off day, though. And I'll be forever thankful that I got back to Detroit in time for it. My wife gave birth to our daughter, Ashley Lyne. As much as I would have been happy to devote my entire time to being thrilled about that blessed moment in our lives, I couldn't. There was still a pennant to be won.

Milt Wilcox was going to be our starter in Game Three. A year ago Milt was wondering if he would ever pitch another game for the Tigers, even doubting it as free agency approached, but now he was pitching the game that could lift us into the World Series. Cortisone was easing the pain in Milt's right shoulder again. But we were never certain how much. He had seven shots of it in 1984. Plus, he always put some kind of therapeutic crap on his shoulder that smelled nasty. This was his moment to shine, though, if he could. Left-hander Charlie Leibrandt, who had won four of his last six starts, would be his counterpart.

We took a 1–0 lead in the second inning when, with runners at first and third, Castillo beat a throw to first that would have completed an inning-ending double-play. Castillo was safe because of "sheer hustle," Craig would say later about the play that indicated just how much we wanted the series to end as quickly as possible. Lemon scored as Castillo beat White's throw to first. Hustle is what we expected from everyone on the team, but this was all Marty. He busted his butt to knock in that run.

In retrospect, Concepcion waited a bit too long for Castillo's grounder to get to him, and his underhand throw to White put pressure on the Royals' outstanding second baseman to make a strong, quick throw to first, which he did, but Castillo beat it by a half-step. "We got so much joy out of doing the little things like breaking up double-plays and running the bases correctly," Evans said.

That play reflected the character of our team—the way we played the game and how we were taught to play the game. Going all the way back to spring training, Sparky had continually emphasized "the little things." He always said they typically end up making the difference in tight ballgames.

Evans, by the way, made the defensive play of the game, stealing a hit away from Wilson in the eighth inning with a great grab at first base, then somehow beating Wilson to first for the out that ended the inning. When Darrell jubilantly thrust his fist into the air after the play, the huge crowd went wild. "I don't know where that burst of speed came from," Evans recalled, "but I got there ahead of Willie. Not by much, but enough."

In any case, we had led 1–0 since the second inning without knowing what the frames ahead of us would bring. "Nobody dreamed one run would hold up," Sparky said.

What the ensuing innings had brought was this: the best game of Wilcox's career. Through the eighth, when he handed the ball over to Hernandez, Milt pitched shutout ball, allowing two hits and two walks. Not once did he allow a Kansas City runner past first base.

When Hernandez was summoned at the start of the ninth, however, Wilcox understood why. The first three scheduled Kansas City hitters were left-handers. "Willie was the man for the job," Milt said.

Hernandez allowed a two-out single to pinch-hitter McRae, but the game ended—with police ringing the field to control the expected celebration—on Motley's pop-up to Castillo at third. "I'm the happiest person on Earth," Castillo said later. "This is awesome. There are probably some other words to describe it, but I can't think of them."

We hadn't done anything more at the plate than score just the one run against Leibrandt—heck, he kept us hitless after the second inning—but it didn't matter. Milt protected the slim lead with all his might. When it was over, someone said that if there was such an honor as a ceremonial first sip of champagne, Wilcox deserved it. I gave Milt a lot of credit. He did whatever he had to do just to be able to pitch. This was Exhibit A along those lines—a great and courageous game for him. "His effort was spectacular," Craig said.

"He's a warrior," Evans added.

"Right now," Wilcox said, "I'm saying this is the biggest victory of my career. Hopefully in a week, I'll be saying that about a World Series win."

Compared to the four-and-a-half cases of champagne when we clinched the division, there were 36 cases waiting for us this time after the final out—enough to drown everyone in the clubhouse. That's because this was a bigger accomplishment. Far bigger. We had just won the American League pennant!

Chapter 15

World Series Game One

What a non-stop whirlwind it had been. Our daughter, Ashley Lyne, was born on Thursday. Then we clinched the American League pennant on Friday. On Saturday we all thought we'd be staying home to host the Chicago Cubs in the first two games of the World Series. But on Sunday after the Cubs failed to finish the job—and after a workout in the rain at Tiger Stadium—we flew to San Diego to get ready for the World Series against the Padres. We'd been off since Thursday. But I was allowed to skip the workout because of my daughter being born. Everybody else had to be there. "The last thing in the world we need is more rest," Sparky Anderson said. "This is the best rested team I've ever had."

Even little Ashley Lyne, whom I picked up at the hospital on Sunday morning, was with us on the charter flight Sunday night from Detroit to San Diego. On Monday we practiced to get ready for the Padres, champions of the National League. And on Tuesday night, in front of a crowd at Jack Murphy Stadium, which was so loud we could hardly think straight, we opened the World Series.

Phew. Did I say whirlwind? Quite the week, I tell you.

To make matters less frenetic, however, when we got back to Detroit for that last homestand of the regular season, a friend of mine, Mike Windiate, had somehow worked his way past security at the airport, telling the guards he was there to drive me to the hospital, claiming it was an emergency. That wasn't true. Arlyne was expecting, but it wasn't an emergency. This was simply an attempt by my friend to rescue me from the huge crowd of fans and get me home faster than I otherwise would.

Arlyne giving birth on that Thursday, October 4, had been strategically planned. She was induced. We had decided that if the baby hadn't already been born—her due date was Friday, October 5—she'd be induced on Thursday, which was the Tigers' off day. It needed to be Thursday because I was determined not to miss any of the postseason games. As for sleep that week, I didn't get much. I got it whenever I could get it.

I admit it would have been fun to play the Cubs. There was a lot of local talk that it would have been a replay of the 1945 World Series, which the Tigers won, and it seemed that most Detroit fans wanted a Tigers-Cubs matchup, but it wasn't to be. "We weren't expecting to play the Padres…didn't really know that much about them," Milt Wilcox said. "It was almost like they advanced by default because the Cubs didn't finish them off."

To be honest, though, you needed to give the Padres credit for the way they came back to win the National League Championship Series after losing the first two games to the Cubs. Even in Game Five, they were down by three runs after the fifth inning but got the job done by rallying in the sixth and seventh. I know Cubs' fans were heartbroken—baseball fans everywhere probably were—but we couldn't think about that. We were facing a challenge to keep our own fans happy with Jack Morris facing lefty Mark Thurmond as the starting pitchers in Game One.

We didn't know much about Thurmond. The 28-year-old was in his second major league season. But we were aware he had an excellent pickoff move and that he had won nine games in the second half of the season. We also knew—and this would be favorable for us if it continued—he'd had more success on the road this season than at home. We were about to find out if that would have any bearing on how we fared against him.

Jack seemed a little jittery at the workout on Monday. He'd also been out of sorts on the flight out to San Diego, so much so that Carol, his wife, asked him why he wasn't having any fun. "Because I'm the guy who has to go out there and pitch the first game!" he barked.

Everyone had to deal with jitters however they could—Jack was a little ornery, anyway—but we had a lot of faith in him. He had overcome whatever was troubling him in the middle of the season after his outstanding beginning and pitched well in his last three starts—not to mention in the playoffs against the Kansas City Royals. We felt he'd be up for the challenge of the World Series. "I like the way I've been throwing," Morris said about his recent appearances.

I told the media he was "in a groove again." And I believed it. After a downhill slide, he had roared all the way back and was throwing the ball really well. As for how we would do against Thurmond, we'd be happy to begin the World Series the same way we had in the playoffs against the Royals—with multiple runs in the first inning. "Ever since I was a kid in Houston throwing baseballs through a tire, I've dreamed about this day," Thurmond said before the first game.

Other than a security guard not recognizing our pitching coach Roger Craig and initially denying him entrance into the ballpark—even though Roger used to manage the Padres—all went well on the workout day in San Diego. We felt we were ready. Despite being from Southern California, I didn't know the San Diego ballpark at all. In fact, I had never been to it. Growing up, I had followed only the Los Angeles Dodgers and California Angels. I'd known nothing about the Padres as a kid. So, for me, as for most of my teammates, it would be a journey into the unknown. Said Sparky, though, trying to keep us upbeat, "I want everyone to treasure every moment."

That was our intention. And I must say, we got off to an excellent start in Game One. Lou Whitaker doubled, then scored on Alan Trammell's line single to left. Both hits came on full counts, so we began the game by making Thurmond work. I just remember thinking that our double-play guys—Whitaker and Trammell—were amazing.

Then we got a little too eager. Due in part to Thurmond's pickoff move, which was known to be excellent, the inning fizzled after we scored. Tram was caught stealing second on a 1–3–6 play, which meant that a pair of

Herndon

Larry Herndon was one of my favorite teammates. Quiet, dependable, he had been traded to the Detroit Tigers from the San Francisco Giants before the 1982 season. His last season in the majors was 1988. In a deal, which strongly benefited us, the Giants dealt Larry to the Tigers for two left-handed pitchers—Mike Chris and Dan Schatzeder—who'd been promising hurlers at one time or another. Chris displayed most of his potential at the Triple A level while Schatzeder, for whom we had traded Ron LeFlore, won 11 games for us in 1980 before slumping to just six wins in 1981. But I'm sure the Giants expected more than the one game the two lefties combined to win for them after the deal.

Herndon, meanwhile, blossomed for us. In his six years with the Giants, he hadn't been a particularly productive hitter. The most home runs he ever hit for San Francisco was eight in 1980, the same year he drove in 49 runs—also a high for him as a Giant. For us, though, he averaged .297 in his first two seasons with an average of 21 home runs and 90 RBIs. For most of those two years, he hit third for us—a spot often reserved for the best hitter on the team.

So, what a great trade it had been.

In 1984, however, Larry just wasn't himself—not at first anyway. He hit just one home run in the first half of the season despite the team getting off to such a fantastic start, and it was because of his struggles, especially against right-handed pitching, that management felt the need to bring in a left-handed hitter to platoon in left field with him. That turned out to be another good development for us because it was Ruppert Jones who was brought in to help. Together, Herndon and Jones combined to hit .306 with 13 home runs and 47 RBIs in the second half of the season.

They didn't have similar personalities, though. Ruppert was more outgoing, whereas Larry was quiet. He never sought attention, never wanted it. "I'm not an ego man," he said.

But we loved him all the same because there was nothing more important to him than doing his job. When he chose not to speak to the media after hitting what amounted to the game-winning home run in the opener of the World Series, we understood. We wanted him to get the credit he deserved, of course, but all the satisfaction Hondo required came from within. He had contributed, which was enough.

There was a quiet dignity to Herndon. Raised in Memphis by his grandmother, he wasn't a boat rocker—on or off the field. Whatever was best for the team was best for him. And he always took as much joy in what the rest of us were accomplishing as he did in his own actions. I remember what he said about the pivotal play in Game One against the San Padres on which we threw Kurt Bevacqua out at third to erase what would have been a leadoff triple late in the game.

Herndon was the left fielder on the play, so it was his job to back up the throw to third, but as the play unfolded—with an accurate throw from Kirk Gibson in right to Lou Whitaker, then another from Lou to Marty Castillo at third—Herndon admired the beauty of its execution. "It was the prettiest thing to see those guys make a perfect play," he said.

But that's what made Larry such a great teammate. He always rooted for the rest of us.

We don't see each other often these days. We talk from time to time but not enough. I miss him. Even more than as a teammate, I admired him as a person.

singles later in the opening inning merely produced a first-and-second chance instead of another run. Barbaro Garbey's grounder to Graig Nettles at third ended the inning.

Despite being nervous Morris retired the first two batters he faced, and it looked like he was off to a good start. "Sure, I was nervous," Jack said. "Show me someone who isn't before his first World Series start."

But two singles and a Terry Kennedy double later, we found ourselves down by a run at 2–1, which was still the score when the fifth inning began. We had put together a first-and-second chance in the third with the help of Trammell's steal of second, but another grounder to third ended the inning. Kennedy came to the plate in the Padres' half of the third, staring at another chance to knock in a run, but he flied out to center this time instead of adding to their lead. Still making Thurmond work (he would throw 117 pitches in his five innings), we gave ourselves a first-and-third opportunity in the fourth, but Whitaker's fly ball to center ended that threat.

I never thought we completely had Thurmond on the ropes. He hung in there with his gameplan, moving the ball around. But we were putting together some scoring chances, so we felt confident we'd get a big hit sooner or later.

We got it in the fifth, as it turned out, but only after Kirk Gibson also was caught off first base by Thurmond on a steal attempt of second. Again, the scouting report had been accurate. Fortunately, my two-out ground-rule double down the line at third extended the inning, bringing up Larry Herndon. Hondo, as we called him, had found his power late in the year. After just one home run in our first 113 games, he hit six in our last 49. Considering that he had hit 43 home runs for us in the previous two seasons, we knew he was fully capable of being a power threat.

Larry had slipped in left field on Kennedy's two-run double in the first inning, so he went up to the plate for his at-bat in the fifth still thinking he had cost us a run—and wanting to make up for it. He also said, "It was just time to do something." Driving me in from second was his hope. Anything more would be a bonus. He added later that a home run was the last thing on his mind. However, our former teammate Enos Cabell had told Herndon that Thurmond would try to keep everything away from him, so that's where Larry was looking for a pitch. And it's precisely where he got one to hit. Not known for his power to right field, Herndon didn't hit a monstrous fly ball but didn't have to. I remember Larry being more of a pull hitter—and sometimes up the middle—but his line-drive home run to right did the job this time, giving us a 3–2 lead.

Tony Gwynn singled and stole second in the bottom half of the fifth inning, but he was stranded at second. The Padres didn't go away, though. In fact, it looked like they intended to cause considerable trouble in the sixth when Nettles and Kennedy, their first two batters, singled. Sparky said later that if one more Padre had reached base that inning, Morris would have been out of the game. "And we would have lost," Anderson surmised.

Until the sixth Jack had been effective since the first inning. With only three strikeouts, though, he hadn't exactly been blowing everyone away—but he soon began to. In fact, he mowed down the next three batters in rapid,

1–2–3 fashion. Bobby Brown, starting in center because Kevin McReynolds would miss the entire series with an injury, struck out swinging on a 2–2 pitch after failing to get a bunt down. Carmelo Martinez also struck out on a 2–2 pitch. And Garry Templeton swung and missed a 1–2 pitch.

As efficiently as that, the Padres' threat in the sixth had been defused. The three consecutive strikeouts would have gone down as the turning point if another play more universally remembered as being the point when the game turned hadn't occurred in the seventh. Just as Herndon wasn't known for hitting home runs to right, San Diego's Kurt Bevacqua didn't have a reputation for hitting triples—anywhere. In fact, he hadn't hit one since 1980. But leading off the seventh for the Padres, Bevacqua sprayed a ball inside the line to deep right. It was going to be a leadoff double for sure—maybe more depending on how much the ball bounced around in the corner. "At worst, it could have rattled around a while," Gibson said, "but, luckily, this one just sat there for me to pick up."

Even so, Bevacqua was three strides past second base when Gibson turned to throw the ball in. Everyone agreed Kurt would made it to third easily—and that the Padres would have been in business with a leadoff triple. I remember it as if it happened yesterday. What followed was one of the best plays of the entire World Series. "If he makes it to third," Morris said, "I figure the game is tied unless I punch out the next three guys again."

Fate intervened on our side, however. "I stumbled," Bevacqua said. "I don't know why I stumbled, but I did. And I'd gone too far to go back, so I just kept going."

"He lost a step or two, but I'm responsible," said Padres manager Dick Williams. "We had him going as far as he could go."

It had been third base or bust, in other words. Suddenly, all the workout hours we had spent on fundamental baseball came into play. It would take two accurate throws—from Gibson to Whitaker, then from Whitaker to Marty Castillo at third base—to cut down Bevacqua. But we got it done. "He didn't fall down, but the stumble cost Bevacqua a couple of feet. So he was definitely out," said third-base umpire Richie Garcia. "Not by a mile, but out."

We welcomed the sight of Garcia's thumb going up, that's for sure. But again it was only because we had worked so hard practicing the little things, like relays, that we threw him out.

"I wouldn't have made that play last year," Gibson said. "I never used to take the time to get the right grip on a ball. I probably would have thrown a 20-foot screwball to Lou."

Years later, when I was managing in the Tigers' organization, I mentioned this very play to Gene Roof, who was our roving outfield instructor at the time. Geno was looking for visual aids to demonstrate cutoffs and relays, so I told him to look for it on YouTube. Roof found it and started using it as proof of perfect execution. I can still remember seeing Bevacqua stumbling around second—at which time I began to think, *We're going to get him. We're going to get him!* It was a great play: Exhibit A of why you work on fundamentals.

That was a turning point for Jack. He didn't allow another hit the rest of the game. When Templeton grounded out to Dave Bergman for the final out of the ninth inning, Game One was ours. Herndon's home run had been the big hit of the 3–2 victory. But he didn't want to discuss it with the media after the game. In fact, while conveying he was sorry for not talking, he had his clothes brought to him in the trainer's room so he could dress there before returning to the hotel.

"That's the way he's been his entire career," Sparky said. "Hondo lets his actions do the talking while he stays in the background."

Larry was a quiet individual. We all knew that. He also hadn't spoken after hitting a home run in the first game of the American League playoffs—but didn't explain until much later. We wouldn't know the reason until much later. "I didn't need the attention," Herndon said of the two times he didn't want to talk. "The pitchers deserved it. Morris deserved it. Both times the credit should have gone to Jack."

And after the World Series opener, most of it did. "His gritty performance showed me a lot of belly," Craig said of Morris.

"None of his pitches were straight," said Gwynn, who had led the majors with a .351 batting average. "One pitch looked like a fastball to me, then the bottom dropped out of it. After that I really didn't know what to look for."

That's because Jack had the same arm action on his splitter as he had on his fastball. Same action, same release point. The bottom fell out of one pitch but not the other. But I can see why a hitter as great as Gwynn would say what he said because that's what made Jack the pitcher he was. It was very difficult to pick up his splitter.

The discussion forever more, though, will be about which play was more pivotal: Lou Brock not touching the plate in the 1968 World Series or Bevacqua stumbling past second base in this game, turning a leadoff triple into an out at third base. Both plays will have their backers. Both plays should. That's how important they were. I can't honestly tell you one was bigger than the other. The first had been at the plate, the latter at third base. I was on the field for one but have only seen the other on television (a thousand times). And even if he had been safe, there's no way of knowing if Bevacqua would have scored from third base. What we can say is that both were huge plays in Detroit Tigers history. We probably should leave it at that.

Chapter 16

World Series Game Two

After winning the first game of the World Series, we naturally wanted to win the second game as well—and we went into it thinking we had a good chance to do so. We were 4-for-4 in the postseason at that point—four wins in four games—and were feeling pretty good about ourselves. If nothing else, going into Game Two, we were on course. Additionally, we had won all five of Dan Petry's starts in September. Plus, he had pitched well against the Kansas City Royals in the American League Championship Series. The game he started in the ALCS was decided in extra innings, so Petry hadn't been the pitcher of record.

But we went into Game Two of the World Series confident he would pitch well again. His counterpart would be right-hander Ed Whitson, a capable pitcher certainly, but one who'd been encountering tough luck. Despite having a 2.93 ERA in his last 11 starts of the regular season, he had won just twice, but he had held the Chicago Cubs to only a run on five hits in eight innings of Game Three, the National League Championship Series game in which the San Diego Padres began their comeback.

So, there was every reason to think Whitson would pitch well against us, though we didn't know much about him. If I had faced him before, for instance, I didn't remember it.

Whitson was a well-traveled pitcher who had been with the Cleveland Indians in the American League, so some of us might have faced him. To that extent he wasn't a complete unknown to us. But we pretty much had to rely on the scouting report about him.

Because San Diego had started a left-hander in the opener of the World Series and was now switching to a right-hander, we went into the game with more lineup changes than the Padres. For instance, Dave Bergman started at first base and Darrell Evans switched to third, bumping Marty Castillo out of the starting lineup. As usual in cases of a left-right pitching change, Ruppert Jones would be in left field for us instead of Game One hero Larry Herndon, and Johnny Grubb would be our designated hitter instead of Barbaro Garbey. In other words, we loaded our lineup with left-handed hitters against Whitson.

The Padres countered by switching Kurt Bevacqua with Bobby Brown in the batting order, but that's all. Instead of hitting ninth, Bevacqua would hit sixth against Petry. It wasn't a move that seemed significant on paper. Bevacqua had one hit in the opener off Jack Morris, the double on which he was thrown out at third; Brown had struck out twice in four hitless trips.

Neither player had hit for much power during the regular season. Brown belted three home runs to Bevacqua's one. But the Padres were searching for offense, so trading slots for those two is what they opted to do.

Petry clearly was nervous to begin the game, but we expected that would be the case. Morris had been nervous in the opener but settled down. We thought the same would be true for Dan. With three runs in the first inning, we tried to give him a quick reason not to be jittery. Poor Whitson, on the other hand, never knew what hit him. He lasted only seven batters. Five of the seven reached base safely with hits. The only routine out that occurred while Whitson was in the game was Jones' pop-up for the second out.

Lou Whitaker began it with a line-drive single to left on the first pitch. Instead of being patient at the plate, which we'd been against Mark Thurmond in Game One, we were aggressive in Game Two. Our first four batters jumped on the first pitch. Our team in general was aggressive, and I'm sure the scouting report was that Whitson would try and get ahead of us with fastballs. So, we were ready for them. After two more singles and my sacrifice fly to foul territory in deep left—it was caught in the bullpen—we led 2–0. Then Evans made it 3–0 by driving in Kirk Gibson from third with a bloop single. It seemed like here we go again.

But when Grubb singled Evans to third with two outs, the Padres made a pitching move, bringing in Andy Hawkins to replace Whitson, and the inning quickly ended at that point on Chet Lemon's grounder to third. We knew the Padres had a good bullpen, but we were headed to the bottom of the first inning with a three-run lead. There was a long way to go obviously; however, we felt we had put ourselves in a strong position.

As nice as it would have been for our lead to remain at three, it didn't diminish our confidence when the Padres scored a run in their half of the first inning on Graig Nettles' sacrifice fly. Petry didn't have the best first inning, but we were confident he'd settle down. With an infield single and a sacrifice, the Padres had made the most of two bunts and a walk. But they didn't hit Dan hard.

Hawkins did an effective job of shutting down our offense after taking over—we couldn't touch him—so the score was still 3–1 heading into the bottom of the fourth. The second and third innings for the Padres had been eventful but scoreless. With the help of a balk, an error, and a walk, they had put a runner in scoring position in both innings but hadn't capitalized. Petry wasn't exactly struggling at that point but didn't look comfortable. He had a live fastball early on but was missing out of the zone, falling behind batters.

Hawkins, meanwhile, continued to shut us down. It took a while for it to sink in that he was kicking our butt. He'd been an ineffective starter during the season, but after a stretch of allowing 16 runs in 11 innings heading into early September, he had finished the season with a stretch of strong relief. Plus, there were times when he simply had outstanding stuff— as he would prove over a longer haul by winning 18 games for the Padres in 1985. Unfortunately for us, this was one of the times his stuff was electric. Despite the quick lead we grabbed against Whitson, we didn't do anything for several innings in a row against Hawkins.

That meant the Padres had time to gnaw away at the lead if Petry struggled. Or if he continued to struggle, depending on how you'd label

Arlyne at the Series

My wife, Arlyne Parrish, on what it like was to travel to the World Series so soon after childbirth:

The challenges of that trip were the obvious, but I got a lot of help from my family. My mom [Grandma Joy] flew from California to Detroit so she could be there for our two boys, who were small and not going to be in San Diego with us because no children were allowed on the team flight. An exception had been made, however, for newborn Ashley. And to help me, my sister Cheryl drove from where she lived in Orange County, California, to San Diego, joining us at our hotel. We got her a room while we all were going to be there.

In San Diego on the first gameday, I nursed the baby in the hotel room during the first inning, then took a taxi to the ballpark, so I could get there without traffic. I stayed at the game until the eighth inning but left before traffic would have gotten heavy again. Then it was time to nurse Ashley again at the hotel.

The routine was different during the second game. My sister packed up the baby at the hotel, then brought her to the ballpark for the bus ride to the airport because we were flying back to Detroit that night. I spent a lot of the time being sore, though, from recently giving birth.

All the Tigers wives were close. We pretty much did everything together, but Barb Trammell played an especially big role in everyone's life. She was so giving and kind.

The day I was released from the hospital in Michigan after Ashley was born was the day it was decided who the Tigers would play in the World Series. I was praying the Chicago Cubs would win because the World Series would have begun in Detroit in that case. But when the Cubs lost and we knew we'd be flying to San Diego instead, I called the doctor to get her permission for me to travel with Lance. She said our baby daughter would be fine, but I would be uncomfortable because of my stitches. If I didn't mind the discomfort, I could go. She was correct. It was an uncomfortable flight for me. But we made it work, not knowing if we'd ever experience another World Series, which we didn't.

For the games in Detroit, I was able to tuck Ashley into a baby carrier I wore on my chest. Our two boys were able to attend the games in Detroit as well. We also had my mother there, and Lance's parents flew in from

California, so we had a lot of helping hands. Our adrenaline was high from the get-go for those games. It was a very exciting time. I was tired, but having been through Coast Guard boot camp where you learn how to override fatigue, I overrode it again during the World Series. We even participated with all our kids, including Ashley, in the postseason parade a few days after it ended.

It probably wasn't smart, though, because weeks later I hit the wall and got very sick. The doctor had told me it was going to be me, not the baby, who would have the rougher time—and she was right. But that's how long it took me to come down from that adrenaline rush at the end of the season.

My training for the Coast Guard was a big help. I enlisted when I was 22 after being turned down three times for a government-insured student loan. It just hadn't been in the cards for me to get one. I'd gone into the fashion industry for a while but got so frustrated with it that one day I decided to go into the military. And soon after, off to Cape May, New Jersey, I went for boot camp. There are no words to describe how demanding it was. But I got through it, then I went to bosun's mate school in Yorktown, Virginia. Why did I enlist? I had come from a broken home, and this was my chance to become self-sufficient by making something of myself. Through the military I would be able to go to college.

I wear it as a badge of honor that I've been recognized from time to time over the years as Lance's wife. When I was in high school, being from a troubled family, I wanted to be a mom. I didn't want to have a business career. I wanted only to be a mom and have a happy family. I don't look at it that Lance got all the attention and I got nothing. To be acknowledged as his wife was, and still is, a compliment. At the same time, it's very strange when I get asked for my autograph, which occasionally happens. I always feel like hugging the person and telling them, "Thank you for your kindness, but don't ask because you're thinking I'm being left out. I'm fine with my life."

What does get awkward, though, is when women have told me over the years that they keep Lance's picture close to them. I understand that they might look at him as an athlete and as a sports hero, but to me he's just my husband.

Patte Freehan had a great impact on my life, especially during the early years when I was a young mom and wife with the Tigers. Patte lived this baseball life before I did, and her friendship, advice, and Godly wisdom were of immeasurable importance to me. The Lord blessed me with her presence in my life at just the right time when I desperately needed it, and she is still an amazing friend to this day.

the quality of his early innings. As Dan would say later, "I couldn't put anything where I wanted to."

He was able to get out of some jams, but eventually trouble caught up to him. That was the case in the bottom of the fourth when Bevacqua led off with a single to left, and with one out, Garry Templeton singled him to third with his second hit of the game. Petry got ahead of Brown with a quick 0–2 count, but on a 1–2 pitch, Brown hit a chopper too slowly to Alan Trammell at short for him to turn a double play. We had to settle for only one out at second base. Bevacqua scored on the play, cutting our lead to 3–2. With our bullpen heating up, especially after Alan Wiggins singled Brown to second for the third hit of the inning, Petry worked his way out of additional trouble on Tony Gwynn's liner to right. That escape meant he'd be around for another inning. So, after four innings we were in front by a run, but Petry was struggling, though Sparky Anderson wasn't ready to replace him. "Not if we're still ahead," he insisted.

True enough, we were ahead and we'd seen Danny settle down in the middle of a game many times. But it was looking as if it would be difficult for us to tack on runs against Hawkins—and through four innings, Petry had allowed eight base runners. When we went down in order in the top of the fifth, Hawkins had retired 13 batters in a row. However, I think the Padres changed their gameplan against us. After Whitson left they began to ride a lot of pitches in on us, trying to tie us up, and it worked. Plus, Hawkins' fastball had good life on it. From his years as manager of the Padres, Roger Craig said he remembered Andy as "a skinny kid" but that he had "blossomed" into a hard thrower. Skinny kids grow up, obviously.

With one out in the Padres' fifth, Petry missed badly on a 3–1 pitch to Nettles, walking him. Then came trouble in the form of a crazy carom on Terry Kennedy's hard-hit grounder to Whitaker. A true bounce on the play might have resulted in a 4–6–3 double-play because neither Nettles nor Kennedy had any speed, and the ball was solidly hit. Whitaker didn't get a true bounce, however. Instead, the ball ricocheted wildly off the hard infield dirt at Jack Murphy Stadium, hitting Lou in the chest, then rolling away for a single—a stroke of bad luck for us but indication the Padres were getting good hacks against Petry and that fielding conditions weren't ideal. "I've already said, 'This is the worst field I've seen,'" Sparky said. "It's harder than a rock. The turning point was the ball that bounced funny on Lou. But it wasn't the field that beat us."

It's what happened next that did. Kennedy's bad-hop single brought up Bevacqua, who seemed to be ubiquitous at that point. After all, it was his leadoff single in the fourth that had led to the Padres' second run after his stumble around second base had been a major attention-getter in the opener. "That's history," Bevacqua said of his Game One stumble following Game Two, indicating it was no longer bothering him.

Still, as a utility infielder who'd been with five other teams, some of them twice—"I've been so many places I have my own zip code," he said—Bevacqua hadn't hit more than two home runs in a season since 1978, so we didn't really view him as much of a power threat, a pesky hitter perhaps but not a slugger. As Tommy Lasorda had said of Bevacqua not long ago, "He couldn't hit water if he fell out of a boat."

But by suddenly driving a hanging 1–0 slider from Petry over the wall in left, he turned the tables on his doubters with a three-run home run that put the Padres two runs in front—the first home run our pitching staff had allowed in 11 games. "I haven't thrown many sliders this year as bad as that one," Petry said. "It was right over the middle of the plate. Just terrible."

I saw it as kind of a middle-in pitch, spinning and hanging right there—if anything maybe breaking right into Kurt's swing. Naturally, the fans at Jack Murphy Stadium went wild. The noise they made was deafening. We also didn't welcome the sight of Bevacqua blowing kisses to the crowd as he trotted down the line from third base—"I hope all the boys saw it," an irritated Sparky said—but it was a big moment for the Padres, and that's one of the ways Bevacqua chose to show it.

Yes, we had noticed it. But that was Bevacqua for you. Some of us had played winter ball with him in Puerto Rico. He was a nut. There was no telling what he would do at any given time. It hadn't been a surprise for him to do something off the wall. But I didn't take it personally.

Aurelio Lopez replaced Petry at that point, but we trailed for the first time since the fifth inning of the opener, so we had our work cut out for us. It was only through some clutch pitching by Aurelio that the Padres didn't add to their lead in the fifth. After Bevacqua's home run, they put runners at second and third by way of a walk, a single, and an outfield error, but Lopez retired Brown on a harmless pop-up to third, then ended the inning on Alan Wiggins' liner to center. Wiggins was 3-for-3 at the time, but Lemon was well positioned to haul in his bid for a fourth consecutive hit.

Down by two runs to a pitcher who hadn't yet—in four-and-a-third innings of relief—allowed a base runner, we faced an uphill challenge, but a leadoff single by Gibson in the sixth was a good omen. At least we thought it was. An out later, however, Gibson was doubled off first on Evans' liner to right because he'd been running on the pitch. Oh well, sometimes it helps to be aggressive; sometimes it backfires.

Not much was going right for us, that's for sure. In the fifth inning, for instance, after giving the sign for a pitchout to Lopez, I had stepped out from behind the plate for the pitch, but Lopez—who insisted he had seen the pitchout sign—fired a fastball down the middle instead, nailing umpire Larry Barnett in a sensitive spot. I told Larry it hadn't been intentional, just a mix-up—and he replied, "Don't worry about it"—but it bothered me because it looked like we didn't know what we were doing. So, I kept apologizing to him for the pitch not just throughout the postseason but all the way to when I saw him at spring training the following year.

The only good news was that with the Padres' bullpen up and throwing it looked like the sixth inning would be the last for Hawkins. Finally. *Now maybe we could get somewhere.*

That was our hope, anyway. But left-hander Craig Lefferts picked up in the seventh where Hawkins left off in the sixth, retiring the side in order. It turned out he would be just as effective.

Bill Scherrer went back out for us in the bottom of the seventh, his second inning of work, and except for another hit by Bevacqua, a line-drive single to left with one out, the Padres caused no trouble. It helped a bit that as Carmelo Martinez was striking out, I was able to throw out Bevacqua at second base on a steal attempt. He had already caused enough trouble for us with his home run. I enjoyed the moment. It was satisfying because I never liked it whenever someone stole a base against me. I got very upset if I didn't throw a runner out. That was my game.

Time was running out, though. If we were going to get anything going, it needed to be soon, and while Trammell's two-out single to left in the eighth off Lefferts was probably our hardest hit ball since the first inning, it led to nothing. When we got to the ninth, we were up against it, knowing that unless we broke through for some runs—"instant runs" as Ernie Harwell used to call them—we'd go back to Detroit with the World Series tied at one victory each. A split is not what we had hoped for, or envisioned, after winning the opener.

It didn't help matters that I took a called third strike on a full count for the first out of the ninth inning. I'd gotten the job done with a sacrifice fly in the first, but it hadn't been the best of nights for me offensively. Most of us probably felt that way, however. As a team we had mustered only two hits—just a pair of singles—since the first inning. And the Padres hadn't issued a walk the entire night. Realistically, it was too late to think anyone could save us when we were down to our last two outs. And sure enough, no one did. The game ended unceremoniously with another strike out and Herndon's foul pop-up.

The Padres had rudely interrupted our championship march with a 5–3 victory. Hawkins had been the difference, most of us thought. Sparky grumbled that we hadn't accomplished our mission. But we hadn't assumed we were going to sweep the Padres. I mean this was the World Series. These guys were for real. They were the best team in the National League. As solace, though, we were headed home.

Chapter 17

World Series Game Three

It was wonderful to be back home, of course. With our daughter being born, followed by a round-trip journey to San Diego for the first two games of the World Series, our family had been through a lot in her first week. Without a workout to attend and no demands on our time, it felt great to catch up on sleep on the off day. I don't even know if anyone went to the stadium. Maybe some of the pitchers did for treatment, but I didn't have to go. It was just good to settle in at home with our baby.

The feeling of being in the World Series was still electric, though, and we knew that Tiger Stadium would be jumping with excitement—and also with media. We were right on both counts. Before Game Three, pitching coach Roger Craig said he couldn't even watch batting practice from our dugout, as was his custom, because of how many reporters were obscuring his view. It was all part of the bustling World Series scene, however, a situation we wouldn't have traded for anything.

If it was a display of baseball artistry the fans were expecting in the game, however, they were going to be disappointed because Game Three was one of missed chances for both teams.

The San Diego Padres kept handing us scoring opportunities—and we kept making the least of them. We could have won this game by a bunch of runs had we managed to come up with a few more hits with runners in scoring position. We eventually won it 5–2, but it took us until the seventh inning before we began to feel even the least bit comfortable.

The pitching matchup was Milt Wilcox for us against lefty Tim Lollar for the Padres. Milt had been superb in the pennant clincher against Kansas City, blanking the Royals on two hits in eight innings while we hung on for a 1–0 victory. He had also finished the regular season strongly with a 6–1 record in his last nine starts. We knew Milt would be up for the challenge of a World Series start. Sparky Anderson didn't hold back on what he thought of Wilcox's toughness, which I, too, held in high regard. "He's the kind of guy you want on your side when it's time to get down and dirty in a fight," Anderson said of Milt.

Lollar had started Game Four against the Chicago Cubs, a pivotal National League Championship Series game the Padres won 7–5, but they didn't win it because of Tim. Trailing 3–2, he was replaced on the mound in the fifth inning because of recurring control problems. According to our scouting report, he sometimes could be, uh…all over the place. To start the Cubs' fourth, for instance, he had walked Gary Matthews before giving up back-to-back home runs with two outs to Jody Davis and Leon Durham. And when Lollar walked two more in the fifth, handing the Cubs a scoring chance with one out, the Padres had seen enough. They made a pitching change at that point to Andy Hawkins, who promptly retired Matthews on an inning-ending double play.

The Padres were accustomed to Lollar's bouts of wildness, however. Nine times during the regular season he had issued five or more walks. Granted, he had good stuff, as a .234 opposing batting average indicated, and he had thrown two shutouts during the regular season—which meant he could be tough on his better days—but control was often his undoing.

In Game Three it would be again—much to our benefit. Lasting for only 13 batters, Lollar allowed four hits and four walks. He also threw a wild pitch. Walks, however, were a constant theme in this game. The difference would be that we eventually stopped issuing them, and the Padres didn't.

The afternoon didn't begin auspiciously for us, though. On a 1–1 count, Alan Wiggins slashed a leadoff double down the third-base line, his fifth hit of the first three games. Wiggins later indicated he wasn't impressed with our pitching staff, saying, "They throw typical American League stuff, a lot of off-speed crap."

First and foremost, I always thought that belief was wrong about American League pitching. Nothing could have been further from the truth. Pitchers threw pretty much the same way in both leagues. But Wiggins could say whatever he wanted. It made no difference to me.

What did make a difference was eventually getting Wiggins out when we needed to. Or having him get stranded on base. He was still at second when Graig Nettles walked with two outs, but both runners were stranded when Terry Kennedy bounced out to Lou Whitaker for the third out of the first inning. Both Alan Trammell and I walked in the bottom of the first, but we, too, were stranded when Larry Herndon flied out to center—not deeply enough to cause trouble.

Lollar wasn't so fortunate in the second inning. With Chet Lemon on third after a single, a wild pitch, and a fly ball to center, the Padres' starter got ahead of Marty Castillo but couldn't put him away. Castillo fouled off two 0–2 pitches, took a ball, then cranked a no-doubter into the left-field seats, giving us a 2–0 lead. Marty wasn't one of the guys you would have expected to go deep with a big home run, so we were thrilled for him but mostly for the entire team. It really had paid off to give him more playing time in the postseason. "Any offense from him was a plus," Wilcox said, "but I think he was probably more shocked than anyone when he hit that home run."

Marty simply replied, "I'm happy to death."

The media made it appear that Castillo was our answer at the plate to San Diego's Kurt Bevacqua, but the fact that both players had hit unexpected home runs was where the similarity ceased. Castillo, for instance, said he gave no consideration to blowing kisses to the crowd while approaching the plate—as Bevacqua had done in San Diego. "I could see myself doing that," Castillo said, "and Goose Gossage knocking me upside the head the next time I came to the plate."

Lemon Aid

One of our secret weapons wasn't so secret at all after the World Series. It was Chet Lemon's defense. Chet's skill at hauling down everything within reach, and sometimes beyond, had been outstanding all season. For all I know, it had been outstanding his entire career, starting with the Chicago White Sox prior to the deal following the 1981 season that brought him to Detroit for Steve Kemp. At the time, I was sorry to see Kemper go. I thought he was one of the building blocks of our future. But it didn't take me long—just a matter of watching Chet play every day—to see why the trade was made. And why it was beneficial.

The bottom line was this: Chet was, without question, a great center fielder. He made outstanding catches often look routine—and he made outstanding catches all the time. The way he chased down Terry Kennedy's bid for extra bases in Game Three of the World Series was a prime example. With two outs in the top of the seventh inning, the San Diego Padres had just reduced our four-run lead to three and still had a runner on third base. Another hit would have made the score too close for comfort. But an extra-base hit would have presented a different problem entirely. After all, in Game Two we had witnessed the Padres' ability to come from behind. And the next batter after Kennedy would have been Kurt Bevacqua, our Game Two nemesis. So, it was time for their half of the inning to end.

On a full-count pitch from Willie Hernandez to Kennedy, Lemon was playing in several steps, thinking that Terry would be concentrating on simply making contact in a lefty vs. lefty matchup. But Kennedy crossed us up with a full swing, resulting in a line drive to deep center. Instantly, we could see this bid for extra bases was going to be a true test of Lemon's ability. Kennedy had hit it squarely, and Chet spun around a little bit in his retreat on the ball. "When he hit it, I knew it was trouble," Lemon said. "I just broke fast, put my head down, and ran. Eventually, I broke the right way and was able to make the catch."

He made it, however, about 420 feet from home plate. With just two innings remaining, it was a play that deflated the Padres. "That one really hurt," Tony Gwynn said.

The catch, though, was not surprising. "It didn't excite me. Chester is going to catch any ball hit to center that doesn't go out of the ballpark. Simple as that," said Sparky Anderson, who despite his high opinion of Lemon had ill-advisedly played him mostly in right field in 1982 while giving Kirk Gibson a chance to prove himself in center.

I had understood the experiment at the time because Gibby was so stinkin' fast we had to find out where he would fit in best. The thought of giving him all that ground at Tiger Stadium to roam around in center field was just so tempting. But I don't think Kirk ever felt as a comfortable in center as he did in right. With Chet, as the Kennedy catch proved once again, he just always got superb, instinctive jumps. No one could argue with that. Least of all the Padres.

"That catch didn't surprise me," said San Diego's Goose Gossage. "I played with Chet in Chicago. I think he's the best center fielder in baseball. From this point on, we need to think: hit it anywhere but center."

Of the challenge facing the Padres after Game Three, Garry Templeton summed it up simply by saying, "We just have to stop hitting the ball to Lemon."

That's how much of a difference maker Chet was, but it also showed how deep of a dent his relentlessly fine defense had made in the way the Padres viewed their diminishing chances after Game Three.

Back then, if you did stuff like blowing kisses, it would come back to haunt either you or a teammate. Someone would pay a price. That's not the case nowadays.

Marty's home run was merely a jump-start for us. It's not where the action ended. After a walk to Whitaker, Trammell doubled to left, increasing our lead to 3–0. Then after a walk to Kirk Gibson, Nettles saved a run by preventing my single from getting through the infield. But we now had the bases loaded with relief pitcher Greg Booker coming in for the Padres. "I just lost it," Lollar would say later of the way he pitched. "The ball didn't go where I wanted it to. Maybe I was trying too hard."

Booker hadn't really had a defined role for the Padres—other than to get out of someone else's trouble. He pitched mostly when San Diego was behind. In fact, the Padres lost 28 of the 32 games in which he worked during the regular season. And the only time he had pitched in the NLCS against the Cubs was for two scoreless innings when the Padres trailed

13–0. Suffice to say, we didn't know much about him because there wasn't much of a file on him—other than the fact that he was the son-in-law of Padres general manager Jack McKeon. Booker won only one game and saved none for the Padres in 1984. But he was a major league pitcher who would eventually last seven seasons with San Diego, so we couldn't afford to take him—or anyone else in their bullpen—lightly.

Fortunately for us, however, Booker picked up where Lollar left off, walking Herndon, the first batter he faced, to force in our fourth run of the inning. We could have blasted the game wide open at that point, but Booker settled down long enough to retire Barbaro Garbey on a fly ball to center, ending the inning.

That didn't mean he had settled down permanently. But he wasn't about to make a Hawkins, who was the bullpen hero of Game Two, kind of relief appearance against us. In fact, Booker walked three of the five batters he faced in the third, giving way to another right-hander, Greg Harris, before the inning ended. The fact we left the bases loaded in both the second and third after the Padres had countered with a run in the top of the third meant two things: one, we were not making the most of our opportunities and, two, we weren't in front by nearly as many runs as we could have been.

Even so, we led 4–1 when Harris entered the game in the third and managed to tack on a quick run against him but only because Gibson was hit on the foot by an 0–1 pitch with the bases loaded. The game seemed sluggishly slow at that point, taking forever to play. It was not shaping up to be a crisp, exciting World Series game. Vin Scully claimed on the telecast that, "The Tigers are one swing away from devouring San Diego." When I nailed a two-out, 3–1 pitch from Harris with the bases still loaded, we thought it might be the productive swing we needed. But Bobby Brown hauled the ball down in left-center to end the third. I had nearly helped the cause a couple of times, but man, oh, man, I just couldn't find a hole. These were opportunities that needed to be cashed in on!

Artistically, because of all the walks and runners left on base (eventually a World Series record of 24 LOBs), the game was probably being viewed as a dud by the national television audience, but we were not judging it on style. We were ahead 5–1 after three innings. That's all we cared about. Despite the lead, Sparky was so upset about the number of runners we were leaving on base that he was heard to grumble about our chances of ending the Series in Detroit, "It ain't going to end here, I tell you. We need to hit better than we have."

Had I heard him make that comment, I would have disagreed. After all, it wasn't like we were behind. The immediate question, however, was whether we could prevent the Padres from bouncing back in Game Three as they had in Game Two.

Getting on base wasn't a problem for them in the first three innings, and with Bevacqua's leadoff single in the fourth, they still weren't having any difficulty. An infield single by Garry Templeton with one out made it another first-and-second chance for them, but a force-out at third, then another at second ended the inning without any damage being done. We even got Wiggins out.

We responded at the plate in the bottom of the fifth with, what else, another pair of walks—our 10th and 11th of the game—but still failed to push across another run. Padres pitching coach Norm Sherry was understandably appalled at what he was witnessing: "It was like a bad dream," he said. "You expect 11 walks in a rookie league, not the majors."

Manager Dick Williams simply moaned that, "Our starting pitching has been very, very bad."

This was a strange game to not only be involved in, but also to be observing. I mean here we were, the best teams in the American and National Leagues respectively, and both of us were getting multiple chances at the plate, but neither team was delivering with runners in scoring position. Not able to get the big hit to blow it open, we went 2-for-9 with runners in scoring position, and both of those hits came in the second inning. The Padres went 0-for-9 but were still trying to cause trouble well into the game. After they put a runner on second with one out, to no avail, in the sixth, the Padres actually got through the bottom of the inning without allowing a walk, the first time that had happened.

We took Wilcox out after the sixth. He'd thrown 100 pitches by then, allowing a run on seven hits. In our eyes he'd done his job despite shoulder problems, so Sparky summoned Bill Scherrer to face the Padres in the seventh. To most, it probably looked like it wasn't Bill's day. But I thought he ran into some bad luck with a deflected grounder for a single and a sinking liner to left that was just out of Herndon's reach. In my opinion, Scherrer didn't throw that badly.

Even so, he allowed a single-double combo with one out to Tony Gwynn and Steve Garvey. Then Nettles drove in Gwynn from third with a fly ball to center. Suddenly, our four-run lead was down to three, and because Scherrer wasn't fooling anyone—to the four batters who had faced him, he'd thrown just five pitches—it was time to call for Willie Hernandez, probably a little earlier than Sparky wanted or intended.

The switch worked but not before a few breaths had to be held for the final out of the Padres' seventh. On a full count, and with a San Diego runner on third, Kennedy hit a liner over Chet Lemon's head in center. This one immediately looked like trouble, but we had learned long ago not to underestimate Chet. And, sure enough, after twisting and turning while retreating the entire way, Lemon hauled down the dangerous drive in deep center. It wasn't the most classic route you'd ever seen, but it was the play of the game, saving us from who knows how much aggravation. "With two strikes on Kennedy in San Diego," Lemon said, "I noticed he was just trying to make contact. So, when he hit it hard this time, I was playing too shallow. At first, I was worried I wasn't going to get back in time to catch it."

It was a *phew* moment for us, to be sure. But, thankfully, the last one of the game. For just the second time, the Padres went down in order in the eighth—and so did we. The game had suddenly changed complexion. After eight innings in which the two teams combined for 30 base runners, was pitching finally getting the upper hand?

It was but not before pinch-hitter Luis Salazar led off the ninth for the Padres with a single off Willie "on the worst screwball I ever saw him throw," Sparky said. I didn't know how Sparky could make a comment like that about a pitch seen from the dugout. But he was right to this extent: Willie did hang it.

With the next three batters making routine outs, however, Salazar never made it to second—let alone beyond. The game had been an ordeal for both teams, lasting three hours, 11 minutes. It was still a fun, exciting atmosphere to have a World Series being played at Tiger Stadium. But the pace had been monotonous. No one could dispute that. The length of the game was only a bother to the team that lost it, though. And we hadn't lost it. So, smile, everyone. Two more victories would get us to the promised land.

Chapter 18

World Series Game Four

Our fans had been cheering for us all year. So, we welcomed a chance to return the favor.

What they did in the ninth inning of Game Four of the World Series at Tiger Stadium earned a special place in our hearts. With two outs and Jack Morris still in control, despite a San Diego runner being at third base in a game we led 4–1, the crowd was neither hushed nor particularly alarmed when Jack suddenly threw a run-scoring wild pitch. Instead, the fans regrouped, took a deep breath, and started chanting, "Who cares?" Followed by "Who cares?"…"Who cares?"

It got so loud and noticeable that Vin Scully and Joe Garagiola mentioned the comical reaction on the national telecast. The crowd also had chanted those two words—"who cares?"—when the San Diego players were introduced before the game, so it was just another sign of how much our fans cared for us. We were their Detroit Tigers, their beloved Bengals, the team they felt was going to get it done. It made us feel good to hear their enthusiasm.

Jack proceeded to get out of the ninth inning and then ended the game allowing a liner to right, so the late run the Padres scored promptly found a home in the harmless file—because harmless is what it had been. Instead of winning 4–1, we won 4–2, but the upshot of the outcome was the same: after four games of the World Series, we held a 3–1 lead over the Padres, which meant we had put ourselves in position to clinch a world champion-ship the next day at home.

When our great fans started chanting "who cares?" in the ninth inning after our lead had been trimmed to two runs with two outs, it was simply their way of displaying their unwavering confidence in us—their acknowl-edgment, so to speak, that they knew we still had the situation under control. And that they also sensed the Padres' run in the ninth wasn't about to matter. It was a saucy manifestation of their joy at being on the cusp of an elusive title, and for that we were delighted on their behalf. It was also an example of a crowd trusting its team, which in turn lived up to the faith the fans demonstrated. In short, everyone, except the Padres, went home happy after Game Four.

But the disturbing truth was that we were still scoring barely enough runs to get by. Our offense didn't exactly explode in Game Four. It hadn't really exploded in any of the World Series games so far—or in any of the postseason games since the opener of the American League playoffs against the Kansas City Royals. But we were doing an efficient job of scoring first, which put constant pressure on our opponents.

Even if you were a confident team, which I'm sure the Padres were trying to be, San Diego had to find it daunting to fall behind early in every game, which it was doing. We had scored in the first inning of the first two games against them and had taken a 4–0 lead in the second inning of the third game.

In Game Four it was a two-run home run by Alan Trammell in the first inning off starter Eric Show. Tram was already having an outstand-ing World Series when he stepped into the box in the first inning against Show, who had allowed five home runs in two wobbly starts against the Chicago Cubs in the National League Championship Series. The longball had become his nemesis.

In turn, the Padres were getting worn down by their disappointing rotation. This start was no exception. Then again, it wasn't Show's fault that Lou Whitaker was at first base when Trammell came up to bat in the first inning. Given an error on the play, Alan Wiggins hadn't cleanly handled

Lou's leadoff grounder to second. It didn't look like a ready-made chance for us to pounce again for some early runs, but factoring in the confidence with which Tram stepped up to the plate, it turned out to be. Show fell behind with a 2–0 count, then threw a pitch Trammell described as "a little slider that didn't do anything."

What happened next? "My eyes lit up," Tram said, "and boom!"

Alan lined the pitch into the left-field seats for a 2–0 lead. And just like that, it had happened again. We had taken an early lead. It was also the start of what Tram would label "the greatest game of my career—no doubt about it."

At that point, however, we didn't know Jack was going to turn in a brilliant performance. That's because he'd had a couple of shaky moments in the second inning. On an 0–1 pitch, for instance, Terry Kennedy took Morris deep to right, an upper-decker, and soon after that, Kurt Bevacqua followed with a double. The hit made Bevacqua 6-for-12 in the series as the Padres' designated hitter. After that Carmelo Martinez gave us a momentary scare with a long foul ball to left, but Martinez hadn't been able to accomplish anything of note the entire series—nor would he this time. The ensuing strikeout would be his seventh in 12 at-bats.

But if Jack was going to settle down, he needed to do it quickly. We led by only a run and when we went down in order in the second, striking out twice, Morris didn't look like the starter who'd been the quicker of the two to find his groove.

If Show beat him to it, however, he did so only briefly. After a stretch of getting seven consecutive outs, the Padres' right-hander ran afoul of the top of our batting order again—namely the same two batters who had given him a headache in the first inning. With one out, Whitaker singled and was able to take second when Tony Gwynn fumbled the hop in right—the second error made by the Padres in Lou's two at-bats.

The blunder handed us another scoring chance. Trammell, it turned out, had been a threat by himself in the first inning and here he was batting again—complete with a sequence of aggressive practice cuts before confidently stepping into the box for his second plate appearance. Show got

In My Children's Words

My daughter Ashley Parrish Hunt, the newborn on the flight to San Diego in 1984, married former Detroit Tigers prospect Kelly Hunt and has spent her entire life close to baseball. My son, David, was a first-round draft choice (of the New York Yankees in 2000). He, too, was a catcher. And my son Matt Parrish is a sergeant in the Orange County, California, Sheriff's Department. Here are their perspectives:

We realized as kids he was a ballplayer when we would get out of school for Easter break, but instead of having one week off, we'd stretch it into two or three to spend time with Dad. Then instead of having a summer vacation at the beach or a lake, we'd be at the ballpark. To that extent our life was different. But I loved it. Maybe when I was in elementary school, I struggled with it because Dad would have to leave so early for spring training. Knowing I wouldn't see him for a while was hard, but we were always very proud of what he did. Even though he was gone a lot, my mother always reminded us that he was the head of the household.

I knew my dad was an avid weightlifter, and that was ingrained in me as well. I work at a gym, and whenever I lift, my work ethic gets complimented. That's something I share with my father. He was very disciplined in that regard. But in the offseason, he'd allow himself to sit on the couch with a package of Oreos—or he would treat himself to a big helping of Baskin-Robbins ice cream. But when it was time to flip the switch and start training again, he'd get right back into it.

Where we differ is that I love big cities, big crowds, which I'm not sure my dad does. I like hustle and bustle. He can do without it. As far as sports were concerned, I played a bit of everything—basketball, volleyball, softball. In college I threw shotput and discus. I'm definitely a baseball fan, however—a Detroit Tiger through and through. The Tigers have a special place in all our hearts. Our loyalty is with Detroit. It's always cool to hear the stories about 1984 when we get together with his former teammates. It's also fun on Facebook to see how much fans still care for that team. I love it. I have fond memories of being a child at Tiger Stadium, sitting in the family section for wives and kids. Someone would drop off cookies and ice cream for us. And the players would throw Bazooka bubble gum from the dugout. Fans sitting around us didn't know we were the players' kids, but the family section was our playground, our summer snack bar. When my dad returned to the Tigers as a coach, I got to know Tiger Stadium all over again, its age, its smell. I was heartbroken when they tore it down.

What does the nickname "Big Wheel" mean to me? First of all, I always think of that big tire by the side of I-94, the road coming in from the airport, in Detroit. I associate my dad with that tire—because nobody was bigger, nobody was stronger.

In my opinion, my dad did a lot to change the game of baseball. I take considerable pride in that. He was one of the first players to lift weights, and as his daughter, I've always wanted him to be recognized for that more than he is. My dad is the quiet type, though. He doesn't seek recognition. He's very humble. And I'm protective of him in that way. To this day, though, I love hearing from fans that they had a poster of The Big Wheel on their wall.

—A.P.H.

I'm sure I bragged about my dad at some point growing up, but I can't tell you when. I know I've always been proud of him. It was a great experience having a father who not only played major league baseball, but also was a good and successful big leaguer. Lord knows he drove himself to be the best he could be. When I was young, it was like having Arnold Schwarzenegger for a dad. Our garage was his gym—filled with nothing but weights.

When I retired from professional ball, I can tell you that what I missed least about being a catcher were the aches and pains of the position. Your body eventually adapts to what you put it through, but that doesn't mean you return to feeling good all the time. My father caught longer than I did, so I'm sure his knees and lower back were affected even more than mine. I didn't want to be a catcher because my dad had been a catcher. And to my parents' credit, they never forced anything on me, such as saying catcher was the position I *had* to play. As I grew up, however, it became apparent my skillset was best suited to catching.

As for my son, who plays Little League baseball, I want him to be whatever he wants to be. If his skills are best utilized with him being a catcher, I can help him with that. His love for the game is growing, but I don't think it's beneficial for any young player to be pigeonholed into one position too early in life. His first name is Briggs—as in Briggs Stadium, the former name of Tiger Stadium. That's where the idea for the name came from. He's not named specifically for Briggs Stadium, but it was a name that appealed to me and my wife.

I remember being a little boy at spring training in Lakeland, Florida, going to games at Joker Marchant Stadium—then to games at Tiger Stadium. Every now and then, I even got to visit my dad in the dugout. From the viewpoint of a kid, that's pretty cool. I was aware of being a player's son; it was normal life for me. He had a job to do, though, and nobody needs children running around when you're trying to do your job. So, the times we were able to participate together in anything on the field, such as a father-son game, stood out as being special. They weren't plentiful, but I loved those games.

Although I was only five, there were bits and pieces I recall of the 1984 World Series. I don't remember any specific events—not even my father's home run off Goose Gossage in Game Five (I wish I did)—but I remember being in the ballpark and feeling the excitement around me. When I got drafted by the New York Yankees, Goose was one of the former Yankees who occasionally threw batting practice to us in spring training. Although I never mentioned the 1984 World Series, I made a point of wanting to hit a home run off him in batting practice. It didn't come close in significance to what my father had accomplished against him in the World Series. I mean hitting a ball into a pond on a back field at spring training can't compare, but it was personally important to me. I never did hit an actual home run off Gossage, just a ball over the fence during batting practice in spring training. Goose, meanwhile, never mentioned my dad's home run to me.

What I admired most about my father's career was how long it lasted. To have the kind of success he had, for as long as he had it—19 years—makes me very proud. To have that kind of career and be the great father he was, and still is to this day, was not some-thing easily balanced. It can be difficult. As a kid, though, there were times my friends were more interested in coming over to my house to be around my father than they were to be around me. That was just something I had to put up with as the son of a major league ballplayer.

My dad and I are similar in a lot of ways, like work ethic and focus, but where we're the most different is in our off-the-field pursuits. For instance, Dad is an avid hunter; I maintain the opposite view. Hunting never caught on with me. And about his days as a young boy in California, he speaks of what he used to bring home from the fields near his house. But you'll never catch me crawling around to catch snakes or frogs. Me? I'd rather go to a beach on vacation instead of chasing after the creatures that always seemed to interest him.

—D.P.

I don't remember anything different than thinking of my father as a ballplayer. I realized it at a very young age because we spent a lot of time together in ballparks, whether it was visiting him in the clubhouse or simply watching his games. It was both a benefit and a drawback to have a ballplayer as your dad. It was a benefit because it was fun going to the games and hanging around big league ballplayers, being a bat boy, or shagging fly balls during batting practice— the kind of things other kids didn't get to do. But it was a drawback because of how much time he was gone during our childhood.

We were super bummed when it came time for him to leave for spring training, meaning the long haul of another season was about to begin. We'd be upset and crying at the house, but my parents would do their best to assure us that we'd visit him soon—and that there would be a lot of phone calls in the meantime. My dad would call and talk to us nearly every day while we were growing up. It would have been great to have Facetime back then, but we still got to hear his voice.

I admired him mostly—not as a ballplayer—but because he was Dad. I thought it was cool that playing baseball was what he did for his job, but looking back at it, baseball is just what he did. I knew nothing different. Only as I got older did I realize how special it really was. He had a supreme work ethic. I know he was always the first one to the ballpark and the last to leave. He instilled that ethic in his children 100 percent.

All I wanted to do when I was a kid was to follow in my father's shoes. The professions of my dad and my grandfather, who worked for the L.A. County sheriff's department, were the only two futures I could envision. If baseball didn't work out for me, then what I'm doing now is what would end up happening.

But my first love, and what I most wanted to do, was to follow in my dad's footsteps as a baseball player. For a while it looked like it might even happen. I signed with the Detroit Tigers as a free agent out of college (Biola University in La Mirada, California,) in 2004. I went to extended spring training, then was called up to the short-season Class A team in Oneonta, New York. In 2005 I played the entire season at West Michigan, then went to spring training with the Lakeland Class A team in 2006. That's where it ended for me.

I always pull for the Tigers, though. I want them to do well not only because my dad played for them, but also because I, too, had the opportunity to play in their organization. I also know that when my father thinks about baseball, he thinks Tigers. He has a stronger love for the Detroit organization than the other clubs for which he played, though he appreciated his time on each team.

I like to think he's viewed as one of the best catchers ever. To me "Big Wheel" was just my dad's nickname while I was growing up. I asked him numerous times what it meant, and he tried explaining it to me once—that *This Week in Baseball* referred to him as Detroit's big wheel, and it stuck. To be honest, though, as a kid I always thought it was because he liked raised trucks with giant wheels.

—M.P.

a breaking ball across for a strike on his first pitch, then missed low with his second. Tram was more than ready for the third pitch, driving it into the upper deck in left for his second home run of the game. In his career Tram had twice hit two home runs in the same game but never before in his first two at-bats. What a great time for it to happen! We now led 4–1. "I'm seeing the ball and hitting it squarely," Trammell said. "I'm no power man, but when you're on a roll, you feel like you'll get on base every time. The bottom line is I am swinging the bat well at the right time. Like so much of baseball, it's about timing."

We, of course, were happy witnesses to it all. Tram and Lou had grown together as hitters. It was a joy to watch them mature. Combined, I think they had nine .300 seasons—and both obviously were capable of coming through with big hits. In this case, it was Alan. He was a very intelligent hitter, always looking for ways to get better. As Sparky Anderson said of Tram, "If he's not named the series MVP, there should be a congressional investigation. But at least he's finally becoming a national name."

When Show allowed a single and a walk in the third after Trammell's home run, the Padres replaced him with left-hander Dave Dravecky. Manager Dick Williams was fed up at that point. "Our starting pitching is what's hurt us," he said of his rotation's 11.70 ERA. "Maybe we should start our bullpen."

Knowing he'd let down his team, Show had no comment.

The other major change in the game, beyond the reality that Trammell's second home run had tripled the size of our lead, was that Jack took charge. He had allowed a run on three hits in the first three innings, but starting in the fourth, the Padres mustered nothing but zeroes. "I would never want Morris to lose his spit and fire," Sparky said. "That's what makes him as good as he is. I told him it's all right to get angry and upset during a season. But let's cut it down from eight times a year to maybe four."

Or as our pitching coach Roger Craig said, "Jack's effectiveness often corresponded to his attitude."

That was a correct assessment, I believe. Jack's attitude had a lot to do with his success throughout his career. There are many words you can use to describe Jack Morris. Most of the time he pitched pissed off, let's put it that way. Maybe that's how he motivated himself. But if he had to pitch pissed off, so be it. It worked. Every once in a while, we had to yank the reins on Jack to get him to re-focus, but Game Four was not one of those times. His concentration was rock solid from the start.

Starting with the final out of the third inning, Jack retired 13 batters in a row before Tim Flannery snapped the streak by leading off the eighth with a single as a pinch-hitter for Martinez. This was a thoroughly dominating sequence of outs for Morris. Of the 13 consecutive batters he retired, only two of them hit the ball out of the infield. Interestingly, it was Kennedy both times with fly balls to left and center, respectively. But he didn't come close to taking Jack deep again—let alone upstairs—as he had in the second inning.

Morris didn't allow any walks in Game Four, but he did throw a pair of wild pitches. The first one didn't hurt him, though. It was a pitch on which Flannery took second with two outs in the eighth but also one that pinch-hitter Champ Summers, our former teammate, swung at and missed before striking out to end the inning. So, even Jack's errant pitches were serving a purpose. A sidenote here: it had once been impressive, but Champ's power was gone by 1984. He hit 40 home runs for us from 1979 to 1981 but had connected only once in the last two years combined for the San Francisco Giants and Padres. The strikeout to end the eighth inning would be his only at-bat of the World Series. In fact, it was the last plate appearance of his career. I liked Champ. As teammates on the Tigers, I often used to ride with him to the ballpark. I think we knew his plate appearance in the eighth might be the only time he'd bat during the World Series, but I'm not sure anyone sensed it would be his last at-bat ever.

Our lack of productivity reared its ugly head a couple of times in Game Four after Trammell's second home run—especially in the fifth inning when we failed to take advantage of a leadoff double from Lou followed by a single from Trammell. That combination had paid off for us all season but not this time. Hoping for a third consecutive home run from Trammell, the crowd at Tiger Stadium gave him a standing ovation when he came up with Whitaker on second—a genuine display of appreciation from the fans but also of anticipation. After all, Whitaker had been on base in Tram's first two at-bats and had scored on both his home runs, so it looked like the stage was set for something historic to occur.

Nothing did, though. On a 2–2 pitch from the lefty Dravecky, Trammell singled sharply to left. For a moment, it looked like Whitaker would score easily from second, and probably should have, but he stopped at third because there were no outs. Lou didn't want to make the first out of the inning unnecessarily. I understood the reasoning. But that proved to be our best scoring chance of the inning. With a pair of strikeouts and a grounder to third, Dravecky escaped. You never think you have enough runs, of course. The more the merrier, so it would have been helpful to add one on Trammell's single. But with no outs, there was no sense trying to force the issue.

The biggest similarity between this game and its predecessors against the Padres was the recurring lack of hitting by both teams with runners in scoring position. We went 2-for-7 in Game Four—not great but considerably better than San Diego's 2-for-29 of the first four games.

I would like to say our pitching was the entire reason for the Padres having so many problems, but to be fair I think they deserved some blame, and we deserved some credit. Sparky was still fretting about our hitting, though. "Before it's over I would like just one day of showing everyone how we can really play," he said.

I wasn't as worried. I mean, it's not like you can blow everyone out in every game you play. We were knocking the stuffing out of San Diego's starters, but their bullpen kept shutting us down. That's because they had a legit bullpen—a big reason why it was only 4–1 as the top of the ninth began. And why, with a pitch count of only 86 through the first eight innings, Jack had a decent chance of pitching a complete game. Having allowed just one hit since the third inning enhanced that possibility as well.

In any case, we took it as a sign of normalcy when Gwynn grounded out to Whitaker to start the ninth inning. Of the 12 ground balls the Padres hit in the game, only two were to the left side. Whitaker alone had seven assists. But it wasn't a sign of normalcy when Steve Garvey doubled off the left-field fence with one out. For one thing, it was San Diego's first extra-base hit since the second inning. For another, we needed to make sure it wasn't a sign that Jack was tiring. He admitted after the game that he might have been, but his determination hadn't weakened.

Having a San Diego runner on second with one out wasn't a reason to be alarmed, however—not with a three-run lead. We pressed on, undeterred, with our starting pitcher. There was no hint anyway that Sparky was close to yanking Jack. "Captain Hook" was taking a breather. With unshaken confidence in Morris, Anderson intended to give him every opportunity to finish it.

That said, we needed two outs. The first one came when Graig Nettles grounded out to second, advancing Garvey to third. At that point I noticed Jack had the same determined glint in his eye that he did in the ninth inning when he was close to finalizing his no-hitter against the Chicago White Sox in April. Then again, he was skilled at rising to an occasion. We were still in good hands, it turned out. Jack was throwing the ball well. He was like a shark in the water with a game on the line. Whenever he smelled blood, he got even more focused while reaching for something extra, meaning he wasn't about to let Game Four slip away. "My concentration was as good as ever," Morris said. Jack had turned to Craig earlier and said, "Don't worry Rog, I'm going to win this game for us."

If anything, Morris tried too hard on his 1–2 pitch to Kennedy with two outs in the ninth. Instead of a splitter dipping over the plate for a third strike, Jack bounced it. That's when the ball got away for a wild pitch, allowing Garvey to score from third base. It was my fault actually. The pitch never should have gotten past me. It's one I should have blocked, a splitter in the dirt right in front of me. It was my job to stop it.

But it was also the pitch that triggered the confident chants of "who cares?" from a Tiger Stadium crowd bursting with anticipation of a game-ending out. The chorus had just subsided when two pitches later the fans got their wish. Kennedy lined out to right.

With a 3–1 lead after four games, we now had a stranglehold on the World Series. After the final out, Morris and Trammell appeared on national TV as Players of the Game. One of them had accounted for all our runs. The other made sure that all our runs had been enough.

Suddenly, it hit us: we were staring down the barrel of realizing our dream. The next game would be for all the marbles, as the saying goes. But in lockstep with another saying, we couldn't get ahead of ourselves. We were well aware that if you let your guard down, even briefly, momentum can change. "Yogi Berra was right about it not being over until it's over," Morris said.

So, we didn't get giddy about being one game away from winning it all. It was almost as if it was still business as usual. Plus our motivational mindset was that we didn't want to return to San Diego. And since we wanted to finish it at home, we dialed up our intensity. I truly believe we had so much confidence in ourselves that we simply were doing what we expected to do. We were a little closer to our goal in other words, but our job was not yet complete.

After Tram's third hit of Game Four, Williams, the Padres' manager, had been shown on television, standing alone, staring at the ground. Years later, I watched a replay of that scene and could almost read his mind that the next step seemed inevitable. When asked later about whether he was going to sleep on how to bounce back, Williams replied, "I'm going to drink on it, then sleep on it."

To everyone involved, it was clear we had reached the threshold of winning it. The Padres hadn't given up, but they were at their wits' end. "We can feel it now," Darrell Evans exclaimed.

Whether the rest of us agreed out loud, I don't remember, but I'm sure we all felt that way. Nailing it down would be the final challenge.

Chapter 19

Champions!

I often think back to the morning of Game Five. If you couldn't feel the excitement of everything swirling around the city at that point, I don't know when you ever would. Or *if* you ever would. As for Arlyne and myself, we were still coming off the birth of our daughter just a few days prior. That took away some of my focus on baseball—but maybe it was a good thing to get my mind off what was going to take place at the ballpark.

The anticipation, of course, was: *This could be it. If we win today, we're world champions.* That thought itself was special because, if it happened, it would be the end of a fabulous season. I know we were hoping to finish it right then and there. Never mind any personal accolades, this opportunity was what you played for and strove for as a team: to end up on top, to be called a world champion. So, to be one game away and to be knocking on that door was a unique moment. But in the back of our minds lurked some concern. "We were scared to death," Kirk Gibson said, "because we knew we'd be thought of as failures if we didn't finish it."

I don't think I was scared to death, so that's probably just the terminology Kirk used to describe the importance of the moment. But we knew the San Diego Padres had come back to beat the Chicago Cubs, so we wanted to put them away. I felt confident we were going to get it done.

Most players will tell you it's not playing the games that's the most stressful. It's getting your family squared away with tickets as well as the schedules of who needs to be where and when. But it's a process you would gladly go through over and over again if you could.

Game Five was slated to begin at 4:45 PM on a Sunday, a strange starting time for a weekend day—or any day, for that matter. But it was a minor matter compared to what would eventually be at stake in the game. All of us were excited to get to the ballpark, so we all got there early.

Dan Petry was scheduled to be our starting pitcher. He'd had a hiccup in Game Two, not pitching as well as he wanted, but we had a lot of confidence in Dan. There was no reason he couldn't bounce back with a strong game. We fully expected he would. But we had no expectations as to what else would take place. We liked the way we had taken charge early in the games against the Padres. Hopefully that would continue. But even if it didn't, we felt there was enough boom in our bats to give them problems. No matter what, we just wanted to provide ourselves with a chance.

In the first inning, Alan Wiggins led off the game with a sharp single to center on a 1–1 pitch. That darn Wiggins. This was his seventh hit of the World Series, and he would get another before it was through. Petry settled down, however, to strike out Tony Gwynn swinging—no easy feat—but on the third strike to Gwynn, Wiggins not only stole second, but he also took third on, I hate to admit, my error. My throw to second hit Wiggins and rolled away, allowing him to move up an extra base. I thought it was a better throw than the result. If it hadn't hit Wiggins on the foot while he was sliding, he would have been out.

So, now the Padres had a runner at third with one out, hoping to grab a quick lead against us. But on a 1–1 pitch that Steve Garvey bounced to Lou Whitaker (whose wife Crystal had given birth to a baby girl that morning), Wiggins aggressively tested Lou's arm by trying to score from third. Lou won the showdown. After Wiggins slid past the plate without touching it, I was able to apply the tag to keep the Padres off the scoreboard. Graig Nettles then bounced out routinely to second—and Petry was out of the first inning unscathed.

What happened on the Wiggins play was that he missed the plate completely while trying to avoid my tag. But my back had been turned to the umpire, Paul Runge, so I didn't know what the call was. I just instinctively went after Wiggins to finish the play in case there'd been no call at all.

Then it was our turn at trying to grab an early advantage—and it wouldn't take long. With one out and Alan Trammell on first base, Gibson picked on the first pitch from starter Mark Thurmond, driving it deep into the upper deck in right-center for a 2–0 lead. Roger Craig had been right when he labeled Gibby "an offensive cloudburst."

Even with a relatively subdued home run trot—probably his most restrained—Kirk thrust his fist into the air three times before reaching first base. The crowd loved it, of course, but we weren't done yet.

Not only did I follow Gibson's home run with a single, I also stole second base—something I hadn't done since May. My other stolen base in 1984 was a steal of home. In all fairness, though, instead of being an example of my great speed, my theft of home was the back end of a double steal. Granted on this play, catcher Terry Kennedy had a problem getting the ball out of his glove prior to making his throw to second, and, though I don't remember if I'd gotten the sign or simply had gone on my own, it went into the scorebook as a stolen base.

When Larry Herndon's fly ball to center dropped in front of Bobby Brown for another hit, it became clear that Thurmond might not last the inning. In fact, he didn't last another two batters—because the next hitter, Chet Lemon, singled me in from third to make it a 3–0 lead with one out. Thurmond had faced only six batters at that point, but because he'd allowed hits to five of the six, the Padres had no choice but to turn to their bullpen. Replacing their starter early was an ordeal the Padres had long since grown accustomed to, however. In the first four games, their starting pitchers had lasted just five-and-one-third innings.

But their bullpen had been stupendous, and we helped it get off on the right foot again when—with Andy Hawkins on the mound—Herndon was thrown out at third on the front end of an attempted double steal. A wild pitch moved Lemon from second to third after that, but Barbaro Garbey, who was still looking for his first hit of the series (he ended up 0-for-12), popped to second for the third out. We led by three runs, though, so it had been a good first inning.

We still led 3–0 when the third inning began. But the Padres began to chip away—not with hits as much as with the help of ground-ball outs. Brown led off the inning with an infield single, hustling to beat Trammell's throw to first, but two infield outs later, Brown hadn't yet scored. He was at third. Garvey's single knocked him in, but even that hit was a ground ball, which Trammell knocked down in the hole. It was enough to trim a run off our lead, however.

So, now it was down to a two-run margin at 3–1.

Once again, we weren't getting to Hawkins in relief of Thurmond. He wore us out the entire World Series. By the time the series ended, Hawkins had allowed just one run in 12 innings, spanning three appearances that pumped renewed hope into the Padres each time.

Hawkins allowed 10 base runners in those 12 innings, but six of those were walks. We had our hands full just hitting the ball hard against him. Of the four hits he allowed, all were singles. In other words, we pecked at crumbs whenever he was in the game. His very presence seemed to revive the Padres' resolve against us because they often were better off when he was finished pitching than when he began. This game was no exception.

By the time we came up to bat in the fourth, in fact, we no longer led. The game was tied at 3–3. That's because the Padres parlayed a leadoff walk and a one-out double into two runs off Petry in the top of the fourth. Garry Templeton and Wiggins (again) provided San Diego's big hits as the Padres tied the game. Templeton doubled in Kurt Bevacqua, who had walked, and Wiggins singled in Templeton. Our opponents were still showing some fight, but the good thing was it didn't faze us. We felt they'd gotten back in the game—temporarily.

Wiggins' hit did more damage than just tying the score, though. It knocked Petry out of the game. So, with both starting pitchers out, the outcome was up for grabs as the game headed into the fifth inning. Bill

Scherrer would be on the mound for us to begin the fifth. Hawkins was still pitching for the Padres, having weathered a bases-loaded jam in the fourth. But at least looked more mortal than usual.

Both managers were on high alert by this time. This game could very well depend on the pitching moves they made. It was no surprise therefore that with a runner on second and two outs, Aurelio Lopez was brought in to replace Scherrer. Getting right down to business, he struck out Bevacqua on a checked swing to end the fifth inning.

Then something quirky took place. It didn't appear to be the best percentage move when the Padres turned to lefty Craig Lefferts to pitch to Lemon in our half of the fifth with two runners on and one out. But it was a move the Padres had to make. Hawkins was out of gas, and Lefferts had been effective in his other postseason appearances. He wasn't immediately sharp this time, however, walking Lemon on a 3–1 pitch to load the bases. I don't think he wanted anything to do with Chet, judging by the way he pitched to him.

Then came the sacrifice fly with which we reclaimed the lead. It wasn't your everyday sacrifice fly, however. Instead, it was one that would be talked about for years because it was a sacrifice fly caught by an infielder. The one-out situation was this: we had the bases loaded with our most aggressive runner, Gibson, at third—an enviable position for us to be in. But we didn't know just how little would be required for Gibson to score. With lefty Lefferts on the mound for the Padres, Sparky Anderson opted to have Rusty Kuntz pinch hit for Johnny Grubb—not a glaringly unusual move in that Kuntz had been 5-for-12 as a pinch-hitter during the regular season. He'd proven he could get the job done. Plus, he wasn't an easy hitter to strike out.

The possibility of a strikeout quickly became a moot point, however, when Rusty lofted the first pitch from Lefferts into shallow right. At first, it looked like the pop-up would be an easy out, freezing the runners where they were. I certainly didn't expect Gibson to score on it.

But with everyone in the ballpark thinking it was his ball to catch, Gwynn in right made a quick gesture to indicate he had lost the ball during its flight, so if it was going to be caught at all, it would have to be second baseman Wiggins catching it, which he did. But while hauling down the ball, Wiggins ended up out of position to make a strong throw home—and with Gibson's speed, plus his alertness in reading the play, the run became one, as Vin Scully said, "the Tigers scored but shouldn't have."

In other words, Gibson's speed enabled us to take advantage of the bungled play. The run had been a gift—one that put us back in front 4–3 after five innings. "When I saw Gwynn wave his arms, indicating he didn't know where the ball was," said third-base coach Alex Grammas, "I knew we had a chance."

There had been some momentary confusion between Gibson and Grammas, however. Alex yelled "Go! Go!" after Wiggins made the catch. Kirk thought he heard "No! No!" But it didn't matter. "I was going to knock the catcher on his ass if I had to," Gibson said.

He didn't have to, as it turned out. Wiggins' throw to the plate was a 15-hopper. Gibby had made it look easy. When I saw it happening, I thought, *No way! Who scores on that ball?* But what an amazing game Gibby played.

Even so, there was plenty of drama left. The sixth inning was quiet for both teams offensively as was the top of the seventh for the Padres. But it can't be understated how valuable those two scoreless innings of relief from Lopez were. We needed to get the upper hand again, to have the game settle down—and with Aurelio's help, it did. "Lopey blew smoke right past the Padres," Craig said.

So, we still were leading 4–3 into the bottom of the seventh when the Padres turned to Goose Gossage to replace Lefferts. With only one previous appearance, Goose had played a surprisingly insignificant role in the World Series. But he was Dick Williams' choice to be on the mound when Game Five headed down the stretch. So be it.

On Gossage's second pitch, as the huge crowd chanted "Goose-busters," I took him deep to left. Some would describe it as a "laser." It was more liner than fly ball, that's for sure, a moment of my career I'll always treasure. In any case we now led 5–3. It wasn't like I had worn out the Goose in my career, so I was pretty pumped about the home run. I just wasn't one to be demonstrative. Clapping my hands a couple of times was the most you'd ever get from me.

We put two more runners on base in the seventh against Gossage—he wasn't dominating us by any means—but the inning ended quietly on Darrell Evans' fly ball to center. With a two-run lead and the clock now loudly ticking for the Padres in the top of the eighth, every out carried us a step closer to our goal. It was an agonizing process—inch by inch—but every inch counted.

Six outs remaining became five when Willie Hernandez retired Nettles on an infield pop-up for the first out of the eighth. Five outs became four when Kennedy lined out to second. Then four became…wait, not so fast. Ever the pest, Bevacqua trimmed our lead down to a run with a two-out home run off Willie in the eighth. I think I muttered to myself about Kurt, "That stinkin' guy, you have to be kidding me."

There was life in the Padres yet. They were still chipping away, obviously not giving up. To get it over with—as in game, set, match—we needed to manufacture a dose of shutdown toughness. We had to punctuate our claim to the title, to take charge once and for all, which we soon did.

Marty Castillo led off our half of the eighth with a walk on a full-count pitch. Whitaker then put down an attempted sacrifice on which the oddest thing occurred. Nettles fielded the ball cleanly at third, then made a quick, accurate throw to second to get Castillo, but Templeton took the throw in front of the bag—not on it—another bungled play by the Padres. So, both runners were safe. That was a weird play. Templeton must have thought the throw from Nettles would go to first base. But not to be on second at such a crucial time—there was no excuse for that. It was a big screw up, but the Padres' defensive lapses were their problem, not ours. For us, it was a welcome opportunity. Instead of having a runner at first with one out, we had two runners on with no outs. Trammell then bunted them over to second and third, setting the table for Gibson.

That's when one of most iconic moments in World Series history took place. With Gibby at the plate, Williams, the Padres manager, wanted him walked intentionally, which would have loaded the bases with one out. Holding up four fingers, Kennedy also seemed to think they were walking Gibson intentionally. It would have been the conventional move, after all. And I would have loved to be hitting with the bases loaded—absolutely. Gossage, however, had other thoughts. "I wanted to go after him because I owned Gibson [seven strikeouts in nine previous at-bats]," he said. "I told that to Dick when he came out to the mound asking, 'What the heck is going on out here?' I said, 'Let's go after him.'"

He answered back, "Okay, all right, go after him."

Being more confident than he should have been and thinking he could either strike Gibson out or retire him without a run scoring, Goose got his way. That's when Sparky memorably shouted out from our dugout to Gibson that, "He don't want to walk you!"

We've all seen it a million times on television. I couldn't believe it. What a bold move it was for Goose to overrule his manager. Craig said, "I feel sorry for him." Dick knew in his heart that walking him was the right move.

But Kirk hadn't ever been successful against Gossage. Going back to their initial encounter, he had struck out against him on three pitches the first time he ever faced him. That said, baseball always offers an any-thing-can-happen chance for redemption. There is always a first time, right?

This was quite a first time. "I knew they wouldn't walk me," Kirk said. "The only hit I'd ever had off Gossage was a broken-bat bunt single. But I couldn't dwell on that. I had to think, *This is my time. I'm going to get you, Goose.*"

Gibson peered into our dugout for a moment, holding up some fingers and saying later he was making a bet with Sparky from the batter's box—wagering his manager $10 that if Goose pitched to him, he was going to "crank him."

That was an interesting back and forth—entertaining, to say the least. I mean, who thinks to make a bet with your manager at a time like that? At the same time, it wasn't a moment Gibby was taking lightly. He was proba-bly the most intense guy I'd ever been around in baseball. There were times

I thought his head was going to explode. That was the fun of playing with him, though. He was such a fierce competitor.

With the meeting at the mound over, the at-bat finally began. Gibson took a ball, but on the next pitch, Kirk was sitting on the fastball, and Scully's words will echo forever: "And there it goes!"

Launching a no-doubter into the upper deck in right, Gibson belted a three-run home run, all but assuring us of winning the World Series. "You ran into a friggin' meatball," Gossage would say good-naturedly to Gibson years later. "But I have lived with it ever since. Even when Dick Williams, whom I greatly admired as a manager, was voted into the Hall of Fame, I said to his wife after she answered my call, 'Hello, Norma, this is the man who should have walked Kirk Gibson.'"

Crossing the plate, then lifting his arms triumphantly over his head, the conquering hero was captured on camera in a pose no Tigers' fan will ever forget. We now led 8–4 instead of 5–4, and it was all over but the shouting. The shouting…the partying…the celebrating—you name it.

Of course, there was still the top of the ninth to wade through before it became official, but with us being 97–0 in games we led in the ninth inning, I felt the result was inevitable. We were going to be world champions. The only suspense remaining was what would be our "McCarver pops up " moment to match the final out of the 1968 World Series. For us, it was Ernie Harwell saying on Gwynn's two-out fly ball to left: "Here comes Herndon. He's there, he's got it! The Tigers are the champions of 1984!"

I'd been creeping out from behind the plate as I watched Larry close in on the ball, but it then seemed like 20 of us arrived at the mound at the same time, mobbing each other. We were like wild horses out of the corral, as Sparky said. The one casualty was that Willie swallowed his chewing tobacco and would be sick in the clubhouse—a small price to pay for a championship. "I've never been out of first place," owner Tom Monaghan exclaimed. "All I can do now is run for president."

And as 50,000 fans streamed out of Tiger Stadium onto the streets, it seemed like 50,000 others took their place, joining the party happening on the field. I was amazed at how fast the field filled up with people. Half the city of Detroit was out there with us, jumping around. After a couple of minutes, you couldn't even move. What a great journey it had been, though—a wire-to-wire achievement. When the last pitch of the 1984 World Series had been thrown and the last out secured, we were what we felt we had been all along. The best team in baseball.

Celebration

During the initial celebration on the field after the final out of Game Five— when we had just won the World Series, in other words—I had my mask in my right hand with my fingers through its bars, but somebody, who had run out from the stands, tried to rip it away from me. He nearly tore my arm off. There I was, trying to congratulate my teammates but fighting with a fan to hang onto my mask. Whoever it was eventually disappeared into the frenzy after I gave him the evil eye, and I rejoined the celebration. But that initial tug on my arm was like: *Holy smokes, man.* Unfortunately, my mask was left in the clubhouse storage room after we left the field, and I never got it back as a souvenir of the World Series.

There wasn't the equivalent in 1984 of Mickey Lolich jumping into Bill Freehan's arms following the final out. When I reached Willie Hernandez on the field, we kind of ran into each other and jumped up at the same time. It wasn't any kind of photographic moment. And no sooner had we collided than all the other players arrived at the mound. We were mobbed by everyone else on the team. So, there was not a memorable jumping-into-my-arms picture. Oh well, I had no issues with how it all transpired; people were just having a good time.

When we wanted to get to the clubhouse, though, it got hectic. There was mass pandemonium as we tried to weave our way to the dugout. Gibby shoved some guy, who'd been in his way. It was so like Kirk to do that. Fortunately, no harm was done. I was obviously very excited, but I don't think I knocked anyone down. It eventually had reached a point on the field that after we were done jumping up and down, there was no room to move. It was every man for himself.

But once we got to the clubhouse, we got into some real celebrating, pouring champagne over each other. That's when we began to absorb what we had just accomplished. The craziness in the clubhouse went on for a while, but we thought it would. We wanted it to. I mean, we were savoring a very special moment.

Eventually I had to go back out to the field for a postgame interview and I took a bottle of champagne with me, so I could salute the crowd from the golf cart that took me to the interview. The fans loved it, I enjoyed it, everyone was excited—yelling and screaming. That went on for quite some time.

But then I went back to the clubhouse where guys were still spraying champagne. This was before anyone wore goggles. So, there were a lot of burning eyes in that clubhouse. It was raucous but also fun. We stayed at the ballpark a long time. There were reports it had become an absolute zoo on the streets outside, so we weren't in a hurry to leave. It was probably safer to stay where we were. When we heard that the Padres team bus was getting rocked back and forth, that's a scene we didn't want to get into.

But except for fans who wanted us to stop and sign, the crowd was polite when I departed with my family. You couldn't stop and sign anything, though, because if you signed for one, you'd soon be signing for everybody. So, we just kind of eased our way through at a slow pace.

We had a condo in Farmington Hills at the time, and I remember the celebration continuing there when we got home. There were people in our front yard and our driveway who had brought over champagne. It was wild in that regard—obviously a time to remember. I didn't get much sleep that night.

The only negative aspect about any of it occurred when we were awarded our World Series rings the next year. On a day the entire team had been looking forward to, I was expecting a keepsake more emblematic of the great year we had instead of a piece of jewelry that looked more like a class ring. After all, we had won a world championship, went wire to wire, won a team record 104 games, and our 35–5 start might never be duplicated. But the Tigers distributed rings of differing values, and not everybody received the top-level ring. Some players, such as Bill Scherrer, were given a less expensive ring, and others, like Randy O'Neal, didn't get any ring at all. I thought Tom Monaghan, who had claimed to be a Tigers fan his entire life, would go all out.

It's not that I was unappreciative—I'm not much into wearing jewelry anyway—but I'll tell you this: I used to wear my World Series ring all the time. Then, one day I was shopping at the mall, and the girl behind the counter saw my ring. The next thing she said was, "Oh, what school did you graduate from?"

What school? So it looked like a class ring to other people as well. That's when I thought, *It's not just me. No one can tell the difference between a class ring and our World Series ring!* At that moment it struck me that the ring we'd been given did not represent the full extent of what we had accomplished.

Chapter 20

Our Pitchers

How did we win the American League East in 1984? For one thing, we had the best pitching staff in the division. The starting rotation won the most games, and the bullpen saved the most games. It would be hard for me to say which of the two was stronger because they were equally effective. The second-place Toronto Blue Jays had the second best rotation in the division but nowhere near as good a bullpen as our maybe even as low as fourth best.

The offensive differences between us and the Jays weren't as pronounced. Though the Boston Red Sox may have had the best offense, we were no lower than second—whereas the Blue Jays were no higher than third, a tad better than the New York Yankees, if at all.

Our starting rotation won 10 more games than the Jays' rotation but also lost four more games. That's a net difference of six victories. Toronto's rotation was strong with Dave Stieb and Doyle Alexander in the No. 1 and No. 2 slots. But Luis Leal didn't match Milt Wilcox as a No. 3 starter, and, though Jim Clancy started 36 games for the Jays as their No. 4 starter—one more than either Jack Morris or Dan Petry started for us—all it meant was that Clancy stayed healthy all season. Clancy actually had a disappointing year. His ERA climbed from the sub-4.00 level of his 1982 and 1983 seasons to 5.12. The Jays were only 15–20 in games he started.

But the bigger difference in the two pitching staffs was the strength of the two bullpens. Led by Cy Young and MVP winner Willie Hernandez and Aurelio Lopez, our bullpen went 27–9 with 51 saves. The Jays' bullpen was 22–28 with 33 saves. Toronto's saves leader had only 10 saves; Hernandez and Lopez combined for 46. As additional proof that the two bullpens weren't the same caliber, the Jays had a 4.26 ERA from the seventh inning on. Our ERA from the seventh on was 2.95. That's not to say the clubs didn't have their standouts. Dave Righetti of the Yankees was an outstanding relief pitcher, but New York couldn't match our starting rotation.

Then again, our rotation was strong in part because of the solid underpinning of our bullpen. Wilcox, for instance, didn't pitch a single complete game all season, but he went 19–1 when he lasted six innings. That's because the bullpen so often finished the job for him. Hernandez alone saved seven of Milt's victories.

The Kansas City Royals, our opponent in the American League Championship Series, felt they could match our bullpen because of Dan Quisenberry's 44 saves, but the Royals' rotation won 18 fewer games (77–59) than ours did. And no other team could match our top three starting pitchers—not even the Baltimore Orioles despite having Mike Boddicker, the only 20-game winner in the American League. Our top three starters won 54 games. Baltimore's top three won 49.

Quite simply, as you can probably deduce from these comparisons, you could look high and low for a better-balanced pitching staff in the American League without finding one. Plus, we always seemed to have the right pitcher on the mound at the right time. I enjoyed catching all of them. There wasn't anyone about whom I said, "I can't believe they're bringing this guy in."

I also found this to be remarkable about our 1984 pitching staff. Yes, we were heavily reliant upon our bullpen, especially Hernandez and Lopez. But in praising the relief pitchers as much as they deserve to be praised, you run the risk of shortchanging our starters. True, none of them had the kind of year Denny McLain enjoyed for the 1968 Detroit Tigers. There wasn't a

20-game winner in the bunch en route to what we accomplished in 1984. But when you examine the numbers, you realize how successful they were.

Keep in mind that because of our bullpen's efficiency, we didn't need complete games. Baseball had changed since 1968. Saves had become a more prominent statistic than complete games. A higher premium was being placed on relief pitching—not only on its effectiveness, but also on its ability to work more innings than it used to. The Tigers' bullpen pitched 26.5 percent of the team's total innings in 1968. In 1984 the percentage was up to 34.1. As a team we didn't require nine innings from our starting pitchers, nor were we looking for nine. We didn't need eight innings. Or even seven. For us six innings was the key to being successful. Of the 162 games we played in 1984, our starting pitchers lasted at least six innings 99 times. That's 61.1 percent of the time—a strong but not an amazingly high number. Toronto's starters lasted at least six innings more often.

It's how well our starters pitched in those six innings that was more significant. They often left us in a winning position. In games that our starter lasted at least six innings, we were 67–17, meaning we won an impressive 78.8 percent of the time. When we didn't get six innings from a starter, we were 37–41 (47 percent). That's a good indication of how helpful our bullpen was in save situations.

Jack led the way, as you might expect. In 35 starts he lasted at least six innings 28 times. In those games, he was 19–6. The trend prevailed throughout our rotation. Dan lasted at least six innings in 24 of his 35 starts, going 15–5. For Milt, who as we pointed out earlier didn't pitch a complete game but still won 17 games, lasting six innings was all important. Milt was 19–1 whenever he lasted at least six innings.

The point is we would most likely win the game if our starting pitcher guided us safely into the seventh inning. Attribute that to the quality of our starting pitchers or to the strong support the starters received from the bullpen. Take your pick, but the combination was good enough for us to win 104 games—and eventually the World Series.

There were three pitchers on our staff who deserve more attention than we've probably given them: Juan Berenguer, Dave Rozema, and Doug Bair.

1968 vs. 1984

The Detroit Tigers were World Champions in 1968 and 1984 due in part to the pitching staffs they had in those seasons. Over the years there've been numerous discussions about which of the two staffs was better, and—to a large degree—it remains an unanswerable question. But here's one look at how they compared.

In 1968, of course, Denny McLain went 31–6, and Mickey Lolich went 17–9. In 1984 Jack Morris went 19–11, Dan Petry went 18–8, and Milt Wilcox went 17–8. But the two championships also showed how much the emphasis of pitching changed from 1968 to 1984. The Tigers had 59 complete games in 1968. It was a starter's world. In 1984 we had 19 complete games. In 1968 they had 29 saves. In 1984 we had 51.

The transformation into a more bullpen-dependent world had taken place. "Yeah, and from the viewpoint of a former starter, today's baseball sucks," Lolich said in 2023 at the age of 82. "But that's coming from me, someone who threw 190 complete games in his career. Back then, we weren't thinking about lasting only seven innings. We were in it to finish it, which we usually did. But the game has changed."

The Tigers didn't have a specified closer in 1968. They had several. If John Hiller is remembered as being their top relief pitcher, as he likely is, it might come as a surprise that Hiller also started 12 games that year and pitched four complete games but had only two saves.

Pat Dobson and Daryl Patterson shared the team lead in saves with seven. But in 1984 the Tiger were heavily reliant on Aurelio Lopez and Willie Hernandez out of the bullpen. Combined, they went 19–4 with 46 saves.

If you take the best of both starting staffs, you end up with McLain, Lolich, Morris, Petry, and Earl Wilson as your starters. The nod here goes to Wilson over Wilcox because of the difference in their earned run averages (2.85 for Wilson, 4.00 for Wilcox), even though Wilcox won four more games than Wilson. Another factor was that Wilson threw 10 complete games and three shutouts while Wilcox ended up with none in both categories. But if your choice is Wilcox because he won 17 games, that's understandable.

There was no such narrow margin to consider in the bullpen, however. Hernandez and Lopez would be your relievers in a combined staff of 1968 and 1984. But it might also come as a surprise that the 1968 bullpen had more wins and a better ERA because of its depth. It went 29–13 with a 2.26

ERA compared to 1984's 27–9 with a 2.74 ERA. Even so, both bullpens were excellent.

Another similarity was that the Tigers allowed 129 home runs in 1968 and 130 in 1984. The 1984 staff was better balanced, however, between home and away (69 home runs allowed at home, 61 away) than 1968 (75 home runs allowed at home, 54 away). As would be expected, both teams had a better record at home than away. In 1968 the Tigers were 56–25 at Tiger Stadium with a 2.80 ERA compared to 47–34 on the road. But they had a better ERA on the road at 2.63. The 1984 team was 53–29 with a 3.15 ERA at home and 51–29 on the road with a 3.85 ERA.

April was the best month for the 1984 staff (18–2, 2.50 ERA). August was its worst at 16–15, 4.57. In 1968 the opposite was true. August was the pitching staff's best month at 20–12 with a 2.57 ERA. That staff didn't have any alarmingly bad months, but July wasn't spectacular at 17–12 with a 3.19 ERA. Those are a lot of statistics to digest. But keep this in mind, the best aspect of both staffs was the most important: they pitched the Tigers to a championship.

—T.G.

They weren't among the leading winners on our team, nor did they appear in the most games en route to garnering the most saves. But all three were valuable pitchers for us. Berenguer went 11–10 in 27 starts. He also pitched four times in relief. He was the No. 4 starter, however, on a team that opted to go with only three in the postseason. Therefore, Juan didn't pitch at all in the playoffs and World Series. I felt badly that he didn't get a chance to contribute in the postseason.

But Juan had at least three outstanding starts that I remember during the regular season.

On June 16 with his only shutout—and with one of his two complete games—Berenguer blanked the Brewers in Milwaukee 6–0. Juan could be overpowering at times. For instance, he had a season-high 12 strikeouts in a game against the Seattle Mariners two months later, but in his shutout of the Brewers, he struck out only one batter. He occasionally was at his best, it turned out, when not ending up with a high strikeout total. Like the game in Milwaukee, he won three games in 1984 when he had just one strikeout. His stuff was comparable to anybody's on our staff. I don't know that anyone threw harder than Juan. He had a great arm and an outstanding curveball. So, his primary pitches were as good as anyone's. It was just a matter of whether he could command them for the entire time he would be in a game. Sometimes he could; sometimes he couldn't. It could be a battle for him, but there were times he was lights out.

His victory in Milwaukee, though, was part of a three-game sweep over the Brewers after we had dropped the last two games of a series in Toronto. So, it came at the right time. Another one of Juan's strong starts was that 12-strikeout game against Seattle at Tiger Stadium on August 18. Berenguer took a 4–1 lead into the ninth inning but had to hand the game over to Willie after issuing consecutive walks with one out. Both runners ended up scoring on a two-out single off Willie, but we won the game 4–3. It was our fourth consecutive victory in what would become a four-game winning streak.

The third game of Juan's worthy of mention was a 1–0 triumph over the Orioles on September 5 at Tiger Stadium. We had scored off tough Mike Flanagan in the first inning, and Berenguer did an outstanding job of protecting the lead until he walked pinch-hitter Joe Nolan with one out in the eighth. In fact, while allowing just two hits, he had outpitched Flanagan. That just shows that on any given day his stuff could be as good as anybody's.

Yet it looked as if the game against the Orioles was going to unravel when upon entering the game after Juan's walk to Nolan, Willie hit the first batter he faced, Gary Roenicke, before throwing a wild pitch that advanced the runners to second and third. But as he so often did, Hernandez regrouped to strike out Benny Ayala for the second out and get Mike Young on a fly ball to right for the third out, stranding the runners. With a runner again at third, Willie also got the final out of the game an inning later. The save went to Hernandez, but the win—and the bulk of the credit—went to Juan. The victory sent us off in a good mood to Toronto, where we swept three straight from the Blue Jays in a crucial late-summer series.

Rozema went 7–5 in 16 starts but also had 13 relief appearances in which he registered a 1.11 ERA. So, I would say his value to the team was his versatility. Sparky Anderson and Roger Craig used him when and where he needed to be used. I think they realized Rosie had kind of a rubber arm. He could do anything that was asked of him. All these years later, he could probably throw batting practice for an hour. Rosie really helped in June and July when he went 6–1 over a stretch of eight starts. It was during that time from June 11 to July 20 that he was at his best.

On July 20 against the Texas Rangers at Tiger Stadium, he pitched his best game of the season, allowing one run on six hits without a walk in eight innings of a 3–1 victory. Only one of the six hits went for extra bases, so it was a masterful performance, coming during a stretch in which we won 11 of 12 games. The victory improved Rozema's record at the time to 7–1 with a 2.97 ERA, so he clearly was pitching effectively. Helping us to remain in the right direction was a big plus.

Although not being called on regularly—he started no games at all in May, for instance—Dave had gotten off to a strong start when he beat the Chicago White Sox 4–1 at Tiger Stadium in his second start of the season on April 21. In that game he blanked the Sox on two hits through six innings, striking out seven, including Tom Paciorek three times. Seven would be his season-high for strikeouts. Rozema would leave that game with a 2–0 lead, after which Bair secured a three-inning save. We were off to a great start as a team at that point. Rozema's gem gave us the second victory (and an 11–1 record) in what would grow to be a seven-game winning streak. Eventually our won-loss record grew to 19–2 before we lost two games in a row for the first time. Rosie was still pitching well by mid-summer. For instance, with another quality start, he beat Milwaukee 7–3 on June 22, allowing three runs on five hits in six innings.

The common denominator in most of Dave's good starts was his control. In the seven starts he won in 1984, he issued just six walks. Also in those seven starts, he allowed only three home runs. From the day I first met Rosie, when we were in the minors together, he would be—if I were ranking all the pitchers I ever caught in my career—the one with the best command. He had pinpoint control with his fastball, pinpoint control with his slider, and a great change-up. Like the splitter was for Jack, his change-up was an out pitch.

Another example of Rosie's effectiveness was a game on July 7 in Texas during which he allowed only one walk while lasting six innings of a 5–2 victory. Instead of occurring during one of our winning streaks, however, this game took place while we were losing seven of nine, so it was more than welcome—and more than needed.

Bair was the unsung member of our bullpen, not accumulating the gaudy numbers of Hernandez and Lopez but a valuable part of it all the same. The third most active pitcher of our bullpen, he was 5–3 with four saves and a 3.75 ERA in 47 games. Multi-inning appearances were Doug's specialty. He worked at least three innings 13 times, going 3–0 with two saves. Twice he pitched more than three innings of relief. That was our coaching staff's understanding of how to best use him, and Doug bought into it early on. He was fine—within reason, obviously—with however long they asked him to remain on the mound, whether it be two innings, three, or maybe even a little more. He was very accepting of his role.

And, for sure, it would be a diversified role. In Boston, for instance, Bair restored a degree of sanity to a slugfest, allowing one run on three hits during four-and-one-third innings of relief in a game we'd win 13–9. That was the game in which we scored eight runs in the first inning, and the Red Sox countered with five—while superstitions of the No. 13 ran rampant at Fenway Park on Friday the 13th. Doug entered that game in the first inning and worked through the fifth, preserving a three-run lead during his appearance. For his performance he ended up as the winning pitcher.

He also was the winning pitcher on September 28 as we tried to regain our edge three days after clinching the division. We had lost the first two games after clinching, but we were in New York in the final series of the regular season—and we needed to get back on track.

With four hitless innings of shutout relief against the Yankees, Bair helped us get there. We beat the Yankees 4–2 that night at Yankee Stadium, finally prevailing on Lou Whitaker's two-run home run in the 12th after we'd been held to two runs through the first 11 innings. Bair, the winning pitcher in that game as well, retired the side in order in the bottom of the 12th.

He might have had a few blowups along the way—no pitcher is perfect—but more times than not, he got the job done. Doug contributed another fine performance on June 10 in the first game of a doubleheader in Baltimore. It's just coincidental that his three best outings of 1984 occurred on the road. In that game against the Orioles, Bair was summoned in the third inning with the score tied at three and then left after the sixth with us ahead 6–3. We eventually won the game 10–4 and would complete the doubleheader sweep over the Birds with an 8–0 complete-game gem from Petry in the nightcap. The sweep helped us recover from a 6–9 slide after our 35–5 start.

Those, anyway, were some of the reasons we enjoyed such a successful season. We made the most of our six-inning starts, we had a wonderfully balanced staff, and everyone—at one time or another—contributed.

Chapter 21

Our Hitters

I previously—and grudgingly—conceded that the Boston Red Sox may have had the best offense in the American League in 1984. That's because the Red Sox led the league in hits, OPS, and total bases— whereas we led the league in runs and home runs. But in the five categories used for this evaluation (runs, hits, home runs, OPS, and total bases) the Sox finished no lower than second in any of them while we slipped a bit in one category, finishing fourth in hits. It was close between us and the Sox for best offense all the same—closer than it was between us and the Toronto Blue Jays for second best. For what it's worth, the New York Yankees had the fourth best offense.

Using the same five categories to determine which Detroit Tiger had the most individual impact offensively in 1984, Kirk Gibson emerged as the winner with Alan Trammell a close second—followed by Chet Lemon, Lou Whitaker, and myself. Gibson led the team in runs scored, OPS, and total bases. Tram led in hits, and I led in home runs (and RBIs). I didn't often walk, though, so the on-base-percentage side of my OPS was low. Consequently, I finished no better than seventh on the team that year in OPS. But it stands to reason that the same five players had the highest production numbers on the team because they had the most at-bats.

We had a strong all-around offense, however. For Trammell it was his second consecutive year of hitting well over .300, and he would enjoy four more seasons of doing so in his Hall of Fame career. Plus, he was deservedly named MVP of the World Series for hitting .450 with two home runs. "The bottom line is I was swinging the bat well at the right time," he said. That comes across as being rather dispassionate, but when we won the World Series, Tram was as emotionally invested in the triumph as anyone, saying, "This is the most important moment of my life."

I was especially happy for Gibson because he had worked so hard to rebound from struggling in 1983. His batting average that year had dipped to .227, requiring a strong two weeks near the end of the season to finish even that high. Gibby was hitting .209 as late as September 9 in 1983 but ended the year with a .372 surge in his last 14 games.

Basically, what Kirk did in 1984 was re-establish himself as a bona fide major league player, proving to one and all that he could turn his career around and live up to his potential. But it had required a lot of introspection for him to do so. A lost soul after 1983, not happy with himself or the direction of his career, Gibson credited the positive influence of Roger Craig for helping him become "someone who believed in himself again."

But Kirk became what the Tigers always hoped he would, an essential cog of our lineup. I think we always knew he had that ability. He was gifted in so many areas as an athlete. I had hoped the on switch would click, and he would become a major contributor, which he certainly did. I give him a lot of credit for rebounding to a spot where he felt good about himself.

Just as I talked about three pitchers who hadn't received enough attention for how 1984 came together, the same approach should be applied to our hitters—specifically to Darrell Evans, Howard Johnson, and Tom Brookens. None of them was a statistical team leader, but each made substantial contributions.

Darrell was a huge addition to our team as a free agent, and I know it thrilled him—after a homerless spring training—to hit a home run in his first regular-season game as a Tiger. That came against the Twins in Minnesota. He followed that with another home run in his first at-bat as a Tiger at Tiger Stadium—a three-run blast off Dave Stewart in the first inning of a 5–1 triumph against the Texas Rangers. He didn't waste any time finding the seats, which had to make him happy. Then again, Darrell was excited just to be on our team.

Hitting .297 in our first 40 games, Evans was a consistent contributor throughout our 35–5 start. But beginning with our visit in May to Seattle—the one in which we were swept by the Mariners—and continuing through the first three weeks of August, Darrell couldn't buy himself a hit. Over the course of 65 games, he batted .168, with more walks than hits. That discerning eye at the plate, though, is something which never deserted Evans. So his 40 walks in those 65 games gave him a respectable .309 on-base percentage even while his batting average caved. We went 15–3 whenever Evans walked more than once. But I know he wasn't contributing throughout the summer as much as he hoped to. Unfortunately, he also struggled during the World Series, in which he went 1-for-15.

Darrell was an essential addition to our team all the same. For instance, he had six games of more than two hits in 1984—and we won all six. That includes the four games in which he had three hits and the two in which he had four. We also won five of the six games in which he drove in at least three runs. Probably his best game of the year was a four-hit performance, including a three-run home run, on August 21 at home against the Oakland A's. It was also the only game of the season in which he scored three runs. That four-hit game took place during our three-game lopsided sweep of the A's in which we scored 37 runs, our biggest splurge of the season. We went from there to taking three of the first four games on a West Coast swing, getting that trip off on the right foot.

Evans' other four-hit game occurred on September 11, a 9–2 victory against the Orioles in the first game of a doubleheader in Baltimore. In that game he had two singles, a double, and a solo home run. Darrell's four-RBI game in 1984 came against the Brewers on June 16 in Milwaukee—a game in which he chipped in with a sacrifice fly and a three-run home run off Don Sutton. Looking back, maybe he should have batted third in the lineup more frequently because he hit .298 while batting third in 1984.

Darrell's value wasn't statistics-based, however. He proved to be a true team leader, always available for advice and guidance, always willing to

In Darrell's Words

The first day I was eligible to sign as a free agent, the Detroit Tigers called me, offering a three-year deal. That was unexpected. No other teams, such as the Los Angeles Dodgers and the New York Yankees, were offering more than two years. I thought the Dodgers might have been a good fit, but they didn't propose anything more than two. I was 36 at the time, going on 37 the next May, so this was going to be my last chance.

It was a different time in that we didn't have cell phones, so keeping track of which team was calling became a challenge, but it was more exciting than frustrating. Having the Tigers in it, though, meant I had to do a bit of research. I didn't know much about them at first, but I discovered they were a hungry, young team with talent, and they soon became my No. 1 possibility. I thought Tiger Stadium would be a great place for me to play.

Bill Lajoie, their general manager, was honest during the negotiations. He said up front, "This is the deal. This is it. This is what we're offering." So, I respected them from the start because they beat everyone to the punch. The three years they offered were more important than anything because I knew they were fully invested in me.

I then called Larry Herndon, who'd been a good friend of mine on the San Francisco Giants before being traded to Detroit, and he said, "C'mon, Darrell, you must do it. This is the best team you'll ever play on. And the fans are the greatest. You'll fit in perfectly."

I'm not saying Larry's the one who talked me into it, but we had an extremely positive discussion. At that point, though, it was decision time. The excitement was incredible because I was getting the vibe from other teams that I was too old. But the Tigers jumped in and said, "No, no, we want you."

So it was a no-brainer. I'm excited just remembering it. I signed with the Tigers about a week before Christmas. It's the best decision I ever made, but I didn't realize what a big deal it was locally. The Tigers had never signed a premier free agent. So when I got off the plane, there were five or six TV stations waiting for me. What also happened was that the people in the airport recognized me and started wishing me well. From the get-go, I was treated like a king.

When I got to spring training, however, I made it clear to Sparky Anderson that I wasn't there to be a full-time designated hitter. I could still play first base, I could also play third, and I wanted to. Sparky replied by telling me about his plans to keep me fresh. Sparky always had to be right.

And that led to some interesting conversations between us before the regular season. I was there to play—not to sit and watch. I don't mean to say we didn't have a good relationship. I always thought we did—Sparky was great—but I was concerned about playing time. I didn't want days off against lefties, for instance.

Then, I hit a home run in my first game as a Tiger and also in my first at-bat at Tiger Stadium the following week. *Are you kidding me?* My teammates were excited about my start because I'd been brought on board mostly for my power. I got another hit when we went to Chicago, but in the Saturday game when Jack Morris pitched his no-hitter, I didn't play because the Sox pitched lefty Floyd Bannister. If it hadn't been a day game, I would have been in Sparky's office bright and early saying, "What the heck are you doing, man? I need to be out there!"

But the magical events of that season were already happening. So I wasn't disappointed at all that I hit only 16 home runs. Big deal. I hit 40 the next year.

The Tigers called me a clubhouse leader. That meant a lot to me, but I always felt it was part of my job as a veteran player to be a leader. The bigger thing is I've never had more fun than that year. Celebrating our championship, jumping up and down with my teammates, and being part of a downtown parade are some of the most beautiful memories of my career. I'll treasure them forever. They went by too fast, but I remember every single second of them. And I wear my World Series ring every day.

—D.E.

listen to whatever any of us needed to discuss. Darrell didn't have his best offensive year in his first season with us, but his contributions were extraordinary away from the field. He was a veteran presence—an experienced player with a lot of credibility, who was not shy at expressing his views about baseball and how to play the game. Everybody on the team appreciated that. We viewed him as someone to learn from. He had no shortage of opinions, including about how often he should be in the lineup. Of the 110 games Evans started for us, by the way, 53 were as our designated hitter, 43 were as our first baseman, and 14 were at third base.

HoJo, meanwhile, started two games at designated hitter, one at short, but 98 at third. He was our starting third baseman for much of the 1984 season but lost the job to Marty Castillo in September and had only one at-bat as a pinch-hitter in the postseason. For us Howard was just a 23-year-old kid with a bright future. Most of that future, however, was realized with the New York Mets for whom he played nine years after being traded for pitcher Walt Terrell following our championship season.

Howard made 12 errors as our third baseman in 1984, so I'm not entirely sure Sparky Anderson ever trusted his defense. But his offensive potential was always held in higher regard than whatever he would accomplish defensively. Therefore, it wasn't surprising that he won two Silver Slugger Awards for the Mets but no Gold Gloves. "Sparky never seemed to warm up a lot to Howard, even though he was a great talent," Brookens said. "It was about his defense."

Johnson had some fine moments for us, however. From May 15 to July 15, he hit .290 with six home runs and 25 RBIs while starting 40 games—and during one 12-game stretch of June—he hit .400 (16-for-40) while we went 9–3. He was capable of carrying the team, in other words. I always thought he was a special talent. In my opinion, we gave up on him too fast.

I would love to have been a fly on the wall during front-office conversations about his pros and cons, the discussions leading up to why we eventually traded him.

Howard obviously had skills. He might not have had the softest hands as a Tiger, but at no time would I have judged him to be an inferior third baseman. More than Sparky not liking him, I think it was that he wanted to go in a different direction because Howard was young. But as with Evans, a good day for Howard usually meant a good day for us. Of the six games in which he knocked in at least three runs, we won five—highlighted by his four-RBI game in Milwaukee on September 25, a 9–1 triumph against the Brewers just five games before the end of the regular season.

In that game Randy O'Neal, who had won our division clincher with seven scoreless innings against the Brewers at Tiger Stadium on September 18, worked another five scoreless against the Brewers at County Stadium for his second victory. It was also our 103rd win, tying the team record set in 1968. Howard hit a grand slam in the first inning of that September 25th game—the last game he ever started as a Tiger.

As had Evans and Johnson, Brookens also played third base for us in 1984, starting 22 games at the position. But he also started 22 games at shortstop while Trammell was out with a shoulder injury—and 19 games at second base while giving Whitaker an occasional rest. To his credit, Brookie played all three positions capably. In all, we had five players who started at third base in 1984: Johnson, Brookens, Evans, Castillo, and Barbaro Garbey. In their entirety, they did a pretty solid job.

Of Brookens' 10 years as a Tiger, he had only one (1979, the season he was called up from Evansville) in which he had fewer at-bats than he did in 1984. One of the reasons for that was Tom's miserable start at the plate. His batting average didn't climb above .200 to stay until June 25. Accordingly, he started only 26 of our first 60 games. "The main reason there was such a traffic jam at third," Brookens said, "was because I didn't hit enough to solidify the job. I'm being honest about that. I played myself out of the position. When you don't hit, they start looking for someone new."

Brookens found other ways to contribute, however. I had a lot of respect for what he brought to the club, on the field and off. On May 6, for instance, with his second sacrifice bunt in extra innings (Tom was always one of our best bunters), he set up the winning run of a game in which we came from five runs down to beat the Cleveland Indians in 12 innings. The unlikely victory gave us a 22–4 record, but it was a game which hadn't seemed destined for our win column. "I guess there's a little magic after all," Brookens said when it was over.

Rebounding from his slow start, Tom hit .297 between June 25 and the end of the 1984 season. We won both of his three-hit games and all four of his multiple-RBI games. His biggest home run was the one he belted in the seventh inning on September 18 against Milwaukee. That home run stretched our lead against Mike Caldwell from 2–0 to 3–0 in the game, which proved to be the division clincher. Slowed by a hamstring problem that limited his role, Tom went 0-for-5 in the postseason, however. "Even with my struggles offensively, I always felt like an important part of the team," Brookens said. "But in a game like that clincher, I was just happy to help in any way I could. About that time, though, I pulled a hamstring, then re-aggravated it near the end of the season. So, I had to tell Sparky I couldn't move as well as I needed to. I didn't want to cost the team any games."

Evans hit 16 home runs in his first season as a Tiger. But he rebounded the next year with 40. In five years with Detroit, he would hit 141 home runs and average 81 RBIs per season. In other words, he had a productive five years with the Tigers. Johnson would live up to the promise he always displayed as a young player, but it would not be with the Tigers. In a five-year stretch from 1987 through 1991, he averaged 31 home runs and 95 RBIs for the Mets, making him one of the most productive sluggers in the majors. HoJo would also play in another World Series—a classic against the Red Sox in 1986, which the Mets won in seven games.

Terrell, the pitcher we received in return for Johnson, won 54 games in his four seasons with Detroit, topping out with a 17–10 record in 1987. He would also make one start in the 1987 American League Championship Series against Minnesota. The Tigers traded Walt to the San Diego Padres following the 1988 season. But overall, it was a balanced trade. Both sides got what they needed.

After 1984, Brookens played four more years for the Tigers, giving him a full decade with the team—"a lot longer than I ever thought I'd last," he said. "But I never had the kind of season that allowed me to waltz into spring training the following year thinking the starting job should be mine."

But the starting job was pretty much his the next season. There wasn't the traffic jam at third for the Tigers in 1985 that there had been in 1984, so Brookens started 134 games the year after we won the World Series. As a ballyhooed rookie, Chris Pittaro started 18 games at third as the starter out of spring training but lost the position in May. Sparky's original plan of having Pittaro take over at second base and bumping Whitaker to third never materialized.

Most of us took that talk with a grain of salt anyway. Chris swung the bat well in spring training and was looking very polished, but when Sparky said he was going to be our starting second baseman, I said to myself, "Wait a minute. I wouldn't go that far." That was Sparky for you, though. But it was Lou at second base when the season began.

Chapter 22

Sparky

S parky Anderson was such a valuable part of what we accomplished in 1984. But other than the games we won—and the fact that we won the World Series—it's difficult to quantify his contributions. So, it's best simply to remember what he meant to the team through the words of those who played for him. There's no denying that as our manager he had a hugely positive influence on the Detroit Tigers of '84 for which we still think of him fondly. In fact, our regard for Sparky after so many years is the most fitting tribute we can bestow upon him.

I thought Les Moss was a great baseball man. He knew the game, he knew how to manage the game, he knew how to manage players,. He was a great teacher. So, I was disappointed when I heard the Tigers were switching from Les to Sparky. Les had played a big role in my development, and I felt the Tigers hadn't given him a chance to show what he could do as a major league manager. It wasn't that I had anything against Sparky. I just thought Les wasn't getting the opportunity he deserved. They were cutting him off at the knees.

Sparky, I know, was a lot more colorful and had a lot to say. I don't know if Les ever would have become quotable, but obviously the Tigers were looking for someone who not only knew how to manage, but also was a smooth talker. Sparky fit that bill. And he did a great job on both counts.

But I would love to have seen what Les might have accomplished if he'd been given that chance.

Let me say this, though: early on in my career after he was hired, even though I had worked closely with Les about the catching position, Sparky injected Bill Freehan into my life. Bill came to spring training to work with me and to help me. We became very good friends. He impacted my career positively. But all that was Sparky's doing. He was the one who made Freehan available, which was great. He even sent Bill a letter to thank him for the work he did with me, adding that it made a noticeable difference.

I never had any major disagreements with Sparky. Then again, I wasn't always certain early on if he even knew who I was. The only time we ever really butted heads was when Roger Craig took over calling pitches, and Sparky didn't adequately explain why at first. After my initial disappointment about the decision, though, it was explained to me to my satisfaction.

Years later, when I ended up leaving, I don't really know what happened when I ended up leaving the Tigers after the 1986 season, however, I don't know if he stuck up for me. I was obviously disappointed by that entire ordeal and I often wondered if Sparky ever spoke up on my behalf. I felt I had played well for him. But did he say, "We need to keep Lance around?" I never did ask him, so I'll never know. That stuck in my craw for a long time. I didn't know if he ever went to bat for me or just kind of let it ride, allowing Jim Campbell to do what he was going to do.

I'm sure there were other times I questioned his decisions. Everybody did that occasionally. I was no exception. I often was defensive about my teammates—when they got rid of somebody, for instance. But I think it would be a fair assessment to say Sparky was shrewd. He knew the game; he knew the right buttons to push. Plus, he knew what to do with his authority. There were times some of what he tried backfired on him, like walking a hitter on purpose and having the next guy hit a home run. That happened a lot, but I never questioned his ability to run a game. He did a great job with that, handling the pitching staff, and giving everyone a fair chance to play.

Plus, he did an excellent job eventually of getting the most out of Kirk Gibson, knowing when to throw him a rope and when to kick him in the butt. But I give Kirk a lot of credit for that, too. Sparky wasn't one to seek a lot of input. He would shoot people down, saying, "Look, I know what I'm doing, I don't need your opinion." He would say his door was always open, as long we were prepared to hear what he had to say as well.

I developed a very good relationship over the years with him, though. Not just me—but my whole family. I had great respect for him—and eventually a great love for him. He was almost like a father figure to me.

What follows are the recollections of several Detroit Tigers on how Sparky steered us to a championship.

ALAN TRAMMELL

When Sparky Anderson was hired by the Detroit Tigers, I was surprised because we thought we were playing pretty good baseball that year under Les Moss. But once I got over the surprise, I was in awe of the fact that Sparky Anderson—*the* Sparky Anderson—was now our manager. He had a built-in presence. I couldn't believe the Cincinnati Reds had let him go. I mean Sparky had won a couple of World Series with arguably some of the best teams in history. Yet, lo and behold, here he was coming to Detroit.

In that first season (1979), Sparky just observed a lot and got accustomed to his new team, figuring out who he liked and who he didn't. Some of the guys weren't bad players, but they didn't fit Sparky's style. He was just laying the groundwork for the following seasons, evaluating what we had. Since he took over in June, a chunk of the season had already been played.

But I think he came away from what he saw thinking, *Okay, we have some young players who are going to be part of our future.* When you look back on it, he was right.

Regarding him as sort of an extension of my parents and having that kind of respect for him, I did a lot of listening to him early on. At the time, I was still very impressionable. So right from the get-go, I was a sponge who wanted to learn. He was the teacher, sharing his baseball knowledge. I loved it. I was totally on board with what he was trying to do. I might have questioned some things, but I never confronted him. Other players might have, but I did not. That wasn't my personality. That's not to say I wouldn't get that scolding look from him once in a while and that finger waggle to make his point. It was some tough love at times. But I respected it.

One of his qualities—and I think most good managers have this—is that he was a people person. The good ones watch, see, and just have a sixth sense about managing. They have that knack. And obviously Sparky knew baseball, so he ended up teaching us the game the way it was supposed to be played. He also coached us on how to conduct ourselves as professional athletes. It was more than just being a player. It's amazing, but even to youngsters today, I convey a lot that Sparky taught us 45 years ago. He pounded fundamentals into us. He totally did, man. It took a couple of years from when he started for it all to sink in, but we needed it to sink in for us to play at a championship level. That's what Sparky gave us. He knew exactly what he was doing, and we're all thankful that he did.

He didn't take losses very well, but he told me numerous times that 1984, the season in which we broke our team record for victories, was the most difficult he ever was a part of. If we hadn't won it all with the kind of start we had, he was afraid that season would have been pushed to the side and forgotten. You didn't see that concern outwardly, but he was feeling it inside that second-place teams aren't long remembered.

I think I would have been able to be a good player anyway. But Sparky got the best out of me. I can't thank him enough now for what he taught me. I know Kirk Gibson is thankful, too. But with that football mentality, it took him a longer time. It wasn't easy for him. Plus, Gibby would be the first person to say he didn't always conduct himself the right way as a young man. But ultimately, with Sparky's help, he did.

KIRK GIBSON

Sparky Anderson was a mastermind who understood how to slow down the game. And he really knew how to push our buttons. He was a very good manager who was fully aware how much the little moments of a game meant. People say the game of baseball isn't fast, but when you're a manager with a three-run lead in the seventh inning and the first two guys get on base for the other team, you have to make a quick decision about what to do.

Sparky once told me, "If you ever manage, make sure to ask yourself two questions each time the game goes to commercial: What do I do if the leadoff man gets on base? What do I do if the first two guys get on? You have two minutes and 25 seconds of commercial time to decide. So if those situations happen, you're ready for them when the game resumes."

He always had built-in alerts like that for himself. That way he'd be ready for any situation he encountered. He was always ahead of every-thing, never getting caught unprepared. But he also was never hesitant to scold if he felt it was necessary—like the time we were in Seattle in 1983 when he sat me down to say I was going to platoon at designated hitter with John Wockenfuss. I went off. But he replied, "I'm going to teach you a lesson, young man, because I don't like the way you're going. So, when the cake-eaters are on the mound, the guys you want to hit against, you'll be sitting here next to me. But when the Hall of Famers are throwing, you're going to be up there batting. At the end of this year, you'll either be a ball-player, or I'll be sending you home to your momma, where you can curl up on her lap like you did as a little boy."

I can still see him wagging his finger at me.

There was another time when we were in the outfield together before a game, and he said he wanted to try covering me like a defensive back covering a receiver. I told him, "Don't do that Sparky. I'll run over your ass."

But he insisted. So we told Dave Rozema to grab a ball and throw it to us like it was a football play. Sparky pretended he was going to jump my route, but I crossed him up, ran into him, and I flat-out crushed him. When he got up, his glasses had come off, so had his cap, and he told Rosie, "That SOB is crazy!"

I told him, "I warned you!"

But that incident was both strategic and well-thought-out. In fact, before Sparky died, he asked me: "Remember that day? You know why I did that? Because I thought I was going to lose you. I had to let you work out

In Jim Leyland's Words

I wasn't part of the 1984 team, but as a minor league manager in the Detroit Tigers' system, I had gotten to know most of their players. I wanted to be on the Tigers' coaching staff when Sparky Anderson was hired, but he had his guys, and I understood that. I wasn't one of them, but I thought if I proved myself at Triple A, maybe I could be added. That never worked out, though.

When the Chicago White Sox asked me to be their third-base coach before the 1982 season, I called the Tigers to see if there was any way they could put me on the staff, even as a bullpen coach. I had a great relationship with Sparky, had all the respect in the world for him, but there just wasn't a spot.

I had spent 18 years in the Tigers' organization, first a player, then as a player-coach, and finally 11 years as a minor league manager. But I realized my time with them wasn't going to end with a major league coaching position. It became obvious to me that if I wanted to get to the big leagues, I'd have to go elsewhere. And after 18 years of riding the buses, I was definitely ready for the big leagues. It was time. But it was nobody's fault. I left on good terms.

In 1984, though, I still knew most of the Tigers really well. I had managed just about all of them. And if I hadn't managed them, I'd had them in the instructional league. I loved them. I had a special feeling for them. They were a great bunch. I was coaching third base for the White Sox when Jack Morris threw his no-hitter in Chicago. And they, in turn, acknowledged my contribution. From that special performance on, it was great to see what they accomplished. I was happy for them. Even now, Dan Petry looks back and says, "I never would have played for Sparky Anderson if there hadn't been a Jim Leyland. He taught me so much about the game."

The Tigers had everything in 1984, though, including, arguably, the greatest double-play combination in the history of baseball. To me, Alan Trammell is the modern-day Mr. Tiger. Plus, they had a a smart manager with a lot of charisma and poise. They were a special team from top to bottom. There've not been many like that before or after.

I don't know, though, that you feel any more pressure as a manager in the World Series than you do at any other time. I think you just realize it's the biggest stage in baseball—like the Super Bowl, the NBA Finals, or the Stanley Cup Finals are in their sports—so there is naturally more excitement.

I always called it "good pressure" because it meant you were playing for all the marbles. And if you're prepared, it's good pressure.

What's key to it is that you really have to manage your time, so there can be no distractions. Outside stuff will drive you nuts when you don't have time to deal with it. The year we won the World Series in 1997 with the Florida Marlins, there were 16 people staying at our house. They were in the pool, having Bloody Marys, enjoying life as they should—but we had a Game Seven to play that night, so I went to the ballpark at 8:00 AM. I couldn't take it. I told them, "I'm trying to win Game Seven of the World Series! I have to get away from this." So I went to my office at the ballpark.

That's the pressure if you let it get to you. The games are the games; they are what they are, but certainly the stakes are bigger. Winning a World Series is something you've worked for all your life. I dreamed as a kid of one day playing in a World Series; I'm not sure I ever dreamed of managing in one, however. You dream of hitting a home run to win it. You don't dream about making out the lineup card or pulling a pitcher, but it's a great experience no matter what.

I'm sure there was added pressure on the Tigers in 1984 because people were expecting them to win it. They were just that good. No matter what, though, when the moment comes that you actually win a World Series, it's a feeling you can't really explain. In my case with the Marlins in 1997, it occurred on a winning single in the 11th inning, and I quickly looked up into the stands to where my family was sitting. Then I ran out onto the field like everyone else. But it's hard to describe unless you experience it. It's unreal. All my life I'd seen other teams celebrate all my life—in other sports, too—then you realize, *Hey, that's what I'm doing now. It's my turn!*

To eventually become the Tigers manager in 2006 was unbelievable for me. I thought the opportunity had long passed me by. I about fell over. I had signed with the Tigers in 1963 and, all these years later, I had finally made it to the big leagues with them. Obviously, I waited a long time, but it was well worth it. Being their manager was everything I expected and more. I loved the fans. And we were fortunate enough to have good teams. Of course, you always regret not getting everything you wanted, like winning a World Series in Detroit, but it was one of the greatest thrills of my life to get that job.

—J.L.

whatever you were feeling about me and get past it. Sometimes you have to take it to save a player if you can."

I tried to do the same thing with a pitcher of mine when I managed the Arizona Diamondbacks. A young guy needed to throw inside but refused to do so. I stepped up to the plate in the cage one day and I told him to drill me in the ribs with a fastball. He said he couldn't do it, but I told him he had to. I was going to take one in the ribs to help him. But when he threw the next pitch, you know where it was? A foot outside. It turned out he couldn't be helped. I said, "Nice guy, but get rid of him."

Years later, I still think of it as an example of what Sparky had meant—but with the opposite result. That's why he was a mastermind.

JACK MORRIS

I was a little nervous when Sparky Anderson was hired because there were two pitchers on our team, Jack Billingham and Milt Wilcox, who warned me about his reputation as Captain Hook—a manager who yanked starting pitchers quickly. But it didn't take long to realize that with me he was the complete opposite. He needed someone to finish games, and I was his guy.

It was a process, though, to understand him as a manager. He had a lot of team meetings in those early years, and some of his bold statements like, "I'm going to weed out the rats" and "Nobody is going to steal the show from me" were kind of off the wall. Ultimately, he got rid of the guys he didn't think would buy into his program and he built the team accordingly.

We didn't have many disagreements initially because we were building a relationship, which took a while, but I had a lot of disagreements with him as the years went by—but that's what I loved most about Sparky. We could agree to disagree and still care about each other. There was one incident in which he aired me out in front of the whole team, but I ended up winning that argument by getting the ball, throwing a shutout my next time out, and quieting him down.

After his phenomenal years with the Cincinnati Reds, I think he came to realize that players make the manager, and if he stayed out of their way, he was going to have success. He never shied away from that. He openly said many times, "I'm really smart when I have great players."

I never saw Sparky feel any pressure during the pennant race of '84. But we were a young, naïve, bull-headed team that got off to a start, which will probably never be duplicated. The pressure, though, if he was going to feel any, was all about how we would finish. We didn't want to hear any questions about what happened. The pressure was also about how to balance the finish with the start. But I think the team understood who we were, what we could do, and Sparky knew how to get the best out of us.

Roger Craig, our pitching coach, was in my corner the whole way. As I reflect on that year, I realize that now, but I probably had more disagreements with Roger than I did with Sparky. He had a unique way of working with Sparky, but we both were stubborn, strong-willed individuals, so I guess it was only natural for us to butt heads occasionally. Roger never pitched the way I pitched, so what he tried to instill in me led to some of our conflicts. For instance, when I would tell him, "This is the way I pitch," I'm not sure he took it very well. Eventually, though, he gave me enough latitude to do my thing, and it worked out.

My fondest memories about Sparky, though, were not about whether he was right or I was right. When I reflect on the years I spent with him, all I can think about is his love for the game—and his love for his players. He also enjoyed taking the media on wild-goose chases, but all of that is what made him beautiful. He was a simple guy, not a rocket scientist from Harvard. Sparky wasn't complicated. But he had all the attributes of a great manager—his love for the game, his passion, his respect for the game and for those involved with it. He never took any of it for granted. One time he told me, "You think you're doing something that will last forever? Let me tell you: you're going to hang up your uniform for the last time someday, but the game will keep on going like you never were there." At the time, I thought, *Gosh, that's not cool.* But he was right on. The game never stops.

If I was changed as a person by Sparky, which I wouldn't dispute, it was for the better. But that goes back to the fact that he cared about us. We were his family. We really were. So, he wanted to bring out the best in us, off the field as well as on. It was natural that his approach to us changed once we got older, through he always cared about us. Suddenly, we had grown into being mature players. That was to be expected. But he absolutely was a positive influence on my career because I know he cared about me, and he knew I could take a lot of feedback from him—even the Sparky-isms. You know what, though? If he yelled at me, or scolded me, or tried to correct me, I never took it personally. I never thought of it as negative. I would think, *All right, maybe he has a point.*

DAN PETRY

I was still in Triple A, of course, when the Detroit Tigers hired Sparky Anderson. I didn't get called up to the majors until about a month later. So other than thinking it was a tough break for Les Moss, whom we had played for and liked, what I mostly remember is meeting Sparky for the first time instead of how I felt when he was hired. I knew all about Sparky and what he had accomplished with the Big Red Machine in Cincinnati. So suddenly, I was like, *Sparky Anderson? He's my manager?* I was sort of shocked at that. But he wanted to get an idea of who the Tigers' prospects were. So I got called up—as did Tom Brookens and Kirk Gibson—before the end of the '79 season.

As soon as you met Sparky, especially as a young player, he commanded immediate respect because of what he had already accomplished. You knew who was in charge. I was an impressionable 20-year-old, and here I was talking to Sparky Anderson. There's a little bit of awe that goes with that. Saying I was scared to death might be too strong, but I certainly didn't want to get on the wrong side of him. I was simply doing whatever I could so that I wouldn't get called into his office to talk to him. If I was talking to him, that meant something was wrong. And I would eventually tell him that, which made him laugh.

Sparky wasn't someone who'd go out of his way to give you compliments, though. He'd say our reward was in our paychecks. He didn't think he had to pat us on the back all the time. Thankfully, I was never in a position of getting yelled at by him—but he sure could yell. My interactions with him were always calm and cordial. We had as good a relationship as a player and manager could have.

I finished 6–5 that first year, which I didn't think was too bad. Eventually, though, the Tigers traded me twice in my career—in 1987 to the California Angels and later in 1991 to the Atlanta Braves. I sort of figured something would happen the first time because my contract was up, and as they approached free agency, some of the guys were starting to leave. I thought at the time I needed a fresh start. So it wasn't devastating. The second time was terrible because our kids were young, and I was going to the National League. That one was awful.

But as I said about Sparky, you knew who was in charge. Roger Craig wasn't afraid to stand up to him—and tell him if he was wrong. There weren't too many people like that, however. But, for sure, Sparky had a major influence on my career in a number of different ways. To this day, whenever I see clips of him, I feel a little bit of denial that he's gone. I don't want to say he was larger than life, but when you see a video of Sparky, it's like you can still feel his presence. I would call him every Christmas, and I would always play in his CATCH golf outings, so our relationship got even better after my playing days were done.

TOM BROOKENS

Sparky Anderson just seemed to know what to do, when to do it, and when we needed just to be left alone. But when we needed a kick in the butt to bring us back down to Earth, he was also pretty good at that, too. Plus, he commanded respect. He had that my-way-or-the-highway-thing going, which sometimes a bunch of young guys, like we were, needed.

More than anything, he was really good at making us respect the game of baseball—playing it right, playing it hard, playing it the way it should be played, going after it every day. It was his feeling that: you're here in the big leagues and you deserve to be here, but don't think the game owes you anything. You owe the game everything. He strongly instilled that in us.

Chapter 23

1985 and 1986

On the heels of our championship, we headed into 1985 with the highest of hopes, of course, accompanied by equally high expectations. I'm pretty sure everyone was confident about winning—rather than just hoping to win. The consensus was that because we were coming off such a strong season we were the team to beat. In fact, we honestly believed, in fact, we'd be able to repeat for a year or two. Therefore, it not only came as a shock to us when we didn't, but it also served as a harsh reminder of how difficult it is to win once—let alone numerous times. "I thought 1985 would be a matter of picking up where we had left off," Tom Brookens said. "I really did. I couldn't identify any reason why we wouldn't repeat."

When 1984 ended, we knew there would be changes. There always are from year to year. Winning didn't change that. But I believe you could label our changes as minimal. Fearing that Milt Wilcox might experience a degree of diminished durability, we traded for Walt Terrell of the New York Mets, but it cost us Howard Johnson. I should say it cost us Johnson's potential because he was on the brink of breaking out, which he did as an annual offensive powerhouse for the Mets.

Johnson wasn't going to figure in our third-base plans, however. In spring training Sparky Anderson became enamored with rookie infielder Chris Pittaro, even considering moving Lou Whitaker from second to third to make room for him. But when Lou balked at the plans, Sparky simply targeted Pittaro for third base instead. When Chris didn't live up to expectations, Anderson pulled the plug on the experiment rather quickly, and Brookens ended up starting 134 games for us in 1985 as our third baseman. I didn't really know what Sparky was trying to accomplish with the Pittaro situation. It was a little ridiculous, to be honest with you. *Moving Lou away from second base?* I thought, *Wait a minute. Let's get a grip on ourselves.* I felt it was distracting. But I suppose it worked out the way it was supposed to.

In another roster development, Ruppert Jones was no longer with us. Seeking a team that would start instead of platoon him, Ruppert signed as a free agent with the California Angels. He found what he wanted with them in that he had more plate appearances in 1985 than in any season since 1982 and he stayed with the Angels another two years, but he didn't ever reach the heights he sought, hitting .231 in '85 with 21 home runs and 67 RBIs. He wasn't as special with California, in other words, as he had been with us.

We also didn't block Dave Rozema's departure via free agency. Rosie signed with the Texas Rangers in December. He'd been valuable for us as a swing man, starting now and then while also having a good year in relief. "But sometimes you have to move," he said. It didn't work out well for him in Texas, starting only four games with the Rangers and going 1–5 in relief. Rosie was still on the Rangers for the start of the 1986 season, but they released him in May. Years later, he would call his time in Texas "a nightmare."

In transactions that received less attention, we also traded pitcher Roger Mason and outfielder Rod Allen. Then in August, because he had compiled an 8.04 ERA in 12 games since June, we released Doug Bair, who had proven quite important in relief for us in '84. But that's it. The core of our championship team was basically untouched.

The team's concern about Wilcox proved to be correct. There wasn't much life left in Milt's arm after he had pushed himself to the limit in '84. Returning as a 17-game winner after two surgeries, he won only one game for us in 1985, beating Texas 4–1 on May 14 with a five-inning start. Wilcox simply couldn't last any longer than that. His last game as a Tiger was on June 3. Milt tried to bounce back one last time for the Seattle Mariners in 1986 but sadly went 0-8. What a gutsy pitcher he had been. "My shoulder was dead, no strength at all," Wilcox told Eli Zaret for the book *'84: The Last of the Great Tigers*. "Two operations had taken a toll—1984 was basically my last year. I pitched my whole life for '84."

The changes we made going into 1985 were magnified by the fact that we didn't win, but at the time, some of us were disappointed that our roster hadn't stayed intact—that they let go of guys from a team as dominant as we had been. To me the biggest surprise was that they let Ruppert leave. I mean everyone can be replaced, but it would have been great to start 1985 with as close to our '84 roster as possible and see where it would have taken us.

As replacements for those no longer on the team, we turned to Terrell and Frank Tanana as starters. Walt was Wilcox's replacement, and Frank— after acquiring him in June for pitching prospect Duane James (who never made it past Double A for the Rangers)—replaced a struggling Juan Berenguer. Genuinely happy to be back in Michigan, Tanana went 10-7 with a 3.34 ERA in 20 starts for us in 1985, finishing with a flourish by winning his last five starts. We still had Juan, but because of a weak second half, it looked like his days with us were numbered, and they were. The day after the 1985 season ended, we traded him to the San Francisco Giants.

Tanana, meanwhile, lasted seven more seasons with the Detroit Tigers. I was always a big fan of Frank's. I had never faced him much when he threw in the upper 90s, but I really came to respect his ability when I caught him. I loved the way he went about attacking hitters without the heat he used to have. I've never seen a pitcher irritate hitters more than Tanana did. If he threw one pitch slow, he'd throw the next one slower. Guys would yell at him heading back to the dugout after they struck out. But he loved that. He fed off it—because you could see that little smirk on his face as they walked away grumbling. Frank outfoxed and outthought hitters. That gave him a great deal of satisfaction.

The newcomer in our lineup, who got the most at-bats in 1985, was Nelson Simmons. He split his time almost equally between the outfield and as our designated hitter. "A big leaguer if I've ever seen one," Anderson said about Simmons.

This was Nelson's chance to live up to that billing after making the team in spring training. But adversity hit him right away. On a throw from the outfield during warm-ups on Opening Day, Simmons felt something pop in his left side. That led to a stint on the disabled list for the first month of the season. Then, after hitting .240 with three home runs in his first 30 games, Simmons was sent down to Triple A Nashville and didn't return until mid-August. With seven home runs and 22 RBIs, his production went up in his last 45 games, but he hit just .239, ending his year with a .140 slide in his last 12 games.

At times, the switch-hitting Simmons showed great power. For instance, in September he became the first Tiger to hit a home run from both sides of the plate in the same game—and he also became the first Tiger in 12 years to clear the 440-sign in center with a home run. For the season he earned Tigers' Rookie of the Year honors. Nelson was a big man, very muscular, and could hit. But he was not a speedy outfielder, and maybe that hurt him because if you can't cover the ground you need to cover as an outfielder, you better hit a ton. He had the ability to hit the ball out of the ballpark, but somewhere along his journey, he fell out of favor. Sparky frowned upon Nelson's weight-training habits, thinking they made him too slow and consequently a sub-standard outfielder—so he didn't make the club out of spring training the following year, which led a disappointed Simmons to say, "It's obvious Sparky doesn't want me around."

We released him on April 29, 1986. General manager Bill Lajoie explained, "We don't think he has a chance of making our club in the near future. This gives him a chance to go somewhere else."

Simmons re-appeared in the majors in 1987 with the Baltimore Orioles, hitting .265 with one home run in 16 games. But his big league career was over by the time he was 23. Nelson wasn't the reason we didn't repeat as champions in 1985, however. Far from it.

So what were the reasons? After all, we got off to another good start, winning our first six games. Granted, it wasn't 35–5, but we were still in first place on April 29 with an 11–6 record. So within the parameters of another storybook April being out of the question, we were satisfied with the way the season had begun.

This was not going to be a carbon copy of 1984 obviously. That much was clear by the time April ended. We had a powerful offense, we hit a lot of home runs, but at the same time, we were not a multi-dimensional offense. We needed those home runs to win. Despite hitting the second most home runs in the American League in 1985, we scored only the eighth most runs. Scoring runs is the name of the game, however, not how many home runs you hit. We were down in hits (ninth), batting average (10th), and on-base percentage (12th) from 1984. Yet, because of our home runs, we were third in the league in total bases. "If that doesn't convince you home runs will never control the game, nothing ever will," Sparky said. "At the end of the year, we couldn't see first place with a telescope."

No matter how you look at the 1985 season, it added up to us having an offense of home runs as the entrée but few side dishes. That's not to say our hitters had bad years. On the contrary, Darrell Evans led the American League with 40 home runs—up from the 16 he hit in 1984. Kirk Gibson was our offensive MVP, leading the team in total bases, OPS, and batting average. I edged him out 98 to 97 for the RBI lead. And Lou Whitaker had a fine year, leading the team in runs scored and hits while hitting what was then a career-high 21 home runs. "I would say we were as good or better offensively than the year before, but it just didn't click," Gibson said. "We tried, we were dedicated, everyone had good intentions, but other teams don't hold back. They come to get you."

Alan Trammell, however, felt he didn't do his part. Tram had a shoulder operation soon after the 1984 season and felt he was behind where he needed to be most of the year. He was still behind deep into the season, hitting .239 the second half. "I was one of the factors why we didn't win it again," he said. "Five days after the World Series, I had shoulder surgery for a labrum tear because my arm had been killing me in 1984. I did

My Health

Alan Trammell's shoulder problem in July, which eventually put him on the disabled list, made many of us reflect on the blessing it had been to stay healthy during the 1984 season. I don't believe I had anything go physically wrong with me the entire year. I was grateful for that, to be sure. But I didn't avoid encountering various health challenges later in my career.

When I was with the California Angels, I got run over by Milwaukee Brewers outfielder Glenn Braggs in 1989, knocking me out of the lineup for about a week, and that started an issue with my knee. Bragg hit me like a ton of bricks, making my knee feel like it was on fire. That injury wasn't long term, however.

But when I was still with the Detroit Tigers, a back situation cost me much of the 1986 season—and eventually dictated the direction in which the rest of my career would go. In spring training I'd had negotiations about a contract extension with the Tigers, but later that spring, I began to have back issues, though I didn't know what the problem was at the time. I thought I could play through it, which I did for a while, but as the season progressed, it got worse. In fact, it got so bad that soon after the All-Star break that year, I had to shut it down because of a sciatic nerve condition that was multiplied by 10 because of the pain. The Tigers flew me out to Los Angeles to see a back specialist, and I remember being alarmed when I saw my X-rays. It looked like my spine was split in two pieces! I thought, *Oh my God, it can't look any worse than that.*

The doctor said I could stabilize the area with physical therapy, but I wanted more than to just stabilize it. I wanted it fixed. He said surgery might repair it but added, "Here's the deal: because it's a nerve condition, if one of the nerves by chance gets nicked during the procedure, your baseball career would be over."

I replied, "Well, in that case, I don't want surgery."

So, he gave me a rehab plan to take back to Detroit based solely on physical therapy. I was at Henry Ford Hospital just about every day from that point on, going through my program. It was part of an effort to stabilize the spine. This is how bad it had deteriorated, though, before rehab: whenever I stood up, it would take only five minutes before I couldn't feel my right leg. I also was able to walk for only a block before having to squat down to relieve the pressure on the nerve. Strangely enough, the only position that provided me with any comfort at all was squatting. It prevented the pinching I felt while I was standing up.

It wasn't until after the season ended that I finally got medical clearance to begin any kind of baseball activity. But the whole thing happened at the worst possible time because I was in the last year of my contract with Detroit. It hadn't been an issue in spring training when we first began talking about a contract extension, but at the end of the season, the Tigers—with Jim Campbell calling the shots—put their foot down and offered me just a one-year deal for the same amount I had made during the 1986 season.

That's when everything kind of got sideways with the Tigers. And the rest is history. I ended up signing as a free agent with the Philadelphia Phillies. Without a doubt it was the worst injury I ever had in my career. But at the time, I looked at it this way: the Tigers had sent me to a specialist whose prognosis was that if I followed the program, I should be fine. Granted, it took me a while to get better because I had inflamed the nerve so badly it was killing me. But, eventually, I recovered. It went away with therapy, and I never felt it again.

However, the saddest part of 1986 for me was that I was probably having my best year production-wise. With my season ending on July 26 because of my back, I missed the last 65 games, but I ended up with 22 home runs and 62 RBIs—better production numbers in a partial season than most catchers had for a full season. That's why I thought the Tigers would pay me what I felt I was worth after that season. Instead, I just kept getting more upset about it because they weren't offering me a raise of any kind—not even $1.

So, I responded, "No way! I'm not doing it."

I was confused by the stance the Tigers took with me and finally grew tired of how aggravating the situation became. I mean, it had become obvious to me I wasn't going to be around anymore as a Tiger. So, we packed up and spent the rest of the winter in California. It was a very difficult time because, as I've often said, I did not want to leave Detroit. I thought I would be a Tiger forever. That's what I had hoped to be. But I wasn't.

everything I could to bounce back, but I was supposed to be one of the go-to guys and while I didn't do badly, I didn't have the kind of year I was hoping to. I place myself at the top of the list as a reason why we didn't repeat. I do."

Nearly all of Tram's offensive stats took a dip in 1985, most of all his OPS from .851 to .692, but as selfless as it was for him to assign himself the blame, we refused to point in the same direction. "That sounds like Tram," Dan Petry said, "but that's not how I view that season. To me it just demonstrated how difficult it is to win once, let alone back-to-back. I mean, even now it hasn't been done since 2000 with the Yankees, I believe. So, you can point fingers and assign a lot of blame, but I would just say repeating is that difficult."

To Jack Morris, it was a matter of being the reigning champs. "I don't think we had the same drive," he said. "A lot of what occurred in 1984, remember, was because of 1983. We came out of that season pissed at Baltimore. They won the World Series, but we felt we were the better team. And we wanted to prove it. That's to say in the world of professional sports: if your hair isn't on fire and if you don't have a chip on your shoulder and a reason to compete every day, it becomes routine. But routine doesn't work. We went to spring training in 1984 with something to prove…However, in 1985 we didn't know what it took to repeat. There was no reason we couldn't have done it. We had the talent. I just don't think we had the same attitude."

To this extent, I disagree with Jack. I don't believe it was a matter of not being hungry enough for another title. Everybody's goal every year is to win a championship. It wasn't a lack of desire, just a combination of various reasons why we didn't win.

Brookens thought it wasn't even about the players. It was about the departure of a coach.

"We lost Roger Craig, which I thought was big," Brookens said. "Roger was a big, big part of our team. He and Sparky worked well together. So, when he didn't come back, it was a huge loss. But I still thought we'd win it again."

In my opinion, Roger had been instrumental in our success. Not only was he a great pitching coach, but he also was the master psychologist of our team. Our whole team missed him when he left.

Without him in 1985 we hung in there for a while. When we beat Texas 5–3 on July 7, for instance, we were only two-and-a-half games out of first place. The only teams within five games of the Toronto Blue Jays were us at 45–33 and the New York Yankees at 43–35, but instead of our best baseball being ahead of us, we began to stumble. After one last fling of playing like the team we knew we could be—a 6–5 victory at home against the Chicago White Sox in which we scored four runs in the ninth followed by a 1–0 gem from Morris the next night—we disappeared, losing eight of the next 10. By the time July ended, we were nine-and-a-half games out. And with a lackluster 31–31 finish, we didn't make another charge at the Blue Jays the rest of the season. They ended up winning the division by two games over the Yankees (who were 42–20 from August 1 on) and by 15 games over us. We went 84–77—some 20 games off our won/loss record of '84.

So, changes were coming after 1985, and we knew it. By the time we went to camp the next spring, Marty Castillo, Wilcox, Barbaro Garbey, Aurelio Lopez, and Berenguer were gone. The championship team had been dismantled. And with collusion becoming an issue, it didn't look promising for those of us with free agency approaching. We made two major additions to our lineup before the 1986 season. Knowing we needed more speed, we acquired Dave Collins from the Oakland A's for Garbey with the intention of using him high in the batting order at all three outfield positions. Collins wasn't young (32) at the time of the trade—he was headed into his 12th major league season—but there were no indications he was rapidly aging. In 1984 for Toronto, for instance, he had stolen 60 bases, then 29 in 112 games for the A's in 1985. We knew he wouldn't lead the league in stolen bases but hadn't made the deal for that purpose. We just wanted to improve our team speed. "He's the kind of player who can make things happen," Bill Lajoie said of Collins.

The other addition to our batting order was third baseman Darnell Coles, whom we acquired from the Seattle Mariners for former first-round draft choice Rich Monteleone. At one point Coles had been considered the Mariners' third baseman of the future, but injuries had intervened. Frankly, I don't think we knew how Coles would turn out for us. It quickly became evident, though, that he had a cannon for an arm. By the end of spring training with Darnell having won the starting job at third base, Sparky was saying, "If we don't win 94 to 96 games with this team, I'll be mighty surprised."

You never knew, however, what the motivation was behind a comment like that from Sparky. He liked making predictions to challenge us. It was his way of saying, "This is how many games I think you can win. Now go out there and do it."

As it turned out, both newcomers did well enough, but they didn't become long-time Tigers. Coles hit .273 with 20 home runs and 86 RBIs. He tied Gibson for the team lead in RBIs, which was a pleasant surprise, and his 20 home runs on a team that led the league with 198 meant that all four of our starting infielders hit at least 20 home runs. "Nice," Coles said, "but it doesn't really mean much because we didn't finish first."

One productive season didn't guarantee his future as a Tiger, though. Hitting just .181 with four home runs in 53 games and having problems on defense, Coles was traded the next August to the Pittsburgh Pirates. "When you make errors," he said, "you don't fit in."

Collins, meanwhile, ended up with 476 plate appearances—second most among our outfielders—and stole 27 bases. But with his skills diminishing, he was released in October.

As far as how our season went in 1986, this should tell you all you need to know: we didn't climb above .500 for good until Jack pitched us to a 5–0 victory against Texas on July 18. At the time, it gave us a 45–44 record. And the most life we displayed all year was when we went 16–7 in our final 23 games. That lifted us from fourth place—13½ games out of first—to a third-place finish, eight-and-a-half games out. But I don't think anybody shut it down early. Before it became a reality that we had no chance, we always thought we'd kick it in gear.

It turned out to be a season of severe injuries for some of us. My season ended on July 26 because of a back issue, the first significant, extremely painful injury of my career. I anticipated it would go away, but it never did. It just got worse. Sometimes it felt like I had a meat hook in my lower back. I'd been having a pretty productive year until one morning I couldn't even get out of bed. It was a sour way for my Tigers' career to end and a bad time for such a debilitating problem to occur—as after the season I found myself mired in a dispute with the front office about my value and ended up leaving for the Philadelphia Phillies as a free agent.

Petry, meanwhile, missed two-and-a-half months—from early June to mid-August—because of elbow surgery. He returned before the end of the season but went 1–5 with a 4.26 ERA in his last nine starts. It was heartbreaking to watch a good friend such as Dan, who'd been a great teammate, struggle because of medical issues. But I'd seen it happen before, beginning with Mark Fidrych. So I knew it was an unfortunate reality of the game that tomorrow isn't guaranteed for anyone. It was also a sad turning point in Dan's career. After 67 victories in his previous four seasons, he went 5–10 in 1986 and would win only 21 more games as a starter before his career ended following the 1991 season. In his time, though, he was a fine pitcher.

The Tigers, to their credit, got it together again to win their division by two games over Toronto in 1987—and they did it with many of the core players from 1984. But not with all of us.

Epilogue

Our Legacy

I looked up the definition of the word *legacy* recently, and this is the what I found: "The long-lasting impact of particular events." Well, I would certainly say that the 1984 season left us with a glorious legacy because 40 years later it is still near and dear to us all.

It's near and dear because I can still remember going to spring training that year, thinking that we had the best team in the American League. I can remember going to Chicago for the second series of the season, and Jack Morris having that look in his eye as out after out went by while his no-hitter drew near…and when he walked Greg Luzinski in the ninth inning how he got upset with the umpire's close call but regrouped to strike out Ron Kittle for the final out against the White Sox.

I remember the joyful anticipation of the crowd at the first home game of the season and how I thought, *Wow, this is going to be a fun ride.* I remember scoring eight runs in the first inning on Friday, April 13th at Fenway Park in Boston, dumping any superstition of that supposedly bad luck day (and of me wearing No. 13) into the harbor. I remember April—with its 18–2 record—and how one game after another went into our win column. I remember thinking, as Willie Hernandez began to look strong and Dave Bergman helped in several ways that, *You know, that spring training trade with the Philadelphia Phillies might have been pretty good after all.*

I remember losing to the Cleveland Indians in the 19th inning for only our second defeat but battling every step of the weary way after arriving home from a road trip to Texas at 6:00 AM that morning. I remember beating the California Angels for our 17th consecutive road win, giving us an unprecedented 35–5 record at the time, then going to Seattle with the hope of extending that streak, only to get swept—and have our lunch handed to us—by the Mariners. And, as June began, there was that wonderful game in which Bergie battled Toronto Blue Jays pitcher Roy Lee Jackson pitch after pitch, finally getting the better of him by hitting a game-winning home run on the 13th pitch of the at-bat.

I remember marveling at the talent we had: Alan Trammell becoming a complete player, Kirk Gibson being such an offensive force, the fluidity of Lou Whitaker as a second baseman and his instinctive intelligence as a hitter, the addition of Ruppert Jones making us even better, Chet Lemon hauling everything down in center, the depth of our starting rotation with Jack, Dan Petry, and Milt Wilcox…not to mention the quirkiness but true genius of Sparky Anderson augmented by the valuable assistance he received from our pitching coach, Roger Craig.

I remember June becoming our first challenge but not giving into it, how July came and went with us weathering seven losses in the first nine games of the month but never coming close to falling out of first. I remember how six of us went to the All-Star game, representing with pride our division-leading team but also how I bit a chunk out of my tongue on a play at the plate. I remember how we beat the Minnesota Twins in consecutive extra-inning games soon after the All-Star break, getting two needed victories while still involved in what we considered to be a nip-and-tuck pennant race, how August wasn't our best but didn't drag us down as the Month of the Dog Days often can. I remember how September began with guarded anticipation of eventually clinching a postseason spot.

I also remember how I began to think my wife's due date for the baby she was expecting might coincide with the start of the World Series if we were fortunate to get that far. I remember how we finally left the bothersome Blue Jays in our wake by sweeping three in a row from them in early September in Toronto. At that point, it was full steam ahead for the destiny that awaited us. I remember how we clinched the division title on September 18 with the help of rookie Randy O'Neal, who had been assigned the start—then never even was given a World Series ring.

I remember how we respected Kansas City as our American League playoff opponent but disposed of the Royals like the determined team we were and how we initially thought we might be facing the Chicago Cubs in the World Series but wound up facing the San Diego Padres instead. I remember how Arlyne gave birth to our daughter, Ashley, on the Thursday before the Sunday we flew to San Diego to prepare for the World Series. Our two boys couldn't go with us because children weren't allowed on the charter flight, but an exception was made for our newborn daughter.

I remember how we won the first game of the World Series, lost the second game but came home to put the Padres away with three consecutive victories at Tiger Stadium and how I homered off Goose Gossage in Game Five but also how Kirk Gibson followed with the iconic moment of the World Series, his "he don't want to walk you" home run off Goose in the eighth inning. I remember how we erupted with joy when Larry Herndon caught the final out and we had completed our journey as CHAMPIONS!

I've thought over the years that going 35–5, winning 104 games, and going wire-to-wire should rank us among the greatest teams ever. I remember how the city of Detroit deserved this championship because our fans had supported us every step of the way, beaming when we won, frowning when we lost, but in the end being able to celebrate. These are the moments I envision and still hold close to my heart—such as being Mickey Stanley's teammate my first two years with the Tigers, creating a link between the storybook seasons of 1968 and 1984. It was a wild, wonderful ride from wire to wire—one that left us with a lifetime of memories—and the legacy we are still enjoying.

Acknowledgments

Forty years is a long time—and when I started working with Lance on this book, I grappled with the fact that because it is indeed a long time, the year of the Detroit Tigers' last (some would prefer "most recent") championship must also have been ages ago.

Then this occurred to hearten me: in the summer of 2023, I attended the induction ceremonies at the Hall of Fame in Cooperstown, New York. At the end of the parade of Hall of Famers, which is a highlight of the annual festivities, I saw only one player refuse assistance to climb down from the back of the pickup truck in which he had been riding.

He refused it, I gathered, because he didn't need it. That player was Alan Trammell.

I thought to myself, *Hey, I know that guy, I know that kid*—because to me Tram is still a kid. And possibly always will be. That's the enchantment of baseball, in my opinion. There's always a place in our hearts for the eternal appeal of yesteryear. So, go ahead, Tram, climb out of that truck without any help as long as you want and for as long as you can.

Every time you do, 1984 seems not so long ago.

Hopefully, this book allows you to relive the magical season of 1984, and I'd like to thank several people who helped with *The Enchanted Season*. Among them my longtime press-box colleague Chuck Klonke, who made his immense collection of baseball literature available to me; Barb Klonke, for tolerating Chuck's basement; Bill Dow, whose knowledge of Tigers' history is vast; Mark Dehem, a business associate who's always ready to help with a phone number or address; Bill McGraw, a former competitor but always a friend; the entire Parrish family, friendly and a joy to work with throughout; the archives of the *Detroit Free Press* and *The Detroit News*; the indispensable statistical help of Baseball Reference; my friend Jim Hawkins for helping to fill in some blanks; the immeasurable resource of SABR; umpire Richie Garcia, who has never forgotten a play; plus former Tigers Trammell, Kirk Gibson, Dan Petry, Jack Morris, Darrell Evans, Tom Brookens, Randy O'Neal, Mickey Lolich, Mickey Stanley, Dick Tracewski, and Jim Leyland.

But most of all, I'd like to thank Lance himself for digging so earnestly into the past for the details of his life and career. He was truly The Big Wheel of this project.

—T.G.

I thank my entire family—past, present, near, far—and every team-mate, coach, and manager I've ever had from my childhood on, from the gridiron to the diamond. I wouldn't have realized any level of achievement without you.

—L.P.

Sources

Most of the quotes from this book came from Tom Gage's direct reporting, but the following sources—especially the *Detroit Free Press*—were particularly helpful:

Wire Services
Associated Press
United Press International

Periodicals
Detroit Free Press
The San Diego Union-Tribune
The Detroit News
The Kansas City Star
The Sporting News
Toronto Star
Toronto Sun

Writers
George Cantor
Bill Dow
Dan Ewald
Joe Falls
Tom Gage
Jerry Green

Jim Hawkins
Lynn Henning
Chuck Klonke
Bill McGraw
Mike O'Hara
Vern Plagenhoef
Eli Zaret

Websites
Baseball-almanac.com
Baseball-reference.com
MLB.com
MLive.com
Newspapers.com
SABR.org (BioProject)
Youtube.com

Books

Anderson, Sparky, *Bless You Boys: Diary of the Detroit Tigers' 1984 Season*, Contemporary Books, Inc. (1984)

Cantor, George, *Wire to Wire: Inside the 1984 Detroit Tigers Championship Season*, Triumph Books (2004)

Craig, Roger, *Inside Pitch: Roger Craig's '84 Tiger Journal*, Wm. B Eerdmans Publishing Co. (1984)

The Magic Season: The 1984 Detroit Tigers, The Detroit News, News Books, International, Inc. (1984)

Zaret, Eli, *'84: The Last of the Great Tigers*, Crofton Creek Press (2004)